# The Embodiment and Transmission of
Ghanaian Kete Royal Dance

# The Embodiment and Transmission of Ghanaian Kete Royal Dance

## From Palace to Academy

Emmanuel Cudjoe

ANTHEM PRESS

Anthem Press
An imprint of Wimbledon Publishing Company
www.anthempress.com

This edition first published in UK and USA 2024
by ANTHEM PRESS
75–76 Blackfriars Road, London SE1 8HA, UK
or PO Box 9779, London SW19 7ZG, UK
and
244 Madison Ave #116, New York, NY 10016, USA

© 2025 Emmanuel Cudjoe

The author asserts the moral right to be identified as the author of this work.

All rights reserved. Without limiting the rights under copyright reserved above, no part of this publication may be reproduced, stored or introduced into a retrieval system, or transmitted, in any form or by any means (electronic, mechanical, photocopying, recording or otherwise), without the prior written permission of both the copyright owner and the above publisher of this book. owner and the above publisher of this book.

*British Library Cataloguing-in-Publication Data*
A catalogue record for this book is available from the British Library.

*Library of Congress Cataloging-in-Publication Data: 2024940683*
A catalog record for this book has been requested.

ISBN-13: 978-1-83999-182-0 (Hbk)
ISBN-10: 1-83999-182-8 (Hbk)

Cover Credit: The Kete Dance

This title is also available as an e-book.

This work is dedicated to my parents, James Ankrah Amponsah Cudjoe and Georgina Akosua Tabuaa Gyimafi Antwi, for instilling in me Akan/Asante cultural heritage and Identity; my wife, Sandra Achiaa Owusu Cudjoe; and my beautiful children, Emmanuella Yaa Tabuaa Gyimafi Cudjoe, Elise Nana Afia Bemah Cudjoe, and our son, Emmanuel Amponsah Cudjoe.

# CONTENTS

*Figures*   xi
*Acknowledgments*   xiii
*Background: The Kete Dance of the Asante*   xv
*Ghanaian Dance-Music Traditions*   xix

1. Odomankoma *Na ɔnwini* Kete!   1
   Shoulders of Eminence   2
   The Context of African Dance: An Orientation to Movement   3
   The Colonial Background   5

2. Royal Dance-Music Origins   9
   Kete Dance Literature Today   12
   Kete Dance, Phenomenology, and Afrocentrism   15
   Afrocentricity: An Imperative Epistemological Framework   20
   Afrocentricity, Language, and Education   22
   Afrocentricity and Kete Movement Analysis   25
   The Melting Pot: Tying the Wisdom Knot of Afrocentricity,
       Akan Symbolisms, and Communication through Kete Dance   28
   Summary   31

3. Afrocentricity: Seeing Clearly the Phenomenon   33
   Kete Dance as Indigenous Knowledge   33
   Holism as an Afrocentric Character   34
   Tracing the Evolution of Kete: Journey from Kumasi to Accra,
       Ghana, and Beyond to North America   36
   Pan-Africanism and Indigenous Dance-Musicking in
       Postindependence Ghana: Legacies of Nkrumah, Nketia,
       and Opoku   37
   Starting the Experiment: Kete Dance-Music as a National
       Repertoire   40
   An Autoethnographic Enquiry into Kete Dance-Music   45

|   | Embodied Afrocentricity: Locating the Black Body in Its Practice and Theory | 47 |
|---|---|---|
|   | Conceptualizing the Kete Body as an Agent of Social Construction and Meaning-Making through Performance | 51 |
|   | Realization and Concept of Kete Dance | 53 |
|   | Kete Performance and Propagation | 57 |
| 4. | African Dance in a Global Context | 61 |
|   | Traditional Dance-Musicking | 61 |
|   | Language and the Shaping of Dance Identities in Ghana | 67 |
|   | Traditional Dance Proliferation and the Postindependence Formulation of "National Identity" | 70 |
|   | Pedagogy, Curriculum Design, and Neo-Traditional Dancing in the Academy | 73 |
|   | Exploring Neo-Traditional Dance Pedagogy Post-1992 Constitution of Ghana and Its Global Implication | 78 |
|   | 2020/2021/2022 Curricula | 81 |
|   | Conceptual Dance Knowledge and Practical Dance Breakdown | 83 |
|   | Addressing Curriculum "Issues" | 84 |
|   | Summary | 85 |
| 5. | From Palace to Academy: An Embodied Journey | 87 |
|   | Fieldwork in Ghana | 88 |
|   | Revisiting Manhyia: Transitioning from Nostalgia to Reverence, Embracing Dance Knowledge as a Researcher | 89 |
|   | Fieldwork in the United States and Canada (Virtual) | 92 |
|   | Navigating Identity through Dance: An Autoethnographic Exploration | 94 |
|   | Navigating Royal Etiquette through Dance: Lessons from Chieftaincy | 96 |
|   | Exploring the Phenomenological Essence of Self | 103 |
|   | Kete as "Artifact"—the Palace as a Museum of Ancestral Legacies | 106 |
|   | Conceptualizing My Bodily Perceptions within the Urban Political System of Fante New Town-Kumasi | 111 |
|   | Transitioning from Royal to Amateur to Academic Kete | 114 |
|   | Rediscovering Myself | 116 |
|   | Summary | 118 |
| 6. | Gendered Aesthetic Appreciation and Evaluation within Asante Kete Dance | 121 |
|   | Clarifying "Traditional and Neo-Traditional Kete" Dance Renditions Today | 126 |
|   | Asante Aesthetics as an Evaluative System | 128 |

|    |    |    |
|---|---|---|
|    | Improvisation in Kete Dance-Music | 132 |
|    | Gendered Drums | 133 |
|    | Kete Dance as Indigenous Epistemological Expression of the Asante People | 135 |
|    | Kete Performativity | 139 |
|    | Issues on Kete Dance Aesthetics within the Academy | 142 |
|    | Summary | 148 |
| 7. | Analysis and Interpretation of Kete from a Holistic Position | 149 |
|    | Personal Experience | 151 |
|    | Revelatory Incident(s) | 156 |

*Postscript: Future of Kete Dance research*     165

*Bibliography*     167

*Index*     177

# FIGURES

1. *Gye Nyame* Adinkra Symbol—Page 30
2. *Adinkrahene*—Page 30
3. *Akofena* Adinkra—Page 31
4. *Kete dancers—Image 1*—Page 53
5. *Kete dancers—Image 2*—Page 59
6. *Dancing Event Table—Figure 1*—Page 64
7. *Department of Dance Studies Course Table*—Pages 81–83
8. *Manhyia palace visit—Image 3*—Page 91
9. *Manhyia palace visit—Image 4*—Page 92
10. *Manhyia palace visit—Image 5*—Page 93
11. *Manhyia palace visit—Image 6*—Page 94
12. *Performing a solo—Image 7*—Page 98
13. *The author's father Nana Amponsah Cudjoe*—Page 101
14. *The author at his father's coronation*—Page 102
15. *Dwannyinimienushia drawing*—Page 105
16. *Akofena, Dwannyinimen, Nyame Dua Adinkra symbols*—Pages 107–108
17. *Author Performing with Abibigromma Theatre*—Page 110
18. *Author performing with Abibigromma Theatre*—Page 110
19. *Author performing at the University of Ghana*—Page 111
20. *Author with Akuaffo Hall Chiefs*—Page 113
21. *Author performing with the Dance Department, University of Ghana*—Page 114
22. *Figure 2: Self-reflection*—Page 118
23. *Kete drums*—Page 134
24. *Kete drums as used by amateur groups*—Page 141
25. *Dancing Kete*—Page 143
26. *Displaying equality gesture*—Page 147

# ACKNOWLEDGMENTS

I would like to thank the almighty God for the gift of life and how far he has brought me. My sincere gratitude goes to Anthem Press for publishing this work and to my mother, Georgina Akosua Tabuaa Gyimafi, who has been my role model and source of constant support. God bless you. I am thankful to my father, James Ankrah Amponsah Cudjoe, and my family, Augustina Cudjoe, for their prayers and well wishes. My life is meaningful because you exist in all my endeavors.

Special thanks to Prof. Molefi Kete Asante, Prof. Mark Franko, Prof. yaTande Whitney Hunter, Prof. Kimmika L. H. William-Witherspoon, and Prof. Sylvanus Kwashie Kuwor.

A special thanks to Manhyia Ketehene in Kumasi and the Ahenemaa Kete groups for allowing me access to their embodied knowledge and the legacies of their ancestors. Special thank you to Kofi Boakye (Alias KB) dance group and Prosper (Gasko) Atsu Ablordey, the leaders of these two groups, who made sure I was comfortable whenever I was in their midst. Your warmth and openness made this publication possible. I also want to thank all the drummers and dancers of these groups who accepted and taught me.

I am very grateful to the School of Performing Arts for not only training me but also placing in me a deeper appreciation of my nation and the cultures that abound within it. Special thanks go to my dance teacher, friend, and mentor, Eugene Kwaku Manu, for his selfless act of adopting me under his wing to train me in traditional Ghanaian dances and life experiences. I also want to thank Dr. Osei Agyeman, Chairman Boboo, Baffour Awuah Kyeremanteng (Yewura) Dr, Sarah Dorgbadzi, Eric Awuah, the faculty of the Department of Dance Studies, the University of Ghana, Dr. Habib Chester Idrissu, and Senyo Okyere for their contribution to this work.

I also thank my research assistants, Mr. Twumasi Ntiamoah, Joshua Benumanson, Mr. Joseph Pieterson, Mr. Bright Anokye, and Mr. Joel Tham. I acknowledge all the spiritual support I received from all my well-wishers, especially my wife Sandra, National Snipers Prayer Army, and my family.

Special thanks to Prof. Sherril Dodds and Prof. Karen Bond. I thank Gloria Scott, Elder Macon, Sister Terry, Lanette Kemp, Roben Kemp, and DeVonne Kemp.

I wish to also express my profound gratitude to my sister, Augustina Cudjoe, upon whose advice and financial support I pursued dance studies at the University of Ghana. To Mama Kariamu Welsh, I cannot thank you enough for the lasting legacy and influence you left in me. For all the wonderful people I have not mentioned in this acknowledgment, it does not mean your efforts go unnoticed. Thank you all very much.

Lastly, to St. Olaf College, the Department of Dance faculty, Ball State University, Theatre and Dance department, the Andrew Mellon ACM Grant-Midwest, thank you for enormous support in making this publication possible.

# BACKGROUND: THE KETE DANCE OF THE ASANTE

Kete is a music and dance form originating from the Asante and also primarily performed by the Akan people of Ghana. Like all indigenous knowledge forms, Kete possesses a nuanced history interwoven with mysticism, sociocultural elements, and historical factors. "The Akan people of Ghana include the Asante, Akwamu, Akyem, Denkyira, and Fante ethnic groups who occupy a large portion of Ghana" Gerry R. Cox and Neil Thompson, "The Akan of Ghana," in *Managing Death: International Perspectives*, ed. Gerry R. Cox and Neil Thompson (Cham: Springer International Publishing, 2022), 85–89, https://doi.org/10.1007/978-3-031-05559-1_9. They primarily occupy the southern part of the country. Within Asante cultural practices, music and movement systems hold a significant place in life. Beyond their communicative functions, these systems act as vital links connecting the past, present, and future. Kete is a traditional dance-music form originally confined to the palace of the Asantehene and subchiefs, who hold the authority to have traditional music and dances in their palaces. The *Kete* dance has gone through many changes since its break away from the older Adowa form, and as Joseph Kaminski (2007) shares, "the music of *Kete* is reputed to possess the power of attracting good spirits […] [Nketia] explains that the surrogated texts extol high moral values through the telling of heroic ideals and a *Kete* dance must be developed with the involvement of symbolic hand gestures reflecting these values. It is danced barefooted and trained male dancers dance with their *Lapa* cloth lowered beneath the chest" ("Asante Kete drumming: music from Ghana," 2007).

There are different accounts attributed to the origins of the Kete Dance form, but this volume employs the two main accounts in my unpublished thesis of 2015 titled *The Contexts and Meaning in Asante Dance Performance: The Case of Kete* by Emmanuel Cudjoe, *The Contexts and Meaning in Asante Dance Performance: The Case of Kete* (Accra, Ghana, University of Ghana, 2015). These two are by no means authoritative over the many other accounts that exist about the dance, but they offer interesting insights into the scholarly departure points this book elaborates. The late Baffour Kyeremanteng (Yewura), an accomplished *Kete* performer who performed in the court of the Ashanti monarch (of blessed memory) Otumfuo Opoku Ware II, shared that *Kete* emanated from the Volta Region of Ghana, even though he agrees and identifies it as an Asante court dance. He states that "even though we do not have a specific root of the name [...] *Kete* happened to be hunters drumming and this is because the original *Kete* is known as *Abɔ foagorɔ*.[1] So we [the Asante's] conquered the *Kete* dance during war [*Kete*-Krachi3]. This is evident of the symbolic cloth used to cover the *Kete* drums known as *sum ne mogya*, meaning darkness and blood. Everything our ancestors did had a meaning. *Sum ne mogya* further explains that if one goes to war and there is no death, there should still be blood" Cudjoe. The other part of the Kete origin story traces its roots to an earlier Asante dance form known as Adowa, from which Kete emerged as a creative extension. Two key observations arise from these accounts, providing deeper insights into Ghanaian traditional dance forms. Firstly, the importance attached to the spoils of war suggests that music and dance were arguably as significant as looted gold, enslaved people, and supremacy over subdued states. This is because a people's music and dance represent their dignity, identity, and authority. Thus, the retention of certain dances, like Kete, within palace courts for royal entertainment underscores their cultural and political significance, reflecting their integral role in maintaining and showcasing the power and prestige of the Asante kingdom. The Ghana Dance Ensemble's first artistic rector, Professor Mawere Opoku, shared that "so great was the value placed by the Asante on [...] art forms that they collected musical and dance forms as part of war booty and displayed them with the captives of vanquished nations during victory parades. The *Mpintin* drum ensemble of large round gourds with skin at the top and straps for tuning, and the *Dondo*, or hourglass drum, which provides music for royal processions, show an Asante link with the *Gonjas*, the *Dagombas*, and other northern ethnic groups." Albert Mawere Opoku, "Asante Dance Art and the Court," in *The Golden Stool: Studies of the Asante Center and Periphery*, ed. Enid Schildkrout and Carol Gelber (New York, NY: American Museum of Natural History, 1987), 192–99. Secondly, the overflow of these court dances to the masses may have been necessitated by the decline of traditional authorities and monarchies during European colonization in Africa. Nevertheless, the dance has adapted to various situations throughout its evolution. Kete, originally a court dance, sparks discussions on power and identity concepts before and after Ghana's

---

1 *Abɔ foagorɔ*—this is made up of two words: *Abɔ fo (Hunters)* and *agorɔ* (Play), so the combination becomes Hunters game.

colonization. Its evolution from an exclusive dance for royalty to a ceremonial performance open to all in contemporary times highlights its shifting role and significance within Ghanaian society. For example, the shift from the *Adowa* dance to Kete illustrates contemporary aesthetics, meanings, and contexts through the expressivity of movement variations in faster tempos. There is much to learn about Kete dance-music, and we have barely scratched the surface. This is just the beginning.

# GHANAIAN DANCE-MUSIC TRADITIONS

Indigenous dance music in Ghana serves peculiar roles in the lives of its practitioners from birth to death. This book explores the role of the Kete dance of the Asante people as an Afrocentric agency of meaning-making. As a dance-music form, Kete is one of the most popular dances in Ghana and a major cultural attraction in the diaspora. Apart from ethnomusicological explorations of its music, not much has been done about its movement element. I theorize Kete as an element of social construction that promotes and sustains cultural/indigenous knowledge through gestures. A performance of Kete in a specific context, such as a funeral, can serve as a lens through which indigenous gender disparities, sociocultural class structures, and embodied agencies for the propagation of indigenous knowledge are exposed. Utilizing a qualitative research methodology that encompasses first-person methods such as autoethnography, along with interviews and audiovisual analysis, I undertake an examination of my personal experience and understanding of Kete as a practitioner since childhood. Additionally, I explore the experiences of selected participants in both Ghana and the United States in providing context for future exploration. The book also serves an advocacy purpose by exclusively aligning with Afrocentricity, a unique feature not previously explored in Ghanaian dance literature. As a reflection of intelligent social structuring, where dancers communicate through gestures, I delve into the transition of Kete from the Manhyia Palace in Kumasi (Traditional Category) to the Ghana Dance Ensemble (Academic and then Professional Category) at the University of Ghana since 1963. Eric Awuah, "A Study of Amateur Groups' Re-Interpretation of Traditional Dances in Ghana: Role on Continuity and Safeguarding" (NTNU, University of Clermont Ferrand, University of Szeged, University of Roehampton, 2014). I aim to explore the impact of neo-traditional structures on the continued proliferation of Kete today. Specifically, my focus is on investigating the agency of the Kete dancer centered within Kumasi and Accra, utilizing first-person methods to understand the structures influencing its proliferation and anticipated future developments. Asante Kete royal court dance music has its origins in the Asante/Akan ethnic group of Ghana, West Africa. The Akan people constitute the largest ethnic group in Ghana, primarily residing in the southern regions of the country. They are characterized by the use of the Twi language and distinct cultural traditions, including their music and dance forms. Kete, dating back to the 1700s, stands as one of the oldest of the Asante court dances. This dance form, along with other traditional music and dance expressions, is associated with the Asantehene (Otumfuɔ Asante king) and the Asante people (Cudjoe 2015; Younge 2011). The term "Kete" encompasses a specific set of instruments, the music produced by these instruments, and the dance performed to that music. Initially confined to the Asante royal court system, Kete has transcended its original context and is now performed and heard in various non-court settings, including funerals, ceremonies, and weddings (Cudjoe 2015; Paulding 2017). Kete, as a dance-music form, intricately utilizes controlled hand and foot gestures to convey specific cultural ideals such as resilience, love, and competition, among others, within diverse contexts. As a subset of the broader Asante/Akan culture, the knowledge embedded in Kete holds both personal and social significance for me. In the realm of community building, Kete plays a vital role, contributing to the preservation of oral heritage through performance. This aspect continues to fuel my fascination with Kete, propelling my commitment to understanding it through dedicated research. For the Asantes, Kete dance events are conduits for the proliferation, preservation, and enshrinement of resilience, bravery, and patriotism that are integral to Asante history. Due to this, dancers who undergo training in the performance of Kete inherently embody Asante philosophies and belief systems. It becomes apparent that any transmission of Asante bodily expressions that disregard traditional structures, including terms and conditions, in performance may pose the risk of "distorting" the consecrated identity markers of Asante culture. The documentation of the Kete dance of the Asante people, particularly as performed in Kumasi, the spiritual capital of the Asante kingdom, serves as the primary focus of this book. This specific location is crucial for understanding the role of Kete in contemporary Ghanaian culture and its integration into a Pan-Africanist politico-cultural strategy promoted by Ghana's first president, Dr. Kwame Nkrumah (1960–1966). This integration occurred through the University of Ghana, the premier educational institution, starting in 1963. Following the emancipation from British colonial rule in the 1960s in Ghana, there arose a necessity to employ indigenous philosophies and approaches to counteract not only the colonial impact on economic development but, more importantly, the emerging discourse on identity politics.

This book serves as a valuable contribution to research on the Kete dance form, offering an analysis of its gestures through a comparative lens, considering both the Traditional Category and Academic Category. It delves into the intricate relationship between dance and politics within the context of the Kete dance form. These explorations lead to two fundamental questions that have been a subject of contemplation for me as a royal, amateur, academic, and professional dancer: What constitutes the political nature of dance? How is politics contextualized within the realm of dance? Does the presence of politics in dance imply the existence of diverse realities and perceptions regarding the nature of dance?

This book is motivated by three distinct circumstances that revolve around the contextual investigation, documentation, and dissemination of Kete and its inherent sociopolitical knowledge, which has resided in oral tradition for decades. Firstly, within Ghanaian dance scholarship, there exists limited documentation employing a critical sociological approach to comprehending the Kete dance form, especially when contrasted with the more prevalent non-ethnomusicological perspective.

Secondly, the use of the first-person voice is not a common practice in Ghanaian traditional/indigenous dance research and writing. Consequently, the field lacks an understanding of individual influences on the form. Even though traditional dance creation and development do not typically attribute specific individuals in the community with choreographic influence, it is evident from neo-traditional renditions in the Professional, Academic, and Amateur categories that certain individuals play crucial roles in making creative decisions and adopting original approaches to the performance of traditional dance-music materials. These individuals encompass drummers, drum makers, dancers, historians, and musicians. To enhance visibility for Kete and illuminate its processes of change over several decades, the voices of these key players must be articulated within the academic realm. Thirdly, there has been a lack of reevaluation of the academic pedagogy of dance from Pan-African and later Afrocentric perspectives, despite these ideologies forming the political and ideological foundations for the 1963 inclusion of dance in university curricula. Kwame Botwe-Asamoah (2005) has critically analyzed Kwame Nkrumah's political and cultural ideas, providing historical and philosophical foundations for the study and promotion of Dance as an element of the African Genius (Nkrumah 1963) trait. This aspect is yet to be thoroughly explored in Ghanaian dance writing. By employing a sociological approach to the use of Kete dance music in both Traditional and Academic categories, this book aims to analyze Kete as a reference point for the examination of other dances in Ghana.

The book weaves together three main themes in the history of Kete dance literature since the establishment of the Institute of African Studies at the University of Ghana: precolonialism, the Ghana Dance Ensemble, and Afrocentric analysis of Ghanaian dances within Ghana. These themes are examined to reflect on their impact on the evolution of dance in Ghana over the years. Given the nature of African historical performance arts literature, which is primarily embodied, there are no written sources validating the origins or earlier beginnings of dances from Africa. The historical data surrounding dances is rooted and validated in African orality. The literary exploration of these artistic mediums and their development in Ghana by Ghanaian researchers in this book begins after 1961, when the Institute of African Studies was established to document Ghanaian and African history. The chapters in this book focus on the role of African Indigenous Knowledge Systems like the Kete dance among its people, the significance of dance in the postcolonial reclamation of African Knowledge Systems central to African living, and the role of dance in higher educational institutions in Ghana's political, cultural, economic, and social development.

# Chapter 1

# ODOMANKOMA *NA ɔNWINI* KETE!

In the beginning, *Odomankoma* created "Order, the Drum/Music, and the Executioner!"[1] According to Asante cosmology played on the *Atumpan* drum, humans are appointed to exist in an orderly world and society, guided by effective communication throughout their lives, and to eventually transition into ancestorshood through death. The pervasive influence of these three elements—Order, the Drum/Music, and the Executioner—on Asante life is undeniable, shaping their interactions with people and the environment, as well as their understanding of spirituality.

The subtitle "Odomankoma na ɔnwini kete!" in Twi language translates to "God assembled Kete dance-music." I selected this chapter title because, as evident in this volume, Kete transcends the physical realm and serves as a bridge between Asante/Akan realities. It is carefully ordered to respond to sociocultural context with its unique movement, visual, and communicative systems. I am cautious not to overly spiritualize this aspect of Kete in my effort to position cultural reverence for this dance-music form. Most importantly, I aim to frame it as an epistemology deserving of more scientific explorations.

I am a Kete dancer, musician, teacher, and lifelong student. My journey and growth are intricately tied, especially to this dance form. Kete offered me my first encounter with self-reflection at a young age, providing a lens through which I could assess my life situations and redefine my focus. It played a crucial role in helping me navigate financial challenges during my primary and senior high school days, contributing to our household income. Even when I received support from my sister to continue my university education, dancing Kete allowed me to save money and supplement the financial assistance. As I pursued my first master's degree at the University of Ghana, Kete provided direction and motivation for my research and thesis. It served as the foundation for understanding movement structure, context, and the function of other cultures during my Choreomundus master's program in

---

[1] This is loosely transliterated from a longer musical stanza played on the Atumpan twin drum found in Akan/Asante musical ensemble.

Europe. When I later gained admission to pursue a PhD in Dance Studies at Temple University, Kete continued to speak to me and drove me toward completion. Today, I share years of experience, practice, and research as a Kete student with the world. I humbly acknowledge that I cannot elevate myself as the sole authority of this form. I owe a debt of gratitude to Kete dance-music, the Asante people of Ghana, the individuals who invested their time and expertise in training me, the masterful dancers who challenged me, and the audiences who encouraged me. My reverence for this art form and those who contributed to my journey is paramount.

## Shoulders of Eminence

African Indigenous Knowledge Systems are modeled on continuity and preservation. People have come before me who have lent their artistic talents to preserving Kete dance. The phrase "shoulders of eminence" here refers to the idea of standing on the accomplishments, knowledge, and contributions of notable and distinguished individuals, known and unknown, traditional/indigenous artists, and academically trained scholars who have made significant strides in Ghanaian dance scholarship. It implies my dedication to building upon the work of those who have come before, acknowledging their achievements, and using that foundation to advance further in the same area of expertise.

In this volume, I stand on the shoulders of my forebears to delve into the realm of Kete dance analysis and research. Drawing from eminent scholars like J. H. Nketia, A. M. Opoku, Ampofo Duodu, Patience Kwakwa, among others, they all agree that dance/embodied movement is intricately connected to all facets of African living. Beyond their contextual uses and functions, dance acts as surrogates for the voices of its people and projects ideals as alternative realities through holistic artistic mediums of propagation. What remains constant is that as societies undergo major changes and develop new technologies, human elements like dancing and their accumulated usefulness have found ways to remain relevant for decades. Kete dance-music is a testament to this. With no verified date of origin owing to the oral nature of African history, Kete has continued to reinvent itself as the people who find it useful employ it in their interactions with people and nature. The significance lies in the fact that within Akan society, contexts, meanings, and aesthetics find validation through the kinaesthetic arrangements of movements in dance. Therefore, dance and its associated elements such as context, aesthetics, and meaning complement each other (Cudjoe 2015).

The book provides a detailed autoethnographic analysis and incorporates anecdotal evidence to trace the transition of Kete dance-music from the Manhyia palace to the Academy (University of Ghana). The aim is to understand the factors in their transmission that have influenced the contemporary perception and performance of Kete. The autoethnographic position is grounded in the author's personal journey as the son of a chief who taught him Kete, offering insights into the evolving nature of this traditional dance-music form.

## The Context of African Dance: An Orientation to Movement

African dance has indeed been a subject of comprehensive exploration for decades from diverse viewpoints, with extensive research shedding light on this culturally rich and diverse form of expression. However, it is crucial to note that historical perspectives on African dance, particularly during the colonial era, were often misinformed or only partially understood. Colonial literature often portrayed African dance forms and the role of the black dancing body inaccurately, contributing to misconceptions about their functions and implications for identity. The devaluation of the black dancing body has persistently obstructed a comprehensive understanding of African performance literature. This issue has been a recurring challenge, particularly for non-African dance researchers, who may struggle to grasp the holistic nature of African dance. The black body serves as a canvas on which various elements such as music, musicality, visual components, and spirituality are vividly expressed. Attempting to isolate the body from these interconnected aspects—music, mythologies, context, and emotional expressivity—results in a fragmented comprehension that fails to capture the integral role of the body in African societies, even in contemporary times. The devaluation is reflective of the Western categorization of "high art" versus "low arts." Hélène Neveu Kringelbach shares that "the body has often been regarded as a still object, as the recipient of illness for example, or as moving according to barely conscious dispositions, as captured in Bourdieu's notion of habitus. Much of what we do is neither entirely conscious nor entirely intentional, but in dancing we are intensely present (if not always entirely conscious), expressive, and often creative."[2]. On the contrary, the body serves as an exceptionally potent medium for achieving a deeper understanding, especially in instances of spirit possession for healing and community cohesion. Additionally,

---

2 Hélène Neveu Kringelbach, *Dance Circles: Movement, Morality and Self-Fashioning in Urban Senegal*, Dance and Performance Studies (New York: Berghahn Books, 2013), https://login.ezproxy.library.ualberta.ca/login?url=https://search.ebscohost.com/login.aspx?direct=true&db=e000xna&AN=665967&site=eds-live&scope=site.

colonialist-written resources often misconstrue, due to their limited perspectives, the significance of dance as one of the most esteemed and privileged forms of expression among African people, a perception that endures to this day. Kringleback describes the misappropriation of the debunked concept of Cartesian dualism by French psychiatrist Henri Aubin in his characterization of African dance forms when he opines that "the multiplicity of circumstances in which under-evolved indigenous peoples dance can be attributed to the fact that dance is a rather elementary activity: motor response, usually rhythmic, responding to stimuli where sensory and emotional data play the main role. Instead of being expressed through complex intellectual representations and a rich vocabulary, their emotional states become actions [...] of which dance is, after all, a privileged form."[3] I find it intriguing that despite the devaluation of the black body, African dance traditions, with their use of dance music, have been employed by communities to heal and redefine themselves throughout centuries of slavery and collective trauma. Historian Toyin Falola contends that the influence of African spirituality, embedded in music and dance and expressed through the body, challenges the epistemological opposition to African arts. He shares that

> [...] [music and dance] have served as agencies of resistance and cultural nationalism during slavery, colonial domination, and thereafter in all places where the black experience has been shaped by domination, oppression, and exploitation. Orisa music and dance assault the entangling indignities brought on by commerce and mammon. In racialized contexts, most notably in the Americas and Europe, they add to how the boundaries of race are created and negotiated—indeed, they even create a moral order for blackness and for castigating oppression and those who participate in it. Through music and dance, Africans have been able to reinscribe their Africanness and identity in hostile, racialized environments, and women have particularly found a source of power to reinscribe their femininity in patriarchal spaces. (Falola 2013, 187)

Movement systems of African origin provide valuable anthropological and ethnochoreological insights into the evolution of African people through performance. Despite historical and contemporary injustices meted out to Africans, these movement systems continue to create avenues to thrive, whether on the continent or in the diaspora, thus captivating the curiosity of many. This volume aims to address fundamental questions about dance, such as where to begin the investigation and why it is necessary. It delves into the importance

---

3 Kringelbach et al. (2013).

of giving the agency of the black dancing body an African re-interpretation and advocates for dancers to speak up. The analysis of movement transmission from palace to academy (school) contributes to the expanding literature of African researchers and scholars who are also practitioners.

## The Colonial Background

British colonialism in Ghana, lasting from 1821 to 1957, had a significant impact on formal education, leading to the erosion of many indigenous knowledge systems among colonized Africans. In response to this historical context, it became essential to integrate Ghanaian indigenous music and dance into educational institutions after gaining independence. This initiative aimed to initiate postindependence educational reforms and reclaim indigenous cultural expressions.

The continuous performance and resilience of indigenous dances in contemporary times suggest that the foundations of an Afrocentric paradigm were established when ancestors began creating and performing the dances that researchers investigate today. The enduring relevance of these dances serves as a testament to their significance in shaping black or African identity and fostering growth. During the struggle for independence, traditional music and dance emerged as powerful mediums for a postcolonial shift toward reclaiming the African self. Ghana's first president, Kwame Nkrumah, played a pivotal role in using these expressive forms to valorize the black African self. The aesthetic qualities embedded in these dances encapsulate indigenous philosophical and cosmological knowledge, which not only survived but continues to thrive today, showcasing a remarkable degree of ontological and epistemological longevity. To comprehend the impact of colonization on indigenous knowledge in Africa and specifically in Ghana, one must examine the key factors that influenced African civilization, including its institutions of indigenous knowledge, economics, arts, and travel. Colonization disrupted these essential elements, leading to agitation among the colonized, which laid the groundwork for postcolonial education in Africa after independence. The schools established during colonization, particularly missionary schools, became influential agents in shaping African identities, often promoting Western ideologies to maintain control over the African populace. This subtle but pervasive influence weakened traditional arts and other aspects of indigenous knowledge, perpetuating a new form of domination. Ghanaian dance scholar Modesto Amegago (2000) stated:

> The Western educational system that has become dominant over the past thirty years has increased the problem of separating African

performing arts under subjects such as music, dance and theatre and the reproduction of new and individual professional artists. This educational system intensifies the alienation of African youths and their ambivalence toward African traditional cultures, including the arts. In addition, the mass commodification of the arts in this contemporary era has affected the educational, communicative and cultural functions of African performing arts and continues to reduce them to a state of entertainment.[4]

Amegago's observations are crucial to understanding the current state of dance scholarship in Ghana and other African states, where the languages of English, Portuguese, French, and Spanish, although lacking the depth and linguistic elasticity to explain movements, concepts, and contexts, were used to describe dances and dancing events of Africans for a long time anyway.

Falola (2013) notes that "western education made it possible to teach [these] languages, but it also began the process of teaching new skills in formal settings, generating occupations that defined prestige, income, and modernity,"[5] thereby displacing the role of indigenous languages and dance in the African way of life. Formal education has nevertheless become important in any analysis of dance knowledge and transmission because it is the context through which decolonization and reclamation of African indigenous knowledge, Pan-Africanism, and subsequently, Afrocentricity, become possible as a paradigmatic intellectual shift for the good of African knowledge. This study illuminates African dance as an enormous affective and intellectual resource that, when explored through the lenses of lived experience, autoethnography, and Afrocentricity, provides an avenue to legitimize and validate its relationship to indigenous knowledge systems, including its teaching, and understanding of its routes of embodiment and transmission.

When traditional dances were included in the Ghanaian higher education curriculum in 1963, it signaled a drastic contextual change from just performing neo-traditional renditions by the newly created Ghana Dance Ensemble (GDE) to becoming a politico-cultural element of the "African personality"

---

[4] Modesto Amegago, 'An Holistic Approach to African Performing Arts: Music and Dance Curriculum Development and Implementation', *ProQuest Dissertations and Theses* (2000).

[5] Toyin Falola, *The African Diaspora: Slavery, Modernity, and Globalization* (Boydell & Brewer, 2013), https://www.cambridge.org/core/books/african-diaspora/99E64922F04FD51 7890F5ABAD0E4C192.

and "African Genius" concepts Nkrumah preached after Independence[6] Traditional dances were adopted into the GDE repertoire, and, subsequently, their neo-traditional renditions became the foundation for further exploration by the School of Music and Drama. Subsequent Department of Dae Studies renditions became neo-traditional renditions, elaborating upon neo-traditional exploration of the GDE. Any attempt to discuss neo-traditional dances in Ghana must include rendition changes. From this interaction, we can see a conscious shift of the body moving from its traditional function into an "[...] intentional cooperation, or of the more or less willing co-optation of the dancer [...] by a bureaucratic state apparatus" (Franko 2006, 5). From Franko's explication of the German dancing body being explored from a nationalist point of view, we see, in less radical forms, the use of the body for nationalist positions in the case of the GDE from 1963.

Therefore, expanding Awuah's neo-traditional dance analysis with the term "neo-traditional" dances of the School of Performing Arts denotes the differences between the ensemble's performance of the African Personality concept and the Department of Dance Studies' further exploration of the same concept through academic design. My view is that dance analysis in Ghana should take the situation of decolonization politics into account. Such pathways would lead to discussions that could address a significant problem in dance transmission in the university where indigenous dance forms such as Kete, with its indigenous name variations and instructional languages, are

---

6 Kwame Botwe-Asamoah, *Kwame Nkrumah's Politico-Cultural Thought and Policies: An African-Centered Paradigm for the Second Phase of the African Revolution, Kwame Nkrumah's Politico-Cultural Thought and Policies: An African-Centered Paradigm for the Second Phase of the African Revolution*, 2005, https://doi.org/10.4324/9780203505694; Falola, *The African Diaspora: Slavery, Modernity, and Globalization*; Sylvanus Kwashie Kuwor, 'Transmission of Anlo-Ewe Dances in Ghana and in Britain: Investigating, Reconstructing and Disseminating Knowledge Embodied in the Music and Dance Traditions of Anlo-Ewe People in Ghana' (University of Roehampton, 2013), https://pure.roehampton.ac.uk/portal/en/studentTheses/transmission-of-anlo-ewe-dances-in-ghana-and-in-britain-investiga; Eric Awuah, 'A Study of Amateur Groups' Re-Interpretation of Traditional Dances in Ghana: Role on Continuity and Safeguarding1', *Acta Ethnographica Hungarica*, 2015, https://doi.org/10.1556/022.2015.60.1.6; Ofotsu Adinku, *African Dance Education in Ghana: Curriculum and Instructional Materials for a Model Bachelor of Arts (Hons.) Dance in Society* (Accra: Ghana Universities Press, 1994); Harcourt Fuller, 'Building a Nation: Symbolic Nationalism during the Kwame Nkrumah Era in the Gold Coast/Ghana' (University of London, 2010), https://login.ezproxy.library.ualberta.ca/login?url=https://search.ebscohost.com/login.aspx?direct=true&db=edsndl&AN=edsndl.oai.union.ndltd.org.bl.uk.oai.ethos.bl.uk.526756&site=eds-live&scope=site; Paul Schauert, 'A Performing National Archive: Power and Preservation in the Ghana Dance Ensemble', *Historical Society of Ghana* 10 (2007): 171–81.

transmitted in English and what the implications of this are on their structure. The problem with the English language being used as an oral medium of instruction,[7] is that it is not expansive enough to capture the depth of the *Twi* language, which has three content components, namely literary, metaphorical, and philosophical components.[8]

---

[7] Obed Mfum-Mensah, 'The Impact of Colonial and Postcolonial Ghanaian Language Policies on Vernacular Use in Schools in Two Northern Ghanaian Communities', *Comparative Education* 41, no. 1 (1 February 2005): 71–85, https://doi.org/10.1080/03050060500073256; Kwasi Opoku-Amankwa, 'English-Only Language-in-Education Policy in Multilingual Classrooms in Ghana', *Language, Culture and Curriculum* 22, no. 2 (1 July 2009): 121–35, https://doi.org/10.1080/07908310903075159; Emmanuel Quarcoo, 'The English Language as a Modern Ghanaian Artifact', *Journal of Black Studies* 24, no. 3 (9 March 1994): 329–43.

[8] Kofi Agyekum, Akan language, movements, and music, Interview, Summer 2021; K. Agyekum, 'The Sociolinguistics of Thanking in Akan', *Nordic Journal of African Studies* 19, no. 2 (2010): 21.

# Chapter 2

# ROYAL DANCE-MUSIC ORIGINS

In Ghana, dance serves a diverse range of purposes and undergoes transformative evolution as individuals and communities progress through various life stages. This chapter will thoroughly explore the landscape of dance scholarship in Ghana, critically examining its theoretical underpinnings from both Afrocentric and Anglo-European perspectives. The analysis aims to assess the profound impact of these viewpoints on dance transmission and scholarly pursuits within Ghana and the broader African context. Special attention will be given to the contributions of indigenous researchers in advancing dance research, with a focus on existing literature addressing Ghanaian dance, particularly the intricate Kete dance form. Throughout this exploration, the chapter will highlight the foundational role of Afrocentric paradigms in shaping Ghanaian dance theory and their crucial contribution to the global recognition of African dances in academic discourse.

The available literature supporting the epistemological exploration of dances from Africa/Ghana by insider/indigenous researchers is limited. Most existing literature from the rest of the world on African dances falls into categories such as historical colonial reports, early anthropological records depicting "primitive societies," neocolonial publications reflecting Western opinions about African dances, and some multicultural ethnomusicological texts. This exploration begins with an overview of the Traditional Kete dance form, tracing its historical roots and contemporary functions. The narrative then delves into the role of dance as a pivotal element in the post-Ghana independence Pan-Africanist revolution. A closer examination follows, scrutinizing the integration of dance into academia and its profound implications for the conceptualization and promotion of the "African Personality" ideology championed by Dr. Kwame Nkrumah.

I support the inclusion of an Afrocentric perspective in the analysis of Ghanaian performance practices, drawing on the deeply rooted practices and philosophies inherent in African indigenous traditions. This validation extends to concepts emerging from African dance-music forms. Initially introduced by Molefi Asante[1] and further championed by scholars like Frances Owusu-Ansah and Bubela Mji in their endeavors to establish the acknowledgment of African knowledge forms, there is a shared understanding of the necessity of adopting an Afrocentric approach. They emphasize the necessity of developing alternative approaches to studying African reality and advocate for steering away from reliance on Western methodologies.[2] This position by Owusu-Ansah and Mji underscores the critical need for African researchers to break away from conventional Western methodologies in their pursuit of understanding and preserving indigenous knowledge. It advocates for a shift toward alternative methods tailored to the African context. The intention is not to discredit established Western approaches but rather to challenge African scholars to explore diverse avenues of inquiry. This shift is crucial for the development and empowerment of African communities, emphasizing the importance of embracing methods that resonate with the unique realities, cultures, and knowledge systems indigenous to the African continent. By doing so, researchers can contribute to a more holistic and authentic representation of African experiences, fostering a richer understanding of the continent's diverse heritage.

This gradual shift toward alternative approaches holds the potential to strengthen indigenous knowledge systems, aligning them with the situational and contextual realities of Africans. It also supports the preservation of collaborative cultural frameworks rooted in the fundamental creative and cognitive capacities of Africans as interactive beings. It is essential to emphasize that Afrocentrism, while not seeking to negate or denigrate Anglo-European methods of inquiry, primarily aims to establish knowledge systems from Africa as intellectually potent. This is particularly important in challenging the theoretical and conceptual positions that colonialist ideologies have held, and continue to hold, over black people and scholarship. The advocacy for an Afrocentric analysis of dance serves as an invitation for researchers and scholars to adopt approaches that illuminate and safeguard indigenous knowledge, such as the Kete dance-music and the many other dance cultures across the continent, before they risk extinction. This approach aligns with the broader goal of preserving and celebrating the diverse cultural heritage of Africa within the realm of academic inquiry. As reiterated by Queeneth Mkabela, "Afrocentric theory and methods are derived from the Afrocentric

---

1 M. K. Asante, *Afrocentricity* (Trenton, NJ: Africa World Press, 1988).
2 Frances E. Owusu-Ansah and Gubela Mji, 'African Indigenous Knowledge and Research', *African Journal of Disability* 2, no. 1 (16 January 2013): 30, https://doi.org/10.4102/ajod.v2i1.30.

paradigm, which addresses questions of African identity from the perspective of African people as centered, oriented, and grounded."[3] This brings forth a crucial question: How can the Asante people assert ownership over the knowledge forms embedded in their music and dance traditions when the preservation methods, beyond embodied performances, are not inherently indigenous? Safeguarding elements that are inherently Twi in language through the medium of English poses a complex challenge.

Mkabela further asserts that Asante's concept of Afrocentricity calls for African individuals to embrace an epistemological standpoint and to traverse historical, economic, social, political, and philosophical dimensions.[4] Asante expands Afrocentricity to include the ideas of geo-political, environmental, and spiritual dislocation, underscoring their importance, as their absence results in a state of being lost. He argues that

> to say that we [African people] are decentered means essentially that we have lost our own cultural footing and become other than our cultural and political origins, dis-located and dis-oriented. We are essentially insane, that is, living an absurdity from which we will never be able to free our minds until we return to the source. Afrocentricity as a theory of change intends to re-locate the African person as subject. [...] As a pan-African idea, Afrocentricity becomes the key to the proper education of children and the essence of an African cultural revival and, indeed, survival.[5]

From this theoretical perspective, Asante argues that Afrocentricity can significantly shape how African researchers perceive their identity and their role in utilizing indigenous knowledge forms for national development. This theoretical framework becomes crucial in establishing connections between nature and knowledge embedded in the construction of Kete dance, for example, as a culturally specific communication tool, particularly through the embodied response of dance. This holistic perspective, as proposed by Ghanaian dance scholar Sylvanus Kuwor, encompasses four key elements: the body (movements and gestures), music (sound and rhythm), visual forms (costumes, shapes, designs, patterns, and colors), and multisensory modalities

---

3 Queeneth Mkabela, 'Using the Afrocentric Method in Researching Indigenous African Culture', *Qualitative Report* 10, no. 1 (1 March 2005): 178–89.
4 Mkabela.
5 M. K. Asante, *Afrocentricity, the Theory of Social Change*. (Amulefi Pub. Co., 1980), https://login.ezproxy.library.ualberta.ca/login?url=https://search.ebscohost.com/login.aspx?direct=true&db=cat03710a&AN=alb.392106&site=eds-live&scope=site.

(kinesthetic senses, including balance and internal feelings).[6] By integrating the Afrocentric paradigm with the holistic outlook and the dancing body, we explore the nuanced components of Kete, identifying it as a significant marker for the Asante/Akan people in Ghana and as an agent of Ghanaian identity in the diaspora. Drawing on my personal experiences as a dancer, teacher, and researcher, I analyze Kete as an embodied agency of representation and communication deeply rooted in Akan/Asante philosophies. Furthermore, I underscore the importance of individual Kete dance practitioners by adopting a hermeneutic phenomenological approach. This represents the initial endeavor in Kete dance scholarship to record their distinctive dance expertise in Kete, providing valuable insights into the structural intricacies practiced both in academic settings and royal palaces. I consider the dancing body as a repository of lived experiences, encapsulating not only my own but also those of fellow Kete practitioners. This viewpoint serves as a manifestation of African Indigenous Knowledge Systems, presented through the lens of the Afrocentric paradigm.

## Kete Dance Literature Today

For more than five decades, there has been a notable absence of a comprehensive study on Kete dance employing a combination of phenomenological, anthropological, and Afrocentric perspectives by an indigenous researcher. In this section, my objective is twofold: first, to employ an Afrocentric framework in justifying Kete Dance as an indigenous epistemology; second, to substantiate the agency of the black dancing body through the lenses of phenomenology and autoethnography. The text incorporates anecdotes from my personal experiences as an embodied Kete dancer and teacher. Finally, the findings will be contextualized within the broader field of dance studies.

Several existing works by both Ghanaian and non-Ghanaian scholars have delved into Kete, but a distinct gap remains as none have exclusively focused on movement analysis. In the 1960s, the esteemed Ghanaian scholar J. H. Nketia delved into the history and sociocultural significance of Kete.[7] His student Ampofo Duodu extended this exploration in 1972, delving into the study of Akan court music and dance with specific attention to the linguistic

---

6 Sylvanus Kwashie Kuwor, 'Understanding African Dance in Context: Perspectives from Ghana', *The Journal of Pan African Studies (Online)* 10, no. 4 (2017): 47.

7 J. H. K. Nketia and A. P. Merriam, 'Drumming in Akan Communities of Ghana', *Ethnomusicology*, 1965, https://doi.org/10.2307/850333.

implications of performance, of which Kete is a vital component.[8] Professor Alberta Mawere Opoku, an esteemed colleague of his and the inaugural choreographer and artistic director of the Ghana Ensemble, also contributed to the literature on Asante court dance etiquette. In his work, he delved into the parameters of movements, considering factors such as social class and knowledge of the form.[9]

In subsequent years, scholars such as Kwasi Ampene and Paschal Younge[10] have contributed to the historical and contemporary understanding of Kete dance, exploring both its traditional roots and performance structures. The period from the late 1950s through the 1960s witnessed a convergence of nationalism, African cultural systems, and the independence of African states from colonial rule, driven by the ideals of Pan-Africanism. This era brought about diverse dynamics in Ghanaian cultural research, with dance playing a pivotal role, notably within the context of the Ghana Dance Ensemble. Researcher Paul Schauert extensively examined the Ghana Dance Ensemble and its connection to nationalism, providing in-depth analyses of the hybridization of traditional dances by professional dance companies in Ghana (Schauert 2007; Schauert 2011; Schauert 2013), thereby enriching existing dance literature. Professor Albert Mawere Opoku[11] made significant contributions by being the first to include a movement description of the Kete dance and, by extension, characteristic feet and hand movements of dances from Asante courts in Ghanaian dance literature. Additionally, Joseph Kaminski,

---

8 Ampofo Emmanuel Duodu, 'Drumming and Dancing in Akan Society: A Study of Court Musical and Dancing Tradition' (Wesleyan University, 1972); Ampofo Emmanuel Duodu, 'Topics in African Dance and the Related Arts', *Legon Journal*, 1994.
9 Albert Mawere Opoku, 'Asante Dance Art and the Court', in *The Golden Stool: Studies of the Asante Center and Periphery*, ed. Enid Schildkrout and Carol Gelber (New York, NY: American Museum of Natural History, 1987), 192–99.
10 Kwasi Ampene, *Asante Court Music and Verbal Arts in Ghana: The Porcupine and the Gold Stool.* (Routledge, 2020), https://login.ezproxy.library.ualberta.ca/login?url=https://search.ebscohost.com/login.aspx?direct=true&db=cat03710a&AN=alb.9087114&site=eds-live&scope=site; K Ampene et al., *Discourses in African Musicology: J.H. Kwabena Nketia Festschrift* (African Studies Center, University of Michigan, 2015), https://books.google.ca/books?id=iDfNsgEACAAJ; Paschal Yao. Younge, *Music and Dance Traditions of Ghana: History, Performance and Teaching* (Jefferson, NC: McFarland & Co., 2011).
11 Opoku, 'Asante Dance Art and the Court'.

Ben Paulding, and James Koetting[12] offered a musicological analysis of the drum music accompanying Kete dance.

In 2015, I contributed to existing literature by conducting a movement analysis of Kete dance as part of my MA African Studies thesis titled *The Contexts and Meaning in Asante Dance Performance: The Case of Kete*.[13] As previously established through the works of J. H. Nketiah, who extensively explored Ghanaian musical cultures, much of earlier literary data on African dance and music forms that gained widespread readership globally were produced by nonindigenous/non-African writers. The omission or lack of proper attention to the nuanced details in the analysis of African dance forms, accompanied by literature in world dance literature by indigenous researchers, has necessitated this work. One significant issue with dance analysis by "others" is the apparent misunderstanding of the meaning of music, dance, or drama to the indigenous Ghanaian and how these are embodied through constant performance. While music, dance, ritual, and dramatic actions are often separated in Western contexts, indigenous cultures, especially in Ghana, intertwine music and dance seamlessly. The essence of music lies in its ability to move people with purpose. Therefore, most African music forms have accompanying dances that share the same name as their musical counterparts. Separating the music alone and drawing conclusions using Western instruments of analysis may gain international recognition, but it does a disservice to the forms in the long run.

I refer to the term "dance-musicking" coined by a Ugandan dance scholar as an apt insider terminology for studying movement systems in Africa. Ronald Kibirige, in a seminar presentation on March 18, 2021, defined dance-musicking within the concept of communal action, reaction, and interactive exchanges. He stated, "Dance-Musicking is a free and non-prescriptive engagement with music for dancing, before, and during the dancing. A

---

12 Ben Paulding, 'Kete for the International Percussion Community', in *Discourses in African Musicology: J.H. Kwabena Nketia Festschrift*, ed. Kwasi Ampene et al. (Michigan: African Studies Center, University of Michigan, 2015), 156–85; Ben Paulding, 'Asante Kete Drumming: A Musical Analysis of Meter, Feel, and Phrasing', *ProQuest Dissertations and Theses* (Ann Arbor: Tufts University, 2017), https://login.ezproxy.library.ualberta.ca/login?url=https://www.proquest.com/dissertations-theses/asante-kete-drumming-musical-analysis-meter-feel/docview/1964391636/se-2?accountid=14474; *Asante Kete Drumming: Music from Ghana* (New York, NY: Lyrichord Discs, 2007), http://www.aspresolver.com/aspresolver.asp?WOMU.

13 Emmanuel Cudjoe, *The Contexts and Meaning In Asante Dance Performance: The Case of Kete* (Accra, Ghana: University of Ghana, 2015).

process of making music through the enaction of dance movements."[14] Much needs to be done to reconcile the conterminous relationship between movement and music in Ghanaian performance research. I propose that indigenous students of Ghanaian dance-musicking be trained to reconcile the role of music and dance in their analysis, providing nuanced perspectives rather than separate analyses of performance forms that serve dual purposes but bear one name. Since considerable work has been done on the analysis of Kete music and history, I intend to add an Afro-phenomenological analysis to demonstrate how a merger could benefit future analyses.

## Kete Dance, Phenomenology, and Afrocentrism

Before my 2015 MA thesis, there was a notable absence of comprehensive data on the movement component of the Kete dance form. Despite its widespread reach and popularity within and outside of Ghana, Kete remains one of the least critically explored dances in both Ghanaian and global dance scholarship, a puzzling gap that this research seeks to address. Ben Paulding acknowledges the notable absence of Kete in international music literature, emphasizing that despite its fusion of rhythm, energy, and intricate combinations of multisensory modalities, there has been limited exploration of Kete music.[15] In reaction to this, this volume contributes movement analysis through phenomenological and Afrocentric lenses, examining how these omissions have hindered the comprehensive and objective study of movement systems both on the African continent and in the diaspora. I examine how these challenges can be reversed by highlighting the agency of the black Kete dancing body.

In my 2015 research on Kete, I explored the context and meanings behind selected movements in the Kete dance form, namely *Tefrɛayiyanda, Dwannyinimienushia a nayehu bɛɛma, Pɛpɛɛpɛ, Nkabom and Ahudedɛ*[16] and through a structural analytical approach, I detailed the performance of these movement variations within the Kete performance, provided their contextual justification and added pictures to aid identification. I previously emphasized the potential origins of the dance, exploring both mythological and historical perspectives. At that time, I did not delve into the authenticity of either,

---

14 Ronald Kibirige, *Inherent Community-Based Agendas in Dancing and Dance-Musicking Traditions in Uganda* (Accra, Ghana: Department of Dance Studies, University of Ghana, 2021).
15 Paulding, 'Kete for the International Percussion Community'.
16 Cudjoe, *The Contexts and Meaning in Asante Dance Performance: The Case of Kete*.

recognizing their varied yet similar nature. During my field research for this project, I coincidentally encountered these origin stories once again, reaffirmed by two distinct informants at different instances. Therefore, it is crucial to reiterate and document these narratives here for reference. Kaminski explores the mythological origin of Kete and states that

> the music of *Kete* is reputed to possess the power of attracting good spirits [...] [Nketia] explains that the surrogated texts extol high moral values through the telling of heroic ideals and a *Kete* dance must be developed with the involvement of symbolic hand gestures reflecting these values. It is danced barefooted and trained male dancers dance with their *Lapa* cloth lowered beneath the chest. ('Asante Kete drumming: music from Ghana.' 2007)

Former Asante court dancer and Kete music and dance expert mentor, Baffour Kyeremanteng,[17] recounts that

> Even though we do not have a specific root of the name [...] *Kete* happened to be "hunters drumming" and this is because the original *Kete* [was called] is *Abɔfoagorɔ*.[18] So, we [the Asantes] conquered the *Kete* dance during war [*Kete*-Krachi3]. This is evident of the symbolic cloth used to cover the *Kete* drums known as *sum ne mogya*, meaning darkness and blood. Everything our ancestors did had a meaning. *Sum ne mogya* further explains that if one goes to war and there is no death, there should still be blood.[19]

These two narratives lend credibility to aspects of Asante cosmology, illustrating the intricate relationship between the spirit and natural realms. Indigenous Asante beliefs embrace the coexistence of spirits alongside human beings, and thus, it's not surprising that one root of the Kete dance, like other traditional dances, mirrors this interconnected reality. The second source emphasizes the significance the Asante attach to spirituality and history, demonstrating how they embody and preserve their narratives through music and dance forms. This underscores the profound spiritual dimension inherent in African worldviews, affirming a nuanced understanding of humans transitioning between the earthly, ancestral, and divine realms. Citizenship

---

17 Passed on to the ancestral world in 2021 before my fieldwork in the summer of 2021. May he rest in peace.
18 *Abɔfoagorɔ* literally translates 'Hunter's play'. *Abɔfoɔ* translates to hunters and *agorɔ* translates into play/music/dance.
19 Cudjoe, *The Contexts and Meaning in Asante Dance Performance: The Case of Kete*.

and pride are deeply ingrained in Asante identity, particularly in their music, dance forms, and overall culture. Akyeampong and Obeng explain that

> the Asante universe was suffused with power. *Onyame* (the Supreme Being) had created a universe impregnated with his power. Power was thus rooted in the Asante cosmology, and individuals and groups that successfully tapped into this power source translated this access into authority if they controlled social institutions. Authority (political power) could be monopolized, but access to power (Twi: tumi:, "the ability to bring about change") was available to anyone who knew how to make use of *Onyame's* powerful universe for good or evil.[20]

This reflection is embodied in Asante music and dance forms, as has been proven through the possible origins of Kete. Further, one sees a close relationship between power and social roles in the performance of most Asante dance forms. Opoku highlights this key relationship by stating that

> the Asante dance experience reflects several aspects of traditional Asante society and depicts its birth and development along with its distinctive methods of expressing commonly accepted ideas and ideals, such as reverence for the elderly and for status. Asante dance is an almost unconscious expression of the religious and spiritual beliefs of daily life, and of Asante's steadfast faith in the achievements of its forebears. It also expresses the Asante's self-confidence, and love for the elegant and sophisticated. There is room too for individualization, for each performer seeks to highlight his personal experience in movement; the dance is a dramatization of traditional Asante customs and of the dancer's individual status in the society.[21]

These result in cultural etiquette that becomes the benchmark for performance in public. Opoku thus affirms that

> Asante etiquette pays great attention to hierarchy: only title holders may dance the court dances with their sandals on and their shoulders covered. Certain gestures are reserved for senior rulers; for instance, placing the right fist atop the left fist indicates one who "sits" on others (that is, belongs to a higher chieftaincy rank) and can only be made by those

---

20  Emmanuel Akyeampong and Pashington Obeng, 'Spirituality, Gender, and Power in Asante History', *The International Journal of African Historical Studies*, 1995, https://doi.org/10.2307/221171.
21  Opoku, 'Asante Dance Art and the Court'.

of that rank. It is not enough, even for a chief, to be an expert dancer; he must also be very conversant with the traditional language of gesture or else he faces censure and, possibly, reprimand and heavy fines.[22]

Ben Paulding furthers this by listing 17 variations of the Kete dance-musicking in his work, including "*Kuokuo Nisuo, Akwduom, Adamrebua, Abofoo, Adabanka, Adowa kete, Adaban, Wofa-Ata, Kyeretwie, Kyremanteng, Apente, Akatape, Ohenko, Akokonobente, Akyakyakuntu, Sresrebidi, and Adinkra.*"[23] Regrettably, none of these variations are reflected in the instructional materials for Kete within academic settings and among numerous amateur groups. This raises a significant concern, prompting the question, "do performers understand the variations they are executing, along with their corresponding meanings and contexts?" It is imperative for competent dancers, particularly within indigenous settings, to comprehend these rhythmic variations and appropriately respond to changes within specific performance contexts. However, the widespread adoption of the "hybrid" Kete by the Ghana Dance Ensemble has led to the emergence of amateur dance groups, often neglecting contextual significance and prioritizing dancing prowess. The incorporation of Kete into the repertoire of the Ghana Dance Ensemble dates back to its early operations in 1963,[24] operating under the authority of the Asante monarchy. During this period, performing Kete required special permission (Adinku 2000).

This permission led to the creation of a hybridized version of the Kete dance and would go on to "alter" how the rest of Ghana and the world would see Kete dance from then till date. Borrowing from Oluwatoyin Olokodana-James' concept of Trans-Sociological Hybridity (TSH) to describe such a two-way relationship between traditional and contemporary culture he

> [...] observes that human environment and culture have taken on new nomenclatures and identities reached via a synergy of diverse systemic juxta positioning of sociological actuality and imaginary conceptual frames operating beyond descriptive or restricted borders. This however is conceptualized as hybridity. As a "postcolonial" concept, "Hybridity" emerged following the migration of humans from one place to another,

---

22 Opoku.
23 Paulding, 'Kete for the International Percussion Community'.
24 Patience Kwakwa, 'Kwabena Nketia and the Creative Arts: The Genesis of the School of Music and Drama, and the Formation of the Ghana Dance Ensemble', in *Discourses in African Musicology: J.H. Kwabena Nketia Festschrift*, ed. Kwasi Ampene et al. (Michigan: African Studies Center, University of Michigan, 2015), 480–506.

and the consequential diffusion of human cultures and values toward the creation of a new form of characterization and identification.[25]

This experimental relationship then served as a precedent for the creation of neo-traditional dance forms, exemplified by the migration of Kete from the Asante Manhyia palace to the University of Ghana. Adinku highlighted that, in certain instances, Opoku, with assistance from Professor J. H. Nketia, who was the Director of the Ghana Dance Ensemble and the Institute of African Studies, had to secure permission from the "custodians" to use the dances. In 1963, the Asantehene, Sir Nana Osei Agyemang Prempeh II, was informed and granted permission to stage the Kete dance. This permission was crucial, as Kete had been exclusively reserved for the Asantehene court.[26] Once permissions were obtained, Opoku bore the choreographic responsibility of integrating traditional concepts inherent in the dance with the new postcolonial Pan-Africanist rhetoric prevalent in the development of Ghana after gaining independence. The dance had to mirror the evolving paradigms of nationalism while simultaneously contributing to shaping a cultural representation that would resonate with all Ghanaians from diverse ethnic backgrounds.

The dance had to reflect the changing paradigms of nationalism and contribute at the same time to shaping a cultural representation that would be endearing to all Ghanaians of different ethnicities. Adinku explains that

> the traditional performance of the *Kete* dance is not as elaborate in terms of movement structure and spatial organization as is found in Opoku's arrangements. The traditional form is often a solo dance or duet accompanied by an orchestra. In Opoku's presentation, a personality emerges which is made up of his different uses of space, line, direction, dynamics, timing, levels and enactment. His brand of *Kete* is a group piece danced by four, six, or eight people arranged in linear and circular paths. These dancers are supported by a group of drummers, flutists, horn-blowers, and such characters as a chief, a queen, an umbrella carrier, and sword—and shield bearers—all grouped upstage centre. Opoku calls this fusion of *Kete* music, dance and pageantry the "Akan Ceremonial Dance Suite.[27]

---

25 Oluwatoyin Olokodana-James, 'Trans-Sociological Hybridity: Conceptualizing African Contemporary Dance Identity', in *Culture and Development in Africa and the Diaspora*, ed. Ahamad Sheuh Abdussalam et al. (London: Routledge, 2020), 95–109, https://doi.org/10.4324/9780429316296.
26 Ofotsu Adinku, 'The Protection of Choreographic Works in Ghana', *Matatu* 21–22, no. 1 (2000): 351–54, https://doi.org/10.1163/18757421-90000338.
27 Adinku.

The success of this type of experiment can even be seen today, with its ensuing philosophical implications being paramount in today's performance of Kete. Today, one can see "group/unison choreographed movement variations" of Kete, which was and is still not the norm in the indigenous performance setting. Mawere Opoku mixed, at random, different music and movement variations in his recreation as artistic director of the Ensemble, but not many practitioners of the dance today are aware of this to the point of even understanding why. What makes Opoku's rendition not easily detected by current neo-traditional propagators of the form today is the lack of understanding of the culture and relevance of music and dance to the Asante's that Opoku had and, most importantly, literature about this experimentation. He, like Nketia, hailed from Asante royal families, and as such, their use of the materials was predicated on their embodied understanding of the forms from their backgrounds. Opoku's exposition of Kete movement systems is a testimony to this. He states that "the distinguishing characteristics of Asante dance are the intricate and subtle manipulation of hands, arms and legs, body sways and tilts in polyrhythmic combinations—expressive miming with rich symbolic undertones and typical Asante hauteur."[28] As such, it can be inferred that performing Kete in Kumasi carried great importance for the individual dancer and the overall theme it conveys of Asante culture and history. As such, selecting Kete as part of the national repertoire reiterated Nkrumah's call for the revitalization of the African glorious past. Allan Lomax averred that "an individual's wisdom, knowledge and self-respect are measured against how much he knows about himself and about the society in which he lives. The individual should also be competent in oral literature and court manners. The dance is composed of those gestures, postures and movements which are qualities most characteristic and most essential to everyday activities, and thus crucial to cultural continuity" (Lomax in Duodu 1994).

## Afrocentricity: An Imperative Epistemological Framework

According to Molefi Kete Asante, Afrocentricity prioritizes African ideals in the analysis of topics related to Africa. Its incorporation into this work is essential to elucidate its role in establishing an epistemic framework that supports and advances dance research scholarship. Positioned as a vital channel, Afrocentricity contributes to the redefinition of African dance performance and representation by emphasizing indigenous knowledge systems as primary sources. It becomes crucial for reevaluating current educational models in

---

28 Opoku, 'Asante Dance Art and the Court'.

Africa and those discussing Africa, reaffirming African knowledge within the global educational discourse through an African-centered paradigm. The urgency in this quest is a result of "African and its cultural heritage like dance and music [becoming] marginalized in their own story portrayed through 'African dances,' [being] held victim by the most ambitious social theorist the West has produced and, as such needing a radical and critical turn-around to liberates Africans from such European gaze."[29] I posit that if African interest in her cultural heritage forms such as dance and music is to be protected from negative "external and globalized" influences, there needs to be an epistemological shift toward conceptual frameworks that can interpret the African elements precisely rather than resorting to "distant" assertions that do more harm to her analysis than good. Kehbuma Langmia's extrapolation of Asante's Afrocentricity helps position the agency of the body in perspective. Langmia avers that Afrocentricity is a framework where phenomena, including dance, can be examined from the perspective of the African individual. It revolves around empowering individuals of African descent to take control of their lives and perspectives on the world. This entails scrutinizing every facet of the dislocation experienced by African people, encompassing culture, health, psychology, and religion. As an intellectual theory, Afrocentricity involves studying ideas and events with Africans as central participants rather than victims. This theory, rooted in an authentic connection to our own reality, evolves into a fundamentally empirical endeavor—African self-assertion intellectually and psychologically, challenging Western dominance in the mind and, by extension, in every other domain.[30]

I employ Afrocentricity here to establish the primacy of African performance and aesthetic experiences. If Asante dance forms encapsulate the visual, vibratory, and multisensory elements of Asante life, attempting to explain them through an "alien" worldview becomes questionable. Afrocentrism critically enhances aesthetic analysis by centering the agency of the black dancing body. Asante dance movement systems become intellectual exercises that foster interdisciplinary connections with symbology and folklore. In African performance practices, the interconnectedness of music, movements, visual elements, and context is crucial to understanding the meaning and functions of the performance forms. For instance, specific organizing principles

---

29 M. K. Asante, *The Afrocentric Idea* (Temple University Press, 1987), https://books.google.ca/books?id=H5txAAAAMAAJ.

30 Kehbuma Langmia, 'Debunking the Truth through a Video Documentary: A Case Study of Henry Louis Gates' "Wonders of the African World"', *Journal of Third World Studies* 31, no. 2 (5 February 2014): 83–99.

in Asante dances reflect politico-cultural beliefs, gender disparities, and gestural leverage, influencing the sociological and scientific habits of a dancer. For instance, court dances such as Kete place a strong emphasis on greetings, a fundamental element woven into the fabric of Akan living. This practice reflects not only respect but also holds deep cultural symbolism within the Akan community. Through the lens of Afrocentricity, these nuanced forms of communication, which are often neglected in the corpus of Kete movement analysis and influences, are validated, dignifying their profound relevance in understanding the history, context, and agency of Asante life. Afrocentricity acknowledges and elevates these cultural intricacies, enriching the exploration of Asante traditions and emphasizing the importance of recognizing and preserving such practices in the broader context of African heritage.

## Afrocentricity, Language, and Education

Within Ghanaian dance scholarship, traditional dances have been documented by ethnographers and analyzed by historians for years, but there has yet to be an exclusive exploration of a dance from an autoethnographic and Afrocentric paradigms. As a music form, however, Kete has been much explored by ethnomusicologists.[31]

I examine not only the personal agency afforded by my lived experience but also that of other indigenous authors, including drummers, chiefs, performers, drum makers, and teachers, who continue to influence the embodiment and transmission of Kete.

To explain the transition of Kete, as with other traditional dance-music forms in Africa, from an indigenous function to national and Pan-Africanist use, I employ Afrocentric theory in this book to situate the agency of the black dancing body as a representation of African knowledge system capable of transforming life and as a conceptual frame for exploring dance traditions in Ghana.

---

31 J. H. K. Nketia, 'The Role of the Drummer in Akan Society', *African Music: Journal of the African Music Society* 1, no. 1 (1 December 1954): 34–43, https://doi.org/10.21504/amj.vli1.225; J H K Nketia, 'The Interrelations of African Music and Dance', *Studia Musicologica Academiae Scientiarum Hungaricae* 7, no. 1/4 (28 September 1965): 91–101, https://doi.org/10.2307/901416; Ampene et al., *Discourses in African Musicology: J.H. Kwabena Nketia Festschrift*; Ampene, *Asante Court Music and Verbal Arts in Ghana: The Porcupine and the Gold Stool.*; Willie Anku, 'Drumming among the Akan and the Anlo Ewe of Ghana: An Introduction', *African Music* 8, no. 3 (28 September 2009): 38–64.

Afrocentricity offers a unique perspective on indigenous African knowledge forms as fundamental to understanding African phenomena.[32] Afrocentricity, as explained by its originator Molefi Asante-Kete, is

> a paradigmatic intellectual perspective that privileges African agency within the context of African history and culture trans-continentally and trans-generationally. This means that the quality of location is essential to any analysis that involves African culture and behavior whether literary or economic, whether political or cultural. In this regard it is the crystallization of a critical perspective on facts. (Asante 2007, 3)

Application of an Afrocentric paradigm in the analysis of Kete dance has been explored extensively by Molefi Kete Asante (1980, 1987, 1988, 2007), who agreed that the illumination of African agency of culture would be a creditable approach to the present study of African intellectual development. Asante adopted the name Kete in Ghana during his visit to a palace, signaling his transition to embodying his African personality and self (Molefi Asante, personal communication, 2021). I noticed from our conversation that this moment may have also emboldened him spiritually to propagate an African indigenous knowledge, a mission he has pursued throughout his academic life. Like Asante, my affinity with phenomena of African agency and indigenous knowledge derives from my Asante heritage and practice as a Kete dance performer, moving me to propagate this knowledge as a cultural responsibility. Ama Mazama notes that within academia, Afrocentricity is best comprehended as "a paradigm [...] [which] must activate our consciousness to be of any use to us."[33] Afrocentricity is rooted in a complex history because it represents "a mixture ('cocktail') of thoughts, ideas and emotions" (Khokholkova 2016, 115). It is apt for this research because of the complex relationship dance has with all of its four categories and their proponents in Ghana.

Considering African dance analysis from an Afrocentric perspective can expand the epistemological tenets of African/Ghanaian dance, dancing, and

---

32 M. K. Asante, *An Afrocentric Manifesto: Toward an African Renaissance* (Wiley, 2007), https://books.google.ca/books?id=4hdyAAAAMAAJ; Asante, *Afrocentricity*; Ama Mazama, 'The Afrocentric Paradigm: Contours and Definitions', *Journal of Black Studies* 31, no. 4 (2001); George Sefa Dei, 'The Role of Afrocentricity in the Inclusive Curriculum in Canadian Schools', *Canadian Journal of Education* 21, no. 2 (1996); Asante, *Afrocentricity, the Theory of Social Change.*; Ana Monteiro-Ferreira, *The Demise of the Inhuman: Afrocentricity, Modernism, and Postmodernism* (Albany: State University of New York, 2014).
33 Asante, *An Afrocentric Manifesto: Toward an African Renaissance.*

dancers as agents of intersubjective communication. Within this, I believe dance students and scholars could situate their discourses within the "African personality" and "African genius" paradigms and draw on these to explain other movement phenomena within traditional dancing in Ghana and Africa as a whole. Such advancements will help to address a significant problem in dance transmission at the university where indigenous dance forms such as Kete, with their indigenous name variations and instructional language, are transmitted in the English language. This is the time to explore the *Twi* language, with its three content components—literary, metaphorical, and philosophical,[34] for the teaching of dances in the University.

For example, Nketia (1986) noted that colonial administrators and historians, although they may have had an appreciation for the forms, fell short in their analysis using western tools. He stated that existing literature from earlier times,

> [...] brings to the foreground some of the difficulties that hindered understanding and appreciation of African music as an art and a mode of communication. These difficulties were created not only by the apparent strangeness of the sounds to some observers but also by the assumption that the aesthetic principles or critical values of western art music provide a valid basis for approaching the music of other cultures. (Nketia 1986, 21)

An Afrocentric paradigm privileges Akan ethnolinguistic elements as crucial to the analysis and propagation of indigenous music and dance forms. My personal experiences performing Kete over the years support the assertion that "many of the cultural institutions [like music, dance, rituals] survived the colonial period [...] the argument in the postcolonial states is that such institutions should even form the basis of contemporary development."[35] This suggests that the significance of work such as this reaches beyond Ghana and will contribute to understanding of Kete, even within the diaspora. Postcolonial theory is applied in this research to examine knowledge forms of "the other," as in the colonized Africans. Like Afrocentricity, postcoloniality reverses power structures and can free the colonized from seeing themselves as lesser beings (Kuwor 2013; 2017; Schauert 2013; Awuah 2015; Kwakwa 2015; Adinku 2004; Cornelius and Iddrisu 2019; Opoku 1987; Nketia 1965; 2019; 2005; Petrie 2015; Young 2004; Fanon 2008; Welsh-Asante 1990).

---

34 Kuwor, 'Understanding African Dance in Context: Perspectives from Ghana'.
35 Falola, *The African Diaspora: Slavery, Modernity, and Globalization*.

## Afrocentricity and Kete Movement Analysis

I posit that an Afrocentric approach to movement analysis extends beyond cultural immersion and the adaptation of tools and methods; it serves as a medium for advocating the interpretation of research data from indigenous African perspectives. In this context, Afrocentricity becomes a powerful lens through which to view and understand the intricacies of movement in a way that aligns with the cultural nuances and lived experiences of African communities. By employing this mode of analysis, the research aims not only to explore movement forms but also to actively contribute to the promotion and validation of indigenous African perspectives in scholarly discourse.[36] An Afrocentric mode allowed me to access deep-layered and contextual primary data through respectful and culturally affirming participant engagement rather than extractive research (Oba 2018). Melanie Carter's assertion that "our stories are our theories and method" (2003, 40) is particularly apt in this context. The movements of Kete not only serve as the foundational elements of analysis but, more importantly, they validate their philosophical efficacy. In embracing the stories embedded in the movements, this research recognizes the profound role narratives play in shaping theories and methodologies. The dance becomes more than a mere physical expression; it becomes a repository of cultural narratives and philosophical insights that enrich the Afrocentric approach to movement analysis. The intertwining of stories and movements serves as a powerful conduit for understanding and interpreting the depth of cultural meaning inherent in Kete. According to Molefi Asante, the "hallowed" concepts and methods from Anglo-European thoughts are inadequate to explain all the ways of human knowing, as "universality can only be dreamed about when we have 'slept' on truth based on specific cultural experiences."[37]

As a Kete performer, it is incumbent upon me not to replicate research methods that treat African culture, specifically Kete dance, as passive objects, but rather as integral subject matter. Given the diverse approaches to qualitative research outlined by scholars such as Margaret Wilson,[38] the emer-

---

36 Asante, *Afrocentricity*; Owusu-Ansah and Mji, 'African Indigenous Knowledge and Research'.
37 Asante, *The Afrocentric Idea*.
38 Margaret Wilson, 'Dance Pedagogy Case Studies: A Grounded Theory Approach to Analyzing Qualitative Data', *Research in Dance Education* 10, no. 1 (2009): 3–16, https://doi.org/10.1080/14647890802697148; Kathy. Charmaz, *Grounded Theory: Objectivist and Constructivist Methods* (Thousand Oaks, CA: Sage, 2000); Norman K. Denzin and Yvonna S. Lincoln, 'Introduction: Critical Methodologies and Indigenous Inquiry In: Handbook of Critical and Indigenous Methodologies Introduction:

gent emphasis on experiential ways of knowing strongly resonated with me. Consequently, I chose to combine this experiential focus with the Afrocentric approach in the context of this work. This approach elevates the lived experiences inherent in Kete dance, aligning with the ethos of Afrocentricity.

Elaborating on the significance of a qualitative Afrocentric approach to data interpretation, Olufunke Oba underscores that "African epistemology offers unique opportunities for knowledge co-creation as well as textured, layered, and contextualized data that quantitative methods may not allow."[39] She contends that qualitative research "focuses on meaning-making about a phenomenon and enables exploration of context and complexity using a variety of data collection sources" (Olufunke 2018). This sentiment is echoed by George Sefa Dei, who emphasizes that "Afrocentric research honors knowledge that resonates with Africans and is based on the philosophical position that we must understand Africa on its own terms."[40] As Afrocentrism aims at cultural reclamation, leveraging African epistemology to redress colonial disruptions is crucial, offering indigenous knowledge as a counter to historical Anglo-American positioning in research.[41] My work affirms the role of indigenous knowledge in the Kete dance form, providing Ghanaian, African, and international scholars with a perspective rooted in the experiences of an indigenous practitioner and researcher.

---

Critical Methodologies and Indigenous Inquiry', 2008, https://doi.org/10.4135/9781483385686; Norman K. Denzin and Yvonna S. Lincoln, *The SAGE Handbook of Qualitative Research*, ed. Norman K. Denzin and Yvonna S. Lincoln, *Choice Reviews Online* (Sage Publications, 2005), https://doi.org/10.5860/choice.43-1330; Michael Quinn Patton, 'Two Decades of Developments in Qualitative Inquiry: A Personal, Experiential Perspective', *Qualitative Social Work* 1, no. 3 (1 September 2002): 261–83, https://doi.org/10.1177/1473325002001003636.

39 Oba Olufunke, *It Takes a Village-Schooling out of Place: School Experiences of Black African Youth in Waterloo Region* (Wilfrid Laurier University, 2018), https://scholars.wlu.ca/etd/2015/.

40 George Sefa Dei, *Indigenous Philosophies and Critical Education, A Reader- Foreword by Akwasi Asabere-Ameyaw* (New York, NY: Peter Lang Verlag, 2011), https://www.peterlang.com/document/1050926.

41 Dei, 'The Role of Afrocentricity in the Inclusive Curriculum in Canadian Schools'; G J S Dei and S Hilowle, *Cartographies of Race and Social Difference*, Critical Studies of Education (Springer International Publishing, 2018), https://books.google.ca/books?id=z559DwAAQBAJ; George Sefa Dei, *Teaching Africa: Towards a Transgressive Pedagogy*, Explorations of Educational Purpose (Springer Netherlands, 2010), https://books.google.ca/books?id=BmjYy-PmEjcC; G. J. S. Dei and M. Lordan, *Anti-Colonial Theory and Decolonial Praxis* (Peter Lang Publishing, Incorporated, 2016), https://books.google.ca/books?id=CyWbDAEACAAJ.

Acknowledging that every knowledge system possesses inherent limitations in both conception and application within diverse contexts, it is imperative to recognize that African indigenous knowledge forms are not immune to such constraints. Nevertheless, it is crucial to emphasize that prior to the introduction of European scientific inquiry methods, African knowledge and practices served as effective guides, continuing to play a significant role in guiding its people across various endeavors and reaffirming their practical efficacy. Dei advocates for the acknowledgment of Indigenous knowledge as inherently legitimate and not in competition with other sources or forms of knowledge. It highlights the influence of power dynamics and ambition in shaping the positioning of bodies within the Western academy, emphasizing the need to recognize the inherent biases of Eurocentric perspectives. The quote contends that evaluating the philosophical grounding and social worth of Indigenous philosophies should not be done using Eurocentric lenses, as doing so would perpetuate a skewed understanding influenced by the dominant Western narrative.[42] The above position emphasizes the impact of power dynamics and ambition within the Western academic context, advocating for a reconsideration of rules set by dominant perspectives. It suggests that evaluating the philosophical foundations and societal value of Indigenous philosophies using Eurocentric lenses is insufficient, emphasizing the importance of an approach that respects the distinctive perspectives and contributions of Indigenous knowledge in its own right. Aligning with the pioneers of Africanist scholarship to affirm the authenticity and efficacy of African knowledge and ways of knowing through embodied practices and storytelling, I underscore the imperative for Afrocentric analysis to center on the body's role in meaning-making.

In Kete dance, the individual body serves as a dynamic storyteller, encapsulating communal beliefs irrespective of body type. Embracing the narrative dimension of human experiences, contemporary social research recognizes personal stories as invaluable sources of experiential data. Life's unfolding is increasingly understood through storytelling, prompting a methodological shift in the collection and analysis of personal narratives. Stories are now scrutinized not only for their content but also for how storytellers and contextual conditions shape the narrative. This evolving approach respects the significance of storytelling while cautioning against an excessive focus on unrestricted narration.[43]

---

42 Dei, *Teaching Africa: Towards a Transgressive Pedagogy*.
43 Jaber F. Gubrium and James A. Holstein, 'Narrative Practice and the Coherence of Personal Stories', 1998.

An integrated approach that combines self-reflection, experiential engagement, and Afrocentric methodologies creates a holistic and comprehensive methodological inquiry. This approach enhances understanding through culturally immersive and participatory research, ensuring an African-centered interpretive schema.

## The Melting Pot: Tying the Wisdom Knot of Afrocentricity, Akan Symbolisms, and Communication through Kete Dance

The Akan/Asante people possess a profound awareness of their surroundings and the factors shaping their daily lives. Prior to the influence of Christianity and Islam, they held the belief, which endures to this day, that humans coexist with spirits. This awareness forms the foundation of every cultural institution governing Asante life, influencing worship, spirituality, nationality, citizenship, and communication protocols. These elements are intricately interconnected, as illustrated in Kuwor's (2017) holistic approach to dance analysis.

Similar to other cultural expressions, Kete dance relies on visual, metaphysical, political, and multisensory elements to fulfill its performative objectives. Essential components of a Kete dance performance encompass the distinctive colors of the drum or musical ensemble, adorned with or without carved Adinkra symbols, and the incorporation of Adinkra symbols into dance costumes, among others. These symbols contribute significance to the dancer's identity, social status, and the contextual setting of the performance, whether it be a funeral or a traditional durbar. The relationship between Kete and Adinkra symbols is closely intertwined, as seen in other Asante music and dance forms like *Fontomfrom*[44] and *Adowa*.[45]

Adinkra symbols expert Kojo Arthur [46] explores Adinkra as a coded system that induces indigenous and contemporary meanings that preserve and present aspects of the beliefs, philosophy, and history of the Asante people of Ghana. Symbols may be derived from proverbs, historical events, human attitudes, animal behavior, plant life, and forms and shapes of inanimate and man-made objects. By their communicative nature, Kete and Adinkra

---

44 This a war dance form of the Asante people.
45 This is a social dance form of the Asante people which is believed to predate Kete dance.
46 G. F. Kojo Arthur, *Cloth as Metaphor: (Re)Reading the Adinkra Cloth: Symbols of the Akan of Ghana*, 2001, https://books.google.com.br/books?hl=pt-BR&lr=&id =DuNFDwAAQBAJ&oi=fnd&pg=PT11&dq=cloth+as+METAPHOR&ots =4LXtHeezin&sig=gydsEMxBkNpI00UOmj667Qo4kus&redir_esc=y#v=onepage &q=cloth as METAPHOR&f=false.

share a relationship through performance. This is important to highlight, as a holistic Afrocentric approach to understanding dances like Kete can support theory-building. For the Akan/Asante/Africans, "[…] symbols are signs that connote meanings greater than themselves and express much more that their intrinsic content. They are invested with specific subjective meaning, Symbols embody and represent wider patterns of meaning and cause people to associate conscious or unconscious ideas that in turn endow them with their deeper, fuller, and often emotion-evoking meaning."[47] Adinkra symbols serve as an iconographic script, encapsulating the philosophies of the Asante people. Consequently, any in-depth analysis of an Asante dance form, such as Kete, is incomplete without an exploration of these symbols. Akan/Asante dances are characterized by layers of complexity and contextuality. Each dance form has both somatic and contextual functionality, with each body part's movements being time sensitive. Moreover, traditional dances and their accompanying songs carry three layers of meaning—literal, metaphorical, and philosophical—according to Kuwor.[48] The study of Kete, without emphasizing its connection to these philosophical foundations, deprives learners of valuable insights into African cultures.

From a performance standpoint, I further delve into the exploration of Afrocentric ideals embedded in Asante dance, with a specific emphasis on depicting human beings within their natural social environment. Emmanuel Ampofo-Duodu observed that "signs and symbolic movements […] have specific meanings to shed light on objects and personalities, and as such, philosophical utterances and ideas that are difficult or risky to proclaim verbally are embodied in symbolic dance movements."[49] He further proposed that Asante dance traditions, such as Kete, communicate thoughts or matters of personal and social significance through the selection of signs and symbols, postures, and facial expressions. Adinkra symbolism, aphorisms, and proverbs are woven into this broader framework of indigenous communication, creating a multilayered tapestry of individual and collective cultural hermeneutics. In this context, Kete dance and Adinkra symbols jointly serve as a multivocal metaphor to interpret the contextual meanings and functional uses of symbols and signs developed by the Akan in their performance practices and other visual media (Arthur 2001).

---

47 Arthur.
48 Sylvanus Kwashie Kuwor, 'Structures of Meaning in Ghanaian Traditional Dance Forms' (Accra, 2019).
49 Duodu, 'Drumming and Dancing in Akan Society: A Study of Court Musical and Dancing Tradition'.

To illustrate, I will now exemplify the intricate connections present in Akan performance aesthetics by exploring two Adinkra symbols and two Kete dance variations.

- **Gye Nyame Adinkra**. This symbol represents a strong knowledge of who God is to the Asante. It places the Akan/African conception of God above everything else and demonstrates dependency on God. *Gye* means *"Except,"* and *Nyame* means God. This is represented by the following symbol:

(Arthur 2001)

- In Kete dance performance, when a dancer points their forefinger to the sky, to the ground, and then to the chest, this means, "except God and Mother Earth, there is nobody besides me in authority." Also, depending on the social status of the dancer, they may have to point their finger symbolically toward a more exalted figure, like a chief or the queen mother, and replace themselves in the equation.

By applying Afrocentric theory, a reevaluation of symbol and movement variations allows for the recognition of a societal framework where God occupies the pinnacle of the hierarchy, succeeded by royalty and the general populace. This tripartite societal structure is intricately linked to Akan numerology, emphasizing the significance of the number three in all numerical considerations. This can be verified through the symbol *Adinkrahene*, which is considered the leader of all symbols.

(Arthur 2001)

According to researcher Kwasi Ampene (personal communication, 2020), in Akan cosmology, this symbol's three concentric circles represent God's creation order, which involves the concept of "Order, Music/Communication, and Death."

- *Akofena* **Adinkra**. This symbol is represented by two Akan state swords crossed together.

(Arthur 2001)

- It symbolizes authority and power and is still utilized for the induction of chiefs today. (In a Kete movement performance of the symbol, a King or subchief points to the left and right with each arm, respectively, holding two swords, and then rotates the lower arm a few inches away from the upper torso—forward in a counter-clockwise direction rhythmically. Finally, both lower arms rest (in an X-crossed shape) on the chest of the chief.) Semiotically, the King is prepared to defend his people and subordinates during war if it occurs, as all authority rests on his chest. This Kete movement was adopted for the 2018 action movie Black Panther as a salute belonging to the people of *Wakanda*. Similar to the analogy on the Gye Nyame symbol, Akofena represents the four cardinal points and symbolizes expansion, which is characteristic of migration.

## Summary

This chapter has underscored the advantages of employing an Afrocentric approach in the analysis of Ghanaian dance, with a specific focus on Kete. By framing Kete as indigenous knowledge, I have elucidated its role in the sociocultural tapestry of the Asante, emphasizing its transgenerational continuity. The discussion has highlighted the paucity of literature on the Kete dance form and underscored the Afrocentric approach's pivotal role in establishing the agency of African dances within global dance scholarship. Through a comprehensive exploration, I have advocated for the adoption of Afrocentric theory as a critical lens for analyzing dances like Kete, illustrating its pertinence in unraveling African aesthetic forms, including Kete dance-music and Adinkra symbols. Serving as both a methodology and a theory, Afrocentricity has the potential to unveil the performative agency inherent in danced embodiment, offering a robust framework for the nuanced analysis of African/Asante dances by engaging with culture-specific elements that constitute the indigenous knowledge of the Asante people.

# Chapter 3

# AFROCENTRICITY: SEEING CLEARLY THE PHENOMENON

**Kete Dance as Indigenous Knowledge**

Kete encapsulates embodied knowledge, undergoing continuous evolution to meet the dynamic needs of its practitioners in an organic and responsive manner.

To expand on this, the Indigenous Knowledge System (IKS) incorporated within the broader framework of Afrocentric theory as advocated by Asante-Kete, is here regarded as an alternative theoretical lens for addressing African artistic developments. An IKS encompasses the entirety of historical and contemporary knowledge, including actions and reactions, grounded in a people's interaction with their environment. Kofi Anthonio shares that "human beings, are defined by the way we socialise, including communal gathering which is representative of the society or its coming together to live as an identifiable entity [...] and that community is not complete without music and dance."[1] I contend that any definitions pertaining to the cultural evolution of African people should be based on their own voices, experiences, and interactions with their history. Meaning and contexts are derived from these activities, supporting social functions and activities that are relevant to a people. This chapter serves as a conceptual exposition of Kete as an IKS within the Afrocentric paradigm.

As espoused first by Molefi Kete Asante (Asante 1988) and later by scholars like Frances Owusu-Ansah and Bubela Mji in their push for recognition of African indigenous knowledge forms, I have recognized, through existing literature, the necessity for adopting an Afrocentric approach in African dance scholarship. Ghanaian dance research has not explicitly utilized Afrocentricity until now. This necessity is echoed by Owusu-Ansah and Miji (2013), who share that in exploring alternative approaches to studying their reality,

---

1 Kofi Anthonio, 'Exploring Indigenous Knowledge Through Music and Dance Practices Of The Aŋlɔ-eʋe' (PhD, Accra, University of Ghana, 2021).

African research must endeavor to diverge from the established Western research methodologies in which many have been trained. This stance does not aim to dismiss or belittle recognized Western investigative methods but encourages African researchers to consider alternative inquiry methods for investigating and preserving indigenous knowledge (Owusu-Ansah and Mji 2013). An Afrocentric method as an alternative approach to existing Western conceptions of dance-music and their functions in African societies is not only necessary but more so needs constant promotion. Historically and presently, Western perspectives on the African body and dance have been sources of fascination and, at times, misunderstanding. Afrocentric theory serves to enhance the presentation of IKS rooted in the body and dance, emphasizing their situational and contextual relevance to Africans. This approach seeks to uphold collaborative cultural frameworks that arise from our fundamental creative and cognitive capacities as social beings. Afrocentricity affirms the intellectual prowess of the black body, challenging colonialist perspectives that have historically exerted influence over the history of black people.

Queeneth Mkabela also shares, "Afrocentric theory and methods are derived from the Afrocentric paradigm, which addresses questions of African identity from the perspective of African people as centered, oriented, and grounded" (Mkabela 2005, 179). The intellectual exposition of African history is multifaceted and requires careful analysis. In the case of Akan/Asante dance-music forms, the following questions arises: How can Asante/African people fully lay claim over their knowledge forms of music and dance when the mediums and tools for their preservation, apart from embodied performances, are not indigenous? How can we safeguard what is philosophically and empirically *Twi* in language through the English language, which may not necessarily deem them so?

## Holism as an Afrocentric Character

The Afrocentric character of holism is evident in its capacity to offer a comprehensive and interconnected perspective based on lived experiences of black people. In the Afrocentric framework, the holistic approach underscores the interconnectedness of diverse elements, acknowledging the contribution of each component to the comprehensive understanding of a phenomenon. Holism, in this context, harnesses the interplay between various elements of African artistic excellence and exploration, enriching the understanding of cultural phenomena, including the Asante Kete dance, with a more complete and nuanced perspective.

As previously discussed, the IKS is holistic and intricately connected to all aspects of African life. This system of knowledge undergoes constant evolution while retaining fundamental characteristics reflective of the associated people. Consequently, attempting to discuss elements of such cultures without incorporating these fundamental components may result in oversights. A notable example is the term "Dance" in English, which, while referring to bodily movement to music across various genres, lacks the depth and nuanced understanding present in indigenous perspectives. In a conversation with the late Ghanaian choreographer Francis Nii-Yartey, a protégé of Mawere Opoku, he conveyed a perspective on traditional dance-music, stating, "we see the music and hear the dance."[2] Despite its paradoxical nature, this statement encapsulates a comprehensive engagement with music and dance distinct from Western interpretations. Adrienne Kaeppler shares that "most researchers simply use the term dance for any and all body movement associated with music, but it should be remembered that dance is a Western term and concept just as is the term music."[3] The varying perceptions and performances of music and dance across cultures highlight the nuanced differences. For Africans, adopting a holistic approach to dances like Kete becomes crucial, delving into the indigenous historical, contextual, and performance perspectives to explore the value, function, and structure of dance-music. This approach acknowledges the multifaceted nature of these art forms, recognizing their cultural intricacies and enriching the understanding of their significance. Kofi Anthonio avers that

Music and dance, as cultural forms, encapsulate strategies vital for sociocultural identity and preservation. Additionally, these art forms may hold the key to Africa's cultural resurgence and global projection. The study of IKS, particularly those embedded in music and dance, contributes to understanding the role of these bodies in motion and in their roles as cultural representation in the diverse landscape of the twenty-first century (Anthonio 2021). Situating Kete dance-music as a paradigm for assessing cultural evolution necessitates continuous rigorous critical examination, providing a foundation for further academic exploration and expansion.

---

[2] Francis Nii-Yartey, 'Introduction to Contemporary African Dance' (Lecture Presentation, Department of Dance Studies, University of Ghana, 2010).
[3] Adrienne L. Kaeppler, 'Dance Ethnology and the Anthropology of Dance', *Dance Research Journal* 32, no. 1 (2000): 116, https://doi.org/10.2307/1478285.

## Tracing the Evolution of Kete: Journey from Kumasi to Accra, Ghana, and Beyond to North America

In 1963, Asantehene Sir Nana Osei Agyemang Prempeh II granted the Ensemble the privilege to present the Kete dance in Accra, marking a significant departure from its traditional setting in Kumasi. The pivotal aspect extends beyond the granted permission, emphasizing the contextual backdrop of the performance. Kete, inherently a court dance for the Asante monarchy, found itself showcased in a nontraditional setting during a politically charged event at the University.

This transposition of traditional authority into an unconventional milieu introduced a noteworthy shift, where specific movements venerating the monarchy were directed toward a broader audience, including ministers of state. Following the transfer of customary power, there ensued a process of restricting and rechoreographing the dance and its movements. Opoku, shouldering the choreographic responsibility, faced the challenge of amalgamating traditional concepts embedded in the dance with the emerging postcolonial Pan-Africanist rhetoric that played a pivotal role in shaping the newly independent nation of Ghana.

The political powerplay surrounding this endeavor gave birth to the neo-traditional Kete renditions witnessed today. These renditions are a direct outcome of the transformative dancing event in 1963, coupled with the royal permission granted and the infusion of afro-contemporary choreography. Remarkably, since 1963, this amalgamation has endured, with many unaware of its paradigmatically Afrocentric character.

The Kete dance had to reflect the changing paradigms of nationalism and contribute at the same time to shaping a cultural representation that would be endearing to Ghanaians of different ethnicities. Adinku shares that Opoku's rendition of the Kete dance diverges significantly from the traditional performance, exhibiting a more intricate structure in terms of movement and spatial organization. In contrast to the customary solo or duet accompanied by an orchestra, Opoku introduces a distinct personality characterized by his innovative use of space, line, direction, dynamics, timing, levels, and enactment. "[...] In Opoku's presentation, a personality emerges which is made up of his different uses of space, line, direction, dynamics, timing, levels and enactment. His brand of *Kete* is a group piece danced by four, six, or eight people arranged in linear and circular paths. These dancers are supported by a group of drummers, flutists, horn-blowers, and such characters as a chief, a queen, an umbrella carrier, and sword—and shield bearers—all grouped upstage centre." Opoku calls this fusion of *Kete* music, dance and pageantry the "Akan Ceremonial Dance Suite" (Adinku 2000). The success of such experimental approaches is evident today in the emergence of group and unison choreographed variations of Kete, a departure from the traditional indigenous performance norms. Mawere Opoku, serving as the artistic director of the Ghana Dance Ensemble (GDE), played a pivotal role in this transformation by incorporating diverse music and movement variations in his recreations. Opoku's innovative approach involved a deliberate mixing of different elements, a practice not widely acknowledged by contemporary practitioners, who may lack awareness of this aspect and its underlying reasons. The subtle nuances that make Opoku's rendition distinct are often overlooked by those promoting neo-traditional forms today. This oversight is attributed to a deficiency in understanding the cultural significance of music and dance in Asante traditions, a depth of knowledge that Opoku possessed. Additionally, the scarcity of literature addressing Opoku's experimentation contributes to the challenge of recognizing and appreciating his contributions. Both Opoku and Nketia, sharing roots in Asante royal families, drew from their embodied understanding of these forms, anchoring their use of materials in a profound cultural context that distinguishes their work within the realm of Kete.

Opoku's detailed exploration of Kete movement systems serves as a testament to his profound understanding, as evident in his statement, "the distinguishing characteristics of Asante dance are the intricate and subtle manipulation of hands, arms, and legs, body sways and tilts in polyrhythmic combinations—expressive miming with rich symbolic undertones and typical Asante hauteur" (Opoku 1987). This insight underscores Opoku's embodied knowledge and appreciation of the nuanced elements inherent in Asante dance.

Performing Kete in Kumasi, as highlighted by Opoku's exposition, carried immense significance for individual dancers and held broader cultural importance for the Asante community. The selection of Kete as part of the national repertoire resonated with Kwame Nkrumah's call for the revitalization of a glorious African past. In this context, Kete became a powerful means of preserving and celebrating Asante cultural heritage, aligning with the broader cultural and nationalist aspirations envisioned by Nkrumah. In examining the exchanges of Kete culture between Kumasi, Accra, the rest of Ghana, and its diaspora in North America, it becomes apparent that certain crucial details have been conspicuously absent from the scholarship on Ghanaian Kete dance until now.

## Pan-Africanism and Indigenous Dance-Musicking in Postindependence Ghana: Legacies of Nkrumah, Nketia, and Opoku

Historian Toyin Falola delves into the profound impact of colonization on African identity formation, illustrating how the upheaval caused by European conquest and violence has left lasting challenges. Falola points out "the current countries created by European conquest and violence have struggled to generate contested nationalities and nationalisms such that a Ghanaian may not have any sense of identification with a Zimbabwean, or a Nigerian may think that he or she has nothing in common with an Egyptian."[4] This observation underscores the enduring struggle to forge cohesive national identities within the boundaries imposed by colonial powers. The disruption caused by colonization not only severed historical connections but also endangered the sense of being and belonging for individuals and communities. The arbitrary drawing of borders and the imposition of foreign ideologies led to a fragmentation of African identities, making it challenging for people from different nations to find common ground. The deliberate discreditation of African knowledge systems during colonial domination further exacerbated this issue. The colonized, influenced by such systematic measures, often internalized a negative perception of their ancestral heritage, hindering the development of a positive historical consciousness and a strong sense of self-identification. In essence, the historical disruptions brought about by colonial forces not only physically altered the African landscape but also inflicted deep wounds on the collective psyche, influencing how individuals perceive their own history and identity. Patience Kwakwa (2015) observed the effects of this disruption during the "awakening era" (2015) before and after Ghana's independence in 1957, stating that

> Much has been written about the activities of colonialists and missionaries on the African continent before independence and their impact on the African way of life. Many people including the elite, even though they may not have accepted totally the developments that took place, abandoned much of their own cultural heritage. They would be indifferent to traditional social and political gatherings, such as traditional marriage ceremonies, funerals, or durbars. If there was a compelling reason for their attendance, they would wear western clothing instead of their African attire. They were often missing at music and dance programmes offered in the traditional settings. English was the language they spoke.[5]

Addressing the significant disruption caused by colonization necessitated an equally profound response to bolster the delicate political stability of the

---

4 Falola, *The African Diaspora: Slavery, Modernity, and Globalization*.
5 Kwakwa, 'Kwabena Nketia and the Creative Arts: The Genesis of the School of Music and Drama, and the Formation of the Ghana Dance Ensemble'.

emerging Ghana. Success in this endeavor depended on individuals committed to prioritizing the national development of Ghana over the interests of a select elite keen on distancing themselves and perpetuating their acquired colonial preferences. Notable figures in Ghana who embodied this nationalistic approach and endeavored to bring traditional knowledge to the forefront included Dr. Kwame Nkrumah, Emeritus Professor J. H. Nketiah, and Professor Albert Mawere Opoku. These individuals played pivotal roles in shepherding Ghana toward a path that celebrated its cultural heritage and prioritized national development over elitist disconnect. Certainly, while acknowledging the significant contributions of drummers and priests who readily shared their knowledge, this research focuses on three key figures who orchestrated a cultural revolution from both political and academic perspectives, which is crucial for the analysis of Kete. Nkrumah, as a visionary leader, propelled the Pan-Africanist agenda, emphasizing the "African personality" capable of self-management with indigenous resources. Nketia, a pragmatic intellectual, structured academic disciplines in music, dance, and drama, creating a foundation to realize this vision. Opoku, on the other hand, exemplified successful collaboration between indigenous systems and modern instruments, showcasing the results through the performance of neo-traditional dance music. This not only aligned with Nkrumah's vision but also instilled hope in Ghanaians for achieving self-sustenance.[6] Together, these three figureheads played integral roles in steering the course of the cultural evolution surrounding Kete.

It has come to my attention that many researchers investigating dances in Ghana often overlook the profound influence of Nkrumah, with both Nketia and Opoku regularly seeking his counsel, obtaining funding, and securing approvals for performances and variations. An illuminating perspective on this matter was shared during an interview with Eric Awuah, where he revealed that renowned Ghanaian choreographer Francis Nii-Yartey personally conveyed to him and his classmates in a 2011 MA dance class named "Dance as Composite Art Form" that specific movement variations in the neo-traditional rendition of Kpanlogo dance were personally endorsed by Nkrumah himself. Hence, it is imperative to recognize Nkrumah's pivotal role when discussing neo-traditional dance music, as he played a significant part in shaping the artistic and choreographic dimensions of performances orchestrated through the GDE, influencing the contemporary dance culture in Ghana. I strongly assert that researchers must duly acknowledge

---

6 Kwame Nkrumah, *The African Genius* (Accra: Institute of African Studies, University of Ghana, 1963).

Nkrumah's impact on choreography and arrangements. His influence was not limited to political and intellectual realms; it extended to the artistic and cultural landscape, leaving an indelible mark on the dance traditions of Ghana today. Moreover, Nkrumah's deep respect for his ancestors' IKS is evident in his doctoral work at the University of Pennsylvania, as recounted by Botwe-Asamoah. This academic endeavor significantly influenced both his intellectual and political approaches, highlighting the intricate connection between Nkrumah's scholarly pursuits and his reverence for Ghana's cultural heritage. Botwe-Asamoah recounts that his study at the University of Pennsylvania influenced his intellectual and political approach.

> It is common knowledge that with a few chapters completed, Nkrumah had a disagreement with his advisor on the content of his dissertation on ethnophilosophy; rather than write and publish material with which Nkrumah disagreed, he left the doctoral program. He had originally proposed "The Philosophy of Imperialism, with Special Reference to Africa," as the topic for his thesis, which his advisor Dr Morrow at the University of Pennsylvania rejected.[7]

Nkrumah's unwavering commitment to nationalistic ideals was evident and transparent, even in the face of challenges. His vision of empowering his compatriots studying abroad to contribute to the reform of the African continent was apparent, illustrating his profound desire for their return. This aspiration materialized in his dream of uniting all Africans in the United States, with the ultimate goal that they might eventually return to Africa to serve. Nkrumah's dedication and extensive efforts culminated in the organization of the first General Conference of Africans in America in September 1943. This historical event reflected Nkrumah's tireless pursuit of fostering collaboration and unity among Africans, both at home and abroad, to collectively work toward the betterment of the African continent.

## Starting the Experiment: Kete Dance-Music as a National Repertoire

The exploration and eventual development of neo-traditional dance music variations in Ghana can be traced back to a seminal moment in 1963, when Nkrumah issued a call during the formal inauguration of the Institute of African Studies. This call marked the inception of a transformative journey

---

7 Botwe-Asamoah, *Kwame Nkrumah's Politico-Cultural Thought and Policies: An African-Centered Paradigm for the Second Phase of the African Revolution.*

that would reshape traditional dance music in Ghana, setting the stage for innovative variations that bridge indigenous roots with contemporary expressions. Nkrumah's initiative played a crucial role in initiating the experimentation that would contribute to the evolution of neo-traditional dance music in the country. He charged the Institute of African Studies (IAS) to

> [...] to study the history, culture and institutions, languages and arts of Ghana and of Africa in new African-centred ways-in entire freedom from the propositions and pre-suppositions of the colonial epoch, and from the distortions of those professors and lecturers who continue to make European studies of Africa the basis of this new assessment. By the work of this Institute, we must re-assess and assert the glories and achievements of our African past and inspire our generation, and succeeding generations, with a vision of a better future. (Nkrumah 1963)

After 59 years of continuous experimentation spurred by Nkrumah's call, Ghana's dance culture remains in a state of evolution. As outlined in Chapter 1, Eric Awuah has identified four distinct categories of folk/traditional/indigenous dance-musicking in Ghana: Traditional, Professional, Academic, and Amateur.[8] In his comparative structural analysis of the Bawa dance from the Upper West Region of Ghana, Awuah illustrates the ideological, structural, and political changes manifested in the performance of the dance by selected amateur groups in Accra. This analysis serves as a clear demonstration of the influence of Nketia and Opoku's artistic interpretation of Pan-Africanism by Nkrumah, which is evident in the contemporary variations of these dances.

In establishing a neo-traditional legacy, Nketia drew inspiration from the "oral way" of the past, expanding both the theoretical and practical exploration of Ghanaian/African dance to represent change. Nkrumah's understanding of the significance of indigenous belief systems, embodied through music, dance, and ritual activities, emphasized their role in serving the purposes of nationalism. This legacy, shaped by the artistic endeavors of Nketia and Opoku, continues to permeate the dance variations witnessed in Ghana

---

8 Eric Awuah, 'A Study of Amateur Groups' Re-Interpretation of Traditional Dances in Ghana: Role on Continuity and Safeguarding' (NTNU, University of Clermont Ferrand, University of Szeged, University of Roehampton, 2014); Awuah, 'A Study of Amateur Groups' Re-Interpretation of Traditional Dances in Ghana: Role on Continuity and Safeguarding1'; Eric Awuah, 'Whose Dance Is This Again?', in *The Book of Everything You Want to Know about Open Air Museum*, ed. Nikola Kristovic (Muzej na otvorenom, Staro selo, 2016), 148–52, https://books.google.ca/books/about/Book_of_everything_you_wanted_to_know_ab.html?id=xB7CzQEACAAJ&redir_esc=y.

today, reflecting a dynamic interplay between tradition, innovation, and the broader sociopolitical context.

At the time of Ghana's independence, the majority of the population was classified as "illiterate" according to colonial standards, even though they demonstrated intelligence by indigenous measures. Nkrumah recognized that the most effective way to connect with the people and create a meaningful impact was through their embodied art forms. Therefore, his strategic use of these performance mediums to reach out to the majority of Ghanaians and promote nationalism was nothing short of ingenious. Paul Connerton's (1989) concept of collective memory provides validation for Nkrumah's embodied approach to nationalism through the artistic visions of Nketia and Opoku. This approach acknowledges the power of shared experiences embedded in embodied practices, such as dance and music, to foster a collective memory that contributes to the forging of a national identity. Nkrumah's foresight in recognizing the potency of these art forms as vehicles for national unity aligns with Connerton's understanding of how embodied practices contribute to the construction of collective memory, shaping the narrative of a nation's identity. Connerton shares that

> our bodies, which in commemorations stylistically re-enact an image of the past, keep the past also in an entirely effective form in their continuing ability to perform certain skilled actions. We may not remember how or when we first learned to swim, but we can keep on swimming successfully—remembering how to do it—without any representational activity on our part at all; we consult a mental picture of what we should do when our capacity to execute spontaneously the bodily movement in question is defective. Many forms of habitual skilled remembering illustrate a keeping of the past in mind that, without ever adverting to its historical origin, nevertheless re-enacts the past in our present conduct. In habitual memory the past is, as it were, sedimented in the body.[9]

Connerton proposes that memory sedimented in the body allows the reenactment of the past in present actions, emphasizing the intricate link between embodied practices and the preservation of collective memories. Recognizing the agency of black dance and indigenous history, Pan-African ideologies find optimal expression through music and dance. Nketia (2015) concurred, stating that for Ghanaians, the preservation and dissemination of indigenous knowledge relied not on literature but on active performance (Kwakwa 2015). This underscores the significance of embodied practices, particularly dance

---

9 Paul Connerton, *How Societies Remember, How Societies Remember*, 1989, https://doi.org/10.1017/cbo9780511628061.

and music, as dynamic vehicles for the expression and perpetuation of cultural heritage in the context of Pan-African ideologies. To test this hypothesis in an academic environment that preferred literature to practice, Nketia argued from an ethnomusicological perspective:

> Ethnomusicology has both a theoretical and a practical side. Over 15 years I had been engaged in the theoretical and not the practical aspect of music, which is visible and helps to give meaning to the theoretical work. At IAS, I had mounted a Higher Diploma course in Music and Related Arts-music with dance, drama, visual arts, poetry praise poetry etc., but it was still academic. All the four students who enrolled in the course had a diploma in western music. Besides, they had to write thesis and sit for examinations. It was still not visible and so the creative part of my research was looking for an avenue for expression. So, with the creation of the School, I had an outlet, a creative outlet I must say. The School of Music and Drama can thus be seen as an institution for realizing Music and Related Arts in practical terms [...] when I wrote to Dr. Nkrumah to set up the School of Music and Drama, he agreed. Nana Kobina Nketia took the letter to him, and it was signed and approved. (Kwakwa 2015)

Nketia's initiative aligns seamlessly with the principles of an Afrocentric paradigm, constituting a movement aimed at integrating African music and dance knowledge into the construction of black identity and knowledge. Molefi Asante, a proponent of this intellectual shift, contends that Afrocentricity should be regarded as a paradigmatic transformation. It serves as a powerful intellectual shift, challenging the hegemonic colonial era by authentically presenting the truth of African knowledge in action. Nketia's endeavors, rooted in Afrocentric principles, contribute to reshaping perspectives and affirming the significance of African cultural contributions in the broader context of knowledge construction and identity formation. In further elaboration of the paradigmatic shift, Asante emphasizes Afrocentricity as a paradigm in the sense that it elevates the centrality of African agency. This paradigm fosters an embrace of African values that goes beyond mere cognitive and structural aspects; it encompasses a functional dimension that activates our consciousness within a revolutionary framework. This functional aspect transcends mere knowledge, emphasizing proactive engagement and transformation in the lives of the oppressed. As Asante contends, the true impact of Afrocentricity lies in its ability to move beyond superficial realms of discourse and effect tangible revolutionary changes.[10].

---

10 Asante, *An Afrocentric Manifesto: Toward an African Renaissance*.

To elaborate, Nkrumah, through executive power, facilitated the widespread acceptance and propagation of the IKS of Ghanaians. Drawing from Nkrumah's evident Afrocentrism and the artistic vision initiated by Nketia and Opoku, it can be inferred that the functional aspect of African intellect emerged, positioning the black individual as capable of progressive and effective self-development. A notable and effective response to colonial influence was found in indigenous and neo-traditional dance-musicking. After 56 years, this response seamlessly found expression again within the Afrocentric theoretical paradigm. Remarkably, no Ghanaian dance researcher has hitherto highlighted the clear connection between black dance, indigenous knowledge, and black intelligentsia through an Afrocentric lens. Previous scholarly explorations have been conducted individually by scholars such as Kuwor (2017), Ampene (2020), Hagan (2015)[11], Botwe-Asamoah (2005), and Kwakwa (2015). By redirecting focus to the agency of the Kete dancing individual as inherently and proudly black, functioning as an intellectual agent that aligns philosophy of personhood with nationhood within indigenous structures, I underscore the relevance of Afrocentric rhetoric harmonizing with African elements like music and dance. I posit that, according to the black body and the intellectual recognition it warrants in black dance literature, prevailing disembodied discussions about black dance and dancing become inconsequential. Within this research, embodiment is presented as the unifying force that both synthesizes and pragmatizes African intellectual capacity and the magnificence of its music and history. When I gesture in Kete dance through my own body, I interpret it as an expression of knowledge passed down from my ancestors. Consequently, my movement to Kete music is not merely an individual act; it symbolizes knowledge systems as enduring as the dance itself. In moving to Kete music, I traverse a timeless space of being with my forebears, and my experience becomes an acknowledgment that we will persist in creating shared experiences as long as the drum continues to produce music.

It is evident that Nkrumah, inextricably linked to the discourse of nation-building and cultural emancipation, propagated the ideology that Africa, as a continent, possessed a rich past civilization deserving emulation. Academic scholars whose erudition aligned with this agenda were sought for consultation to establish a platform for intellectual and political expression—the GDE. It is important to note, however, that Nketia and Opoku, in shaping

---

11 George Hagan, 'Dondology: Music, Mind and Matter', in *Discourses in African Musicology: J.H. Kwabena Nketia Festschrift*, ed. Kwasi Ampene et al. (Michigan: African Studies Center, University of Michigan, 2015), 456–77.

the ensemble, engaged in a syncretization of cultures. Their familiarity with Euro-American choreography and performance, coupled with the initial dance-focused nature of the GDE, contributed to a nuanced fusion of diverse cultural elements. Nevertheless, to Nkrumah, music and drama could not be severed from the awakening he intended to spark in Ghana. Nkrumah noted that "the School of Music and Drama will link the University of Ghana closely with the national theatre Movement in Ghana. In this way the Institute can serve the needs of the people by helping to develop new forms of dance and drama, of music and creative writing, that are at the same time closely related to our Ghanaian traditions and express the ideas and aspirations of our people at this critical stage in our history. This should lead to new strides in our cultural development" (Botwe-Asamoah 2005). The quote underscores the profound connection envisioned between the University of Ghana's School of Music and Drama and the national theater movement in Ghana. It emphasizes the Institute's role in meeting people's needs by fostering the evolution of innovative forms of dance, drama, music, and creative writing. Crucially, these artistic expressions are intended to be deeply rooted in Ghanaian traditions while articulating the ideas and aspirations of the people during a crucial period in the nation's history. The quote envisions a symbiotic relationship between cultural preservation and progress, anticipating that this collaboration will propel Ghana's cultural development to new heights.

## An Autoethnographic Enquiry into Kete Dance-Music

My approach to Kete dance research utilizes an embodied perspective derived from my extensive experience as a dancer since childhood. By employing autoethnography with an emphasis on phenomenology, I bring a first-person, reflective dimension to my exploration of Kete dance. My analysis is personal, drawing on my lived experiences within the four distinct categories of Traditional, Professional, Academic, and Amateur Kete dance renditions in Ghana (Awuah 2014). I delve into my personal performance journey across the four dance categories in Ghana. Firstly, as an indigenous performer in the Traditional category; secondly, as a student-dancer at the School of Performing Arts, University of Ghana; thirdly, as a dancer within three professional dance companies in Ghana—the Ghana Dance Ensemble, the National Dance Company of Ghana, and the Abibigromma Theater Company; and lastly, as a dancer with various amateur groups in Kumasi and Accra, notably my initial group, the Ahenemma Kete Group in Kumasi.

My multifaceted engagement, from indigenous performances and academic pursuits at the University of Ghana to professional roles in various dance companies and participation in amateur groups, provides a rich foundation for a comprehensive and authentic understanding of Kete dance in Ghana. The self serves as an analytical agent in my research, employing autoethnography with a deliberate reliance on phenomenology—a first-person approach to elucidate my lived experiences as a Kete dance practitioner and researcher. Merton's statement validates my position when he states that "you can only tell me who I am, and I cannot tell you who you are. If you do not know your own Identity, who is going to identify you? Others can give you names and number, but they can never tell you who you really are. That is something you yourself can only discover within."[12]

Merton's insightful statement underscores the inherent personal nature of identity, emphasizing the profound and intrinsic journey of self-discovery as an introspective process within the individual. Recognizing my role as an active agent within all four categories enables a retrospective exploration of the self, which is crucial for contextualizing movement structures. This is particularly significant given the distinct transmission structures and embodied politics inherent in the performance practices of the four categories in Ghana. Many dance researchers in Ghana adopt individual perspectives when addressing traditional dances, but emerging scholars, including myself, acknowledge the importance of cross-sharing movements and ideas between these categories in shaping our conceptualization of indigenous and neo-traditional dance forms and their evolution. Therefore, the justification for this autoethnographic approach lies in its capacity to allow for a comprehensive experiential exploration of the forms and structures used in both the Traditional and Academic categories. Kemal Nance highlights three key components of self-reflection, such as "auto (the self), ethno (community) and graphy (process)."[13] From this, I am able to meaningfully weave different knowledge together with my passions, experiences, and embodied individuality in my life.[14] My personal narratives and those of my informants

---

12 N. K. Nketsia, *African Culture in Governance and Development: The Ghana Paradigm* (Ghana Universities Press, 2013), https://books.google.ca/books?id=dRDFoAEACAAJ.

13 C. Kemal Nance, 'Brothers of the "Bah Yáh!": The Pursuit of Maleness in the Umfundalai Tradition of African Dance', *ProQuest Dissertations and Theses* (Ann Arbor: Temple University, 2014), https://login.ezproxy.library.ualberta.ca/login?url=https://www.proquest.com/dissertations-theses/brothers-bah-yáh-pursuit-maleness-umfundalai/docview/1617432728/se-2?accountid=14474.

14 Karen Barbour, *Dancing Across the Page: Narrative and Embodied Ways of Knowing* (Bristol: Intellect Books, 2011), https://login.ezproxy.library.ualberta.ca/login?url=https://search.ebscohost.com/login.aspx?direct=true&db=e000xna&AN=1135592&site=ehost-live&scope=site.

underscore the relevance of the body and dance as important in the meaning-making process for communities.

## Embodied Afrocentricity: Locating the Black Body in Its Practice and Theory

In emphasizing the crucial intersection between anthropology and critical postcolonial dance theory and practice, researcher Ojeya Cruz Banks underscores the profound role of the body and dance in both historical and contemporary contexts. Drawing inspiration from scholars like Barbara Browning and Yvonne Daniels, who frame dance as a potent form of resistance and embodied knowledge, Cruz Banks contends that dance serves as "social medicine," impacting power dynamics, community relationships, and affirming identities.[15] Acknowledging the historical vilification of the African dancing body under colonial rule, this exploration focuses on the Akan/Assante dancing body, seeking to restore its agency and recognize it as a carrier of generational legacies through traditional dance routines.

In amplifying this epistemological reality of the body, I infer the "realization and concept" theory of Ethnochoreologists Egil Bakka and Gedimina Karoblis[16] and Afrocentricity[17] to situate the black dancing body as an intellectual element of indigenous knowledge. Bakka and Karoblis explore the importance of embodied knowledge in making it possible for one to perform a dance, whereas Afrocentricity serves as a paradigmatic theoretical shift from western understanding that situates the body within a holistic, interconnected indigenous environment.[18] This is influenced by an inquiry into the role of the performing body in the quest for political and cultural independence, which addresses both the liberation from colonial rule and the assertion of cultural autonomy by projecting indigenous knowledge on national and international stages. This exploration delves into how the body, through performance, became instrumental in shaping the narrative of political and cul-

---

15 Ojeya Cruz Banks, 'Of Water and Spirit: Locating Dance Epistemologies in Aotearoa/New Zealand and Senegal', *Anthropological Notebooks* 16, no. 3 (2010): 9–22.
16 Egil Bakka and Gediminas Karoblis, 'Writng "a Dance": Epistemology for Dance Research', *Yearbook for Traditional Music* 42 (3 August 2010): 167–93.
17 Asante, *An Afrocentric Manifesto: Toward an African Renaissance*; Mazama, 'The Afrocentric Paradigm: Contours and Definitions'.
18 Kuwor, 'Transmission of Anlo-Ewe Dances in Ghana and in Britain: Investigating, Reconstructing and Disseminating Knowledge Embodied in the Music and Dance Traditions of Anlo-Ewe People in Ghana'; Kuwor, 'Understanding African Dance in Context: Perspectives from Ghana'.

tural identity during pivotal historical moments. In addressing this inquiry, it is essential to trace the role of the body in the evolution of Pan-Africanism as both a political and cultural concept, culminating in the establishment of the GDE. A crucial acknowledgment is that neo-traditional dances, while representing an indigenous iteration of culture, seemingly "conform" to Western standards through theatrical conventions. These dances reflect the artistic exchange of their time, embodying a blend of cultural forms where movements and musical expressions migrate consciously or unconsciously. This complexity challenges the characterization of neo-traditional forms as strictly Pan-Africanist or Afrocentric, as they incorporate elements of Western conventions. However, examining this conundrum necessitates consideration of political motivations, performance structures, and contemporary contexts, which are crucial for situating independent artistic expressions from Africa. This exploration underscores the intangible yet potent psychological legacies of colonial occupation, surpassing the physical remnants left by colonialists. The path taken by Dr. Nkrumah was for psychological reformation through the same structures of colonialism supported by the Pan-Africanist rhetoric. Years later, as this rhetoric temporarily declined, there was a need for new theoretical lenses that explored the challenges from evolving contextual perspectives and, hence, Afrocentricity as a conduit for action. Positioning the body as the focal point of analysis enables African researchers to delve into the intricacies of cultural "decenteredness." This approach becomes paramount as there is a considerable gap in comprehending our indigenous philosophical and cosmological sources. By prioritizing the body in the analytical framework, researchers can unravel the complexities of cultural identity and unearth the profound connections between embodied practices, indigenous knowledge, and the quest for a comprehensive understanding of African heritage. Afrocentricity, as a theory of change, endeavors to reposition the African individual as a subject. Serving as a continuation of Pan-Africanism, Afrocentricity assumes a pivotal role, especially where the impact of Pan-Africanism on the continent through formal education fell short. According to Asante (1980), Afrocentricity emerges as the cornerstone for the proper education of children, embodying the essence of an African cultural revival and survival. The revitalization and endurance of Ghanaian and, by extension, African cultures hinge on the epoch of performance through the body. Understanding the environmental implications of the body rhetoric is imperative to discern how African art forms can wield a more significant impact on youth amid evolving modernization.

    I reference anthropologist Harry Silver's perspective, suggesting that the emerging art scene in newly independent African states faced the challenge of catching up under the influence of modernization. Silver characterizes modernization as a Western force of change, depicting the "tribesman" as seemingly powerless to resist, ultimately succumbing to its effects. This viewpoint reflects the complex dynamics between traditional African cultures and the sweeping changes brought about by modernization, raising questions about the preservation and adaptation of indigenous artistic expressions in the face of external influences. He stated that "today's tribesman faces the very real challenge of living in a modern nation. The forces of change and tradition tear at the sinews of contemporary African life; changing circumstances demand effective adaptations for survival. I will show that messages conveyed in modern secular art provide a cognitive route to adaptation that may well serve as a model for similar passage at the economic and political level."[19] Silver highlights the contemporary challenge faced by individuals in Africa, referring to them as "today's tribesman," who grapple with the dual forces of modernization and tradition in the context of living in a modern nation. According to Silver, the interaction between modernization and tradition exerts pressure on various aspects of contemporary African life, requiring effective adaptations for survival. He proposes that modern secular art serves as a means of conveying messages that act as a cognitive route for adaptation. Silver suggests that these artistic expressions could serve as a model for navigating similar challenges at economic and political levels. However, this perspective, offered 17 years after Nkrumah's African Genius speech, may inadvertently lack respect for indigenous culture, portraying it as succumbing to modernization rather than recognizing its resilience, regenerative capacity, and functionality. The statement reflects a potential bias that continues to influence Western analyses of African movement systems, considering them "low arts" due to perceived notions of cultural hierarchy. This was a problem after independence and continues to resurface in different ways generationally. Kuwor observed that

> in 1960, Nkrumah saw the need for resurgence in African culture and personality and the creation of institutions that would give expressions to the intrinsic values of Africa. He saw these "as part and parcel of the socio-economic emergency of Ghana, and later on, of course, of the African continent," [...] Nkrumah had a grasp of the perpetual Euro-American ethnocentric hegemony that had marginalized the African and reduced him to an object. As Asante notes, Nkrumah, more than

---

19 Harry R. Silver, 'Beauty and the "I" of the Beholder: Identity, Aesthetics, and Social Change among the Ashanti', *Journal of Anthropological Research* 35, no. 2 (14 January 1979): 191–207.

any of his contemporary political colleagues, wanted to see our [cultural] views translated into political power.[20]

As outlined by Asante, Nkrumah's ambition to align cultural perspectives with political influence is met with resistance and assertion in contemporary Ghanaian and African art forms through the lens of Afrocentricity. Despite criticisms branding Afrocentricity as racist or militant, its core objective is unequivocally pro-Africa. Originating from the yearning of the first transported slaves to return to their homeland, Afrocentricity confronts the phenomenological implications of historical injustices on the evolving African, including the traumatic experiences of lynching and decapitation. While sociopolitical and historical narratives have been extensively explored, the application of Afrocentric thought to dance and the body provides a unique perspective, allowing for a deeper understanding of personal experiences, training, performance, and the transmission of cultural legacies. Afrocentricity facilitates the positioning of the dancing body within the context of Pan-Africanist struggles from the 1960s to the present, acknowledging the enduring influence of political ideologies on the performance of traditional and neo-traditional forms.

The dearth of indigenous epistemological investigations into dance-musicking by Africans, including myself, raises concerns. Existing studies primarily offer basic sociocultural explorations, leaving a hunger for more critical analyses. I contemplate whether I am a "lynched or decapitated" explorer of indigenous Ghanaian dance knowledge, a concept coined by Asante. The decapitated African intellectual examines culture from a detached perspective, while the lynched intellectuals lack historical and intellectual knowledge of the continent, despite having cultural links. Recognizing the limitations of an Afrocentric approach, articulated by writers like Tunde Adeleke, is essential to understanding its relevance and challenges in dance analysis.[21] In his critical exploration of Pan-Africanism and Afrocentricity, he poses the following questions—"can black Americans truly claim African identity? Do they really share common interests and challenges with Africans? Have they been drawn together historically by shared experiences? In other words, has there always been a Pan-African tradition? If so, how old is it? These are

---

20 Kuwor, 'Understanding African Dance in Context: Perspectives from Ghana'.
21 Asante, *An Afrocentric Manifesto: Toward an African Renaissance*; Mazama, 'The Afrocentric Paradigm: Contours and Definitions'; Tunde. Adeleke, '"Black Americans and Africa: A Critique of the Pan-African and Identity Paradigms." *The International Journal of African Historical Studies* 31, no. 3 (1998): 505–36; Tunde Adeleke, *The Case against Afrocentrism*, *The Case Against Afrocentrism*, 2009, https://doi.org/10.5860/choice.47-7019.

pertinent questions whose answers compel a reconceptualization and reassessment of the historical focus of the relationship and experience of Africans and black Americans."[22]

These questions are critical, especially as an African in the USA among African Americans. The shared goal for the development of the continent remains a complex issue, with cultural and sociological differences evident in interactions. While Adeleke's inquiries are valid, my encounters with passionate African Americans, both intellectuals and others, devoted to protecting, promoting, and developing Africa challenge this conception. Despite the questions raised, the Afrocentric paradigm remains influential in shaping my understanding of African dance, projecting the African body as an agent of knowledge, whether in the diaspora or on the African continent. Dancing in neo-traditional forms becomes a shared expression of geographical and political black identity for Africans and African Americans alike. Afrocentricity serves as an epistemological anchor for the black body, whether navigating the struggles of slavery and civil rights in America or confronting imperialism on the African continent. This theory instills a historical and political awareness of perpetual black identity, empowering the body as an agent to shape black reality and narratives. In response to Adeleke's consideration of the timeline for shared experience validity, performing traditional dances becomes a means to move communal knowledge, fostering mutual embodiment. The prevalence of African neo-traditional dances in predominantly black American communities reflects shared experiences in the struggle for independence, resisting Western hegemony, and transmitting black knowledge globally. Through these dances, African philosophies and knowledge are shared, creating theories grounded in our experiences for future generations.

## Conceptualizing the Kete Body as an Agent of Social Construction and Meaning-Making through Performance

The Kete dancing body, within the Afrocentric paradigm of agency, emerges as a crucial subject for the study of black dance in Ghana and the diaspora. This indigenous knowledge form, deeply embedded in Akan cosmology, serves a multifaceted role in traditional and contemporary societies. Beyond its cultural significance, Kete plays a pivotal role in decolonizing the black dancing body within Ghanaian dance scholarship, a dimension previously overlooked. Through Kete, the body becomes a medium for the critical

---

22 Adeleke, "'Black Americans and Africa: A Critique of the Pan-African and Identity Paradigms." *The International Journal of African Historical Studies* 31, no. 3 (1998): 505–36.'

exploration of social construction within the Pan-Africanist and Afrocentric movements.

Kete, as a performing art form, offers a unique conduit to comprehend Akan culture, transcending the limitations of sociological and anthropological methods. It intricately weaves together cosmological tenets with movements, gestures, music, and performance. Its relevance extends to the decolonization agenda of the 1960s and continues to contribute to contemporary Ghana. The neo-traditional variation of Kete, introduced during the Pan-African experimentation of the GDE, has surpassed expectations, becoming a popular representation not only of the Akan people but of Ghana as a whole. Exploring the complex role of Kete in cultural relevance and social construction, this work delves into the nuanced nature of the dance through an embodied perspective, drawing on personal practice, family history, revelatory incidents, concept realization, and propagation. Through these categories, the intricate tapestry and connections of Asante culture and sociocultural power systems are revealed through the lens of the Kete dance. Building on Dewey's pedagogic creed, I propose an embodied, centered, and functional approach to understanding Kete dance. If education is viewed as a fundamental process of living, as stated by Dewey[23] then Kete, as an indigenous agency of knowing and an educational avenue for understanding cultural phenomena, becomes a functional medium for assessing indigenous knowledge in an Afrocentric context. Kete, with its functionality, serves as an Afrocentric means of evaluating indigenous knowledge reflective of communal understanding of movement systems. In this context, the body serves as the medium of assimilation, centered within an indigenous community that functions in musical, visual, and multisensory dimensions. This firmly situates Kete within the realm of Akan living, strategically employed to navigate and enforce social roles. A centered body is consciously attuned to environmental needs and societal expectations. A Kete dance body, irrespective of its social and cultural hierarchy, emerges as a political body projecting socially functional knowledge essential for daily living. This prompts the question: What is the indigenous body without its relevance to the totality of knowledge systems that give it identity and meaning among a people like the Asante?

---

23 K. Asafo-Agyei Okrah, *Nyansapo (the Wisdom Knot): Toward an African Philosophy of Education.*, African Studies (Routledge, 2012), https://login.ezproxy.library.ualberta.ca/login?url=https://search.ebscohost.com/login.aspx?direct=true&db=cat03710a&AN=alb.8775617&site=eds-live&scope=site.

**Image 1** Kete dancers displaying their cultural knowledge with their dancing bodies.
Source: Photograph by Nana Twumasi-Ntiamoah & Joshua Benumanson.

## Realization and Concept of Kete Dance

I begin this analysis by quoting Nana Ketehene's words on the performance of Kete today.

> This generation has trivialized the Kete dance in many ways. A clear example is with the colors of the drums where most performers of today different furniture materials to drape the drum. I say this because originally Kete is full of aggression and sorrow and that is why it is called Kete. It uses two significant colors which is black (*besi*) and red (*nkrawo*). These colors should set the tone for performance and so any other colors affect the meaning and context of the performance. Traditionally, the playing of the Kete signals to people that the Asantehene or king is already seated in state either at a social occasion or especially at a funeral or the *Akwasidae* festival. This means the Kete is not played as and when it pleases people. The deviation from this practice by most performers outside of the palace is as a result of "alien" concepts that appeal to the masses more than the owners of the dance. This has led to most people treating the Kete ordinarily which should continue because of its value. If even the current Asantehemaa was taught Kete in this house/

palace, during the reign of Otumfuo Pokua. (Transliterated from Twi to English)[24]

The above statement highlights important elements in the performance of Kete in Ghana that need further exposition. The statements are basically a conceptual foundation for the understanding of a Kete dance event, which includes the knowledge needed before the actual dancing of Kete. I draw on Kuwor's holistic analysis of indigenous dance forms to highlight the connections that make the dance and even a composite knowledge system of the Asante for all participants and onlookers in the event. Kuwor highlights the "visual, bodily, musical, and multisensory modalities" as key indicators to understanding dances. However, Nana Ketehene's first point of criticism is directed toward the visual elements "required" in the performance of Kete. He singles out the red and black colors required for draping Kete drums, which in turn, in the case of a funeral event, is the dominant color set and represents loss/sorrow (red/blood) and despair and pain at the departure of the dead to the spirit world (black/darkness). This visual and musical connection is helpful in setting the mood of the whole function or event, for it is linked with the reason(s) for gathering, the costumes on display, and the music that is required from the Kete ensemble. When connected to the body and the mood of the occasion, the color combinations and established concepts for the event then set up or dictate the required gestures and movement variations that are needed at that particular function. Moreover, within the same function, the music of Kete, as Ketehene explains, alerts people to the presence of the king or chief who is at the occasion. The music conditions all participants, consciously and unconsciously, about the social hierarchy at that particular event. Therefore, the visual, bodily gestures, and musical combination set the mood for the performance of identity. I argue that Kete as a holistic art form can singlehandedly communicate so much in a space of minutes more than words or sentences can in the same time frame. It transcends the gestures and combines historical, social, and political information just by the stroke of the *kwadum* and the swipe of a dancer's hand from left to right to order/tie together a whole cultural process of meaning-making that is not easily identifiable by an outsider. In another performance context, I learned that apart from specific musical variations for royals, there are others for specific demographics among the Asante people. He shares that

> there is a drum that is played here in the palace that is reserved solely for the king, his children, and the executioners-*abrafuɔ* . No matter how

---

[24] Nana Kwadwo Boateng, *Kete with KeteHene of Manhyia Palace* (Kumasi, Ghana, 2021).

appealing it is to any outsider apart from this category of dancers, one is not allowed to dance. Breaking that rule comes with repercussions like a fine of least four sheep for atonement known as ɔdwanputua in addition to monetary fees known as *sika ɔdwan*. There are even specifications about the type of sheep required for the atonement. This penalty is called *Parade* which prevents others from dancing to that particular tune.[25]

The prescribed use of specific Kete rhythms, such as the one reserved for the king, his children, and the executioners (abrafuɔ), reinforces the hierarchical structure within Asante society. The stringent penalties for unauthorized participation, including fines and specified rituals for atonement, contribute to maintaining the exclusivity of certain dances, affirming the authority of the king. Additionally, the mention of rhythms like "Adabanka" for older women and "Agogomu" for little people illustrates how Kete serves as a platform for diverse expressions, acknowledging and celebrating various segments of the community based on age and physical attributes. He shared that there is a particular rhythm which derives its name from a specific drum called "*Adabanka* which when is played, only old and weak women are expected to dance. It has a relatable tempo for their age. Most of the aged use the opportunity to communicate proverbs to younger onlookers and this brings to the fore, the concept of respect as practiced among the Asante. *Agogomu* is another type of Kete variation that is reserved for midgets/little people."[26]

Respect holds significant importance within Asante culture, extending to various realms of social interaction. In the context of Kete dance, respect is a foundational principle, emphasizing reverence toward authority figures such as parents, the elderly, strangers, and those in positions of authority, particularly within the monarchy. The adherence to this concept is evident in the meticulous gestures of Kete dance, where any deviation from the norms of respect can disrupt the delicate balance of social harmony. Notably, the cultural expression of respect is symbolized by refraining from wearing slippers when dancing in the presence of a king, especially for individuals of common status, reflecting a deep understanding of societal norms and maintaining the equilibrium of mutual respect. An illustrative example is the significance attached to the traditional slippers, known as *chaochao*. When the king and subchiefs, adorned in these slippers, preside over a function, a dancer's refusal to remove their slippers can be interpreted as an attempt to equate their status with the royal figures—a gesture deemed inappropriate. In the male

---

25 Boateng.
26 Boateng.

performer's protocol, the initial step involves carefully folding their clothes at waist level while the music plays. Subsequently, the removal of slippers signifies an understanding and acceptance of the respect code, allowing the performer to proceed. This nuanced action becomes a tangible expression of indigenous respect within the cultural milieu.[27]

Also, the role of a chief or king extends beyond mere ceremonial presence; it encompasses a profound connection with indigenous music, positioning them as the "owner of all traditional music and dance." Competence in this domain is not only measured by a comprehensive understanding of history but also by an acute grasp of the meaning behind rhythms and gestural variations. This proficiency is showcased during dances, where the king must demonstrate precision, hitting every note and responding adeptly to calls from the drums. This multifaceted mastery underscores the integral link between leadership, cultural knowledge, and musical expression in the monarch's daily duties. For instance, the ceremonial movements of the Otumfuɔ (Asantehene) are intricately linked to specific music variations, each holding distinct significance. The Fontomfrom music accompanies the Otumfuɔ when he is in a palanquin, emphasizing the regal procession. As he proceeds to his seat, the Mpente variation sets the tone for this transition. However, it is the Kete music that takes precedence when the Otumfuɔ is seated, marking the pinnacle of the ceremonial musical expressions. Additionally, whether attending a funeral or other occasions, the Asantehene may choose between Kete and Fontomfrom music. The Asantehene's personal Kete ensemble is known as Mpesetea, while the Asantehemaa's is named Manhyia Kete. This orchestration of music and movement underscores the nuanced role of music in royal protocol and ceremonial events within the Asante cultural context.[28]

The intricate relationship between music and dance is deeply embedded in Asante culture, reflecting a holistic understanding of these art forms. In the context of Kete, indigenous dancers are encouraged to have a comprehensive knowledge, at least rudimentary, of Kete drumming, fostering a symbiotic connection between the dancing body and music. This reciprocity is encapsulated in the local saying, "a good dancer is also a good drummer," and vice versa, emphasizing the interdependence of these skills. Interestingly, the hierarchical structure of the Kete musical ensemble challenges common misconceptions based on drum size. Contrary to expectations, the smallest drum, the Aburukuwa, holds the utmost significance and seniority, even played before the larger Kwadum. This nuanced understanding showcases

---

27 Boateng.
28 Boateng.

the depth of indigenous knowledge in Kete drumming, extending beyond mere physical attributes to hierarchical importance and ritual roles.[29]

## Kete Performance and Propagation

The intricate nature of Kete dance reveals an interconnected relationship with Asante history and their understanding of the body's agency in conveying social, cultural, and political roles. While I've explored communal aspects of Kete performance, my informants' subjective experiences add another layer. Over years of researching movement systems, I've observed that dances evolve with changing bodies and expectations, challenging the notion of static traditions. Informants advocating for traditional standards sometimes admit to personal choreographic liberties, highlighting the dynamic nature of Kete. Despite Kete's popularity, scholarly research on its historical and choreographic development has been lacking, contributing to challenges in preserving its structural integrity outside its native context.

The Kete dance form, primarily a solo dance in traditional settings, relies heavily on the symbiotic relationship between the dancer and the master drummer. This relationship sets the aesthetic expectations for the entire performance, as audiences, upon recognizing this dynamic, anticipate specific responses to cues. The audience in a traditional setting, which Ofotsu Adinku refers to as the personal audience, consists of people familiar with the dance, deeply connected to their culture. They judge the performance harshly if the original meaning and symbolism are not adhered to. In settings like Manhyia Palace, the performer's expectations are higher than in university or social functions in Accra. At Manhyia, dancers are not just expected to dance beautifully but consciously. The conscious state derives from understanding the dance, identity, and social hierarchy. Structural arrangements in Kete performance encompass not only spatial and directional leverage but also the extent of leverage through gestures. A dancer's interpretation of their identity, location, and actions, combined with technical know-how, allows them to meet expectations in Kete performance. Neo-traditional Kete performers face fewer pressures and embodied consciousness requirements, as their audiences lack traditional Asante authority dictating specific expectations. Nana Ketehene's emphasis on Asante identity underscores the role of music and dance in forming the foundation of allegiance to ethnicity. In the traditional setting, Kete dance and gestural phrases of praise are directed toward God, the ancestors, the monarchy, and esteemed community members. In

---

29 Boateng.

the neo-traditional setting, protocols are more relaxed, allowing for improvisation. Dancers may direct attention and praise to individuals based on their likelihood to provide monetary gifts, irrespective of high social and cultural standards.

The propagation of Kete dance depends on its performance a lot more than just costumes or gestures alone would. Performing Kete is performing philosophical ideals of living and Asante symbolisms. For example, Kete performer Nana Kyei Baffour demonstrated to me a "concept of unity" that is allowed within most performance contexts because of its meaning and also the facial expression that goes with it. He stated that "when I perform the *Tefre ayiyanda*, it also means *times change*. When I raise my two hands up and then in bringing them back down, I put them together [prayer hands] towards another person or people, it means *unity*, or I wish for unity among us. When I switch immediately to moving my right palm across my left hand in a slicing motion, it could stand for attack or threat of slashing you with a weapon. The latter example is normally associated with the royal executioners known as *Abrafour* whose duties include killing."[30]

In Kete performance, adherence to context is crucial for the propagation of the form. Often associated with funerals, Kete is performed to evoke sorrow and loss. Specific rhythms are crafted for distinct groups, ensuring that the intended participants, based on social hierarchy or role, join the dance when the corresponding variations are introduced. Nana Boakye explains that

> the *Adaban* is a very 'dangerous' rhythm. When a king dies in times past, it was required for the *Abrafour* to decapitate any person who broke a stipulated curfew enforced for several days as part of the funeral events. As such the Kete *Adaban* was only played at night to warn indigenes of what was afoot at night and the fact that the chief or king was dead. So, to demonstrate their assignments, they imitate slashing of heads or body parts by using the straitened palm. Therefore, a king does not dance to the *Adaban* but reserved for the executioners and royal guards known as *ahenkoa*.[31]

Furthermore, the performance of Kete serves as a vehicle for expressing key indigenous concepts related to beauty and marriage. In Asante culture, dancing has been integral to life to the extent that, in the past, individuals

---

30  Nana Kwame Kyei Baffour, *The Role of Kete in Asanteman* (Accra: Fieldwork in Ghana, 2021).
31  Nana Boakye, *Kete with Nana Boakye* (Accra, Ghana, 2021).

selected spouses based on their dancing abilities. Maidens would embellish themselves with beads and ornamental jewels on specific body parts—ankles, knees, elbows, and heads—to draw attention to these areas, considered synonymous with overall beauty. Mothers, especially, were tasked with teaching their daughters to dance, enhancing their prospects for marriage. The Asantehemaa, the queen mother, is known to assist her courtiers in finding husbands within her palace. This cultural significance was highlighted during an interview with Nana Ketehene, where our conversation shifted after a young woman greeted him and walked by. At that moment, we were discussing the role of the courtiers, making the incident with the young woman particularly relevant to our conversation. He shared that

> the girl who just passed by served as a courtier—*Nkyemkyemfour* to the Queen mother from a younger age. When they get to the marriage stage, the Asantehemaa trains them in family and marriage matters and supervises their dancing lessons after which creates opportunities for male suitors to engage in courtship and if everything goes well according to tradition, then marriage. Those who are obedient and meet all the standards after years of training come highly recommended for marriage. Such women are difficult to find nowadays because society has changed so much. Their training included being messengers for the queen and during the *Akwasidae* festival, you would have seen them here run errands for the *Asantehemaa*. These women are very protected, men were forbidden to touch them inappropriately or even attempt to

**Image 2** Kete dancer displaying passage of knowledge to the younger.

woo them with special permission from the queen. If any man committed such an offence there are huge penalties to pay and even to the extent that your village chief is summoned to the queen mother's court to answer on the perpetrator's behalf. The *Nkyemkyemfour* are identified by a special haircut called *Amele*.[32]

This detailed account establishes the criteria for the dancing of Kete in specific situations where beauty is assessed and appreciated. Whether performed with or without these underlying concepts, Kete provides a balanced assessment of structures within neo-traditional and traditional dancing circles. By considering the philosophical parameters of the structure and variations of the dance form, a more assertive exposition of tradition from an embodied perspective is achieved, moving beyond mere mechanical repetition of movements to music.

---

32 Boateng, *Kete with KeteHene of Manhyia Palace*.

# Chapter 4

# AFRICAN DANCE IN A GLOBAL CONTEXT

This chapter delves into the foundation of Ghanaian dance scholarship, emphasizing traditional and indigenous dances and their significance in the Indigenous Knowledge Systems of various communities. It explores postindependence dance categories and their progressive changes, drawing on Awuah's (2014) categorization to analyze their characteristics, dancing structures, rules, and aesthetics. The transmission of Kete in the Traditional category, with its move from Kumasi to the University of Ghana in 1963, reflects its unique role in community life. The chapter highlights the official decree from the Asantehene allowing Kete's use in the academy for academic and nationalist purposes, marking it as a distinctive knowledge system within the ensemble's repertoire. The approval and support from both the Asantehene and Dr. Nkrumah contribute to Kete's significance in the broader context of Ghanaian dance scholarship.

## Traditional Dance-Musicking

Traditional dances in Ghana serve to navigate the communal lives of the people who engage in their performance.[1] Traditional dances, crucial to community life, involve creators, custodians, and practitioners of artistic elements in dance-musicking across time. They embody an intellectual expression,

---

[1] Opoku, 'Asante Dance Art and the Court'; Albert Mawere Opoku, 'Thoughts from the School of Music and Drama', *Okyeame* 2, no. 1 (1964): 51; Paul Schauert, 'A Performing National Archive: Power and Preservation in the Ghana Dance Ensemble', *Historical Society of Ghana* 10 (2007): 171–81; Younge, *Music and Dance Traditions of Ghana: History, Performance and Teaching*; Kuwor, 'Transmission of Anlo-Ewe Dances in Ghana and in Britain: Investigating, Reconstructing and Disseminating Knowledge Embodied in the Music and Dance Traditions of Anlo-Ewe People in Ghana'; Amegago, 'An Holistic Approach to African Performing Arts: Music and Dance Curriculum Development and Implementation'.

revealing how individuals interpret their identity and relationships within indigenous Ghana. In the 1960s, Ghana pioneered the integration of professionalizing traditional music and dances into academic practice. This facilitated further exploration, connecting cultural forms with other state elements, shaping not just art but also influencing knowledge production and the conception of the African self. Understanding traditional music and dance requires exploring connections in movements, music, visual forms, multisensory modalities, audience engagement, and dancing events within Ghanaian/African traditions.[2]

There should be a distinction between the dancing activity and the dancing event. One must understand that the dancing activity, herein referred to as the "realization,"[3] is only made salient within the event it is perpetuated in. Hence, it is the dancing event that creates the contexts and validates the movement variations, music, and its historical antecedents. "A dancing event is a kind of an open or restricted occasion in a place and time, where and when dancing is in the focus."[4] In many indigenous communities, dance events are intricately linked to economic, religious, or political activities, using dance-musicking as a central element to convey meaning. Social dance events may serve as a source of enjoyment and merriment, while ritual dance events become a form of worship. These dance events often extend beyond their immediate context, connecting to other activities that contribute to the overall significance. For instance, in the Asante Adae festival, traditional forms like Kete are featured in various suboccasions within the broader celebration. Movements and gestures in Kete, though consistent across contexts, take on distinct meanings based on the specific subevent within the larger festival. Rituals and esoteric activities, although not public, play a crucial role in shaping the context and meanings derived from dance events, influencing attire, facial expressions, songs, and movements. Analyzing Ghanaian dance research without considering the connection to the dancing event and its broader community associations may dilute the nuanced nature of the term "context." I contend that a loose use of "context" in scholarly analysis risks undermining its role in the meaning-making process. If context is viewed as the surrounding circumstances that encompass any indigenous dance event

---

[2] Kuwor, 'Understanding African Dance in Context: Perspectives from Ghana'; Kuwor, 'Transmission of Anlo-Ewe Dances in Ghana and in Britain: Investigating, Reconstructing and Disseminating Knowledge Embodied in the Music and Dance Traditions of Anlo-Ewe People in Ghana'.
[3] Bakka and Karoblis, 'Writng "a Dance": Epistemology For Dance Research'.
[4] Egil Bakka, Andrée Grau, and László Felföldi, *The Dance Event* (Trondheim: Choreomundus Master, 2013).

and dancing activity, I propose to conceptualize it as an integral part of the dance "concept."[5] In this sense, context becomes, for the indigenous individual, the knowledge that shapes the perceptions, imagery, and expectations of the learner/performer. It plays a crucial role in the know-how process that enables a dancer to perform Kete. Therefore, lumping the "concept" with the "realization" without critically connecting it back to the cultural dancing event that necessitated its "naming" in the first place only presents half of the holistic information of the dance. There is a need to clarify the agency of the event, its created subagency of context, and the agency of the body that is performing the act. This, I argue, helps us to understand the contextual discourses surrounding dancing in the academy, professional settings, and among the Amateur category because each category, in one way or another, redefines its own dancing events, their corresponding contexts, and movements use.

As a practitioner and emerging scholar of Ghanaian dance, I reflect on my practice and scholarship to argue that even the term "Neo-traditional dancing" needs to be interrogated. Neo-traditional dance-musicking was an offshoot of political rejuvenation in Ghana after independence in 1957. The first republic that created the avenue for its thriving development was ousted from power in 1966. Although there is no written document on what changes the Ghana Dance Ensemble and the Institute of African Studies went through, it is not hypocritical to hypothesize that successive governments after the first republic may have made changes. There is a probability to this because, much like indigenous dances in rural communities' propensity to adapt to situations, so was neo-traditional dance responsive to changes until the 1992 constitution was drawn and the end of military juntas became a reality. Unfortunately, there are no written records of any changes. Therefore, to use the word largely after Kariamu Welsh-Asante's use in her extensive scholarship without much interrogation within Ghanaian dance history is quite difficult for emerging scholars like me. Interrogating the term and its role in contemporary dance events, including the academic use of music and dance material, affords us the opportunity to trace our history and understand what dance-musicking has truly contributed to Ghanaian national identity. In my perspective, dance-musicking stands out as one of the most vital and enduring elements in Ghana, retaining its relevance for individuals like me today. The image below illustrates the interconnectedness between the dancing event and the dancing body in traditional/indigenous dance practices in Ghana.

---

5 Bakka and Karoblis, 'Writng "a Dance": Epistemology For Dance Research'.

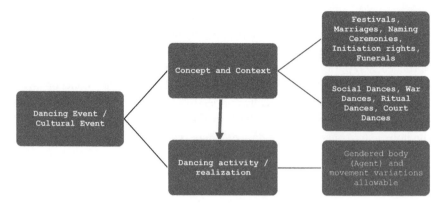

**Figure 1** The dancing event: a breakdown of cultural elements.

Traditional dancing in Ghana stands out as one of the most recognizable and enduring elements of ethno-cultural development, playing a pivotal role in knowledge transmission within society. While the origins of many dances may lack authentication due to their oral and performative nature, their significance in shaping social, religious, and political developments is evident. Awuah's (2014) category analysis, akin to Raymond Williams's (Williams 1977) concept of social formation, underscores the Traditional category as the most dominant and influential in creating and disseminating indigenous music and dance knowledge within Ghana. This category, as its name implies, serves as the originator and creator of indigenous dance and music forms, crafted to fulfill specific functions within the cultural life cycle, including birth, puberty, initiation, marriage, and death.[6] Their significance in Ghana extended to their indispensable role in shaping the foundation of the "new nation" under Kwame Nkrumah. Trevor Wiggins, in his examination of the establishment of the Arts Council of Ghana, echoed the sentiments of certain parliamentarians who emphasized the vital role of rural communities in sustaining cultural forms, including music and dance, and thereby contributing to the broader goal of nation-building. Wiggins highlights that

---

6 Nketia, 'The Role of the Drummer in Akan Society'; Opoku, 'Asante Dance Art and the Court'; Paschal Yao Younge, 'Enhancing Global Understanding through Traditional African Music and Dance: A Multicultural African Music Curriculum for American Middle Schools', *Dissertation Abstracts International Section A: Humanities and Social Sciences* (2008); Younge, *Music and Dance Traditions of Ghana: History, Performance and Teaching*; Kuwor, 'Transmission of Anlo-Ewe Dances in Ghana and in Britain: Investigating, Reconstructing and Disseminating Knowledge Embodied in the Music and Dance Traditions of Anlo-Ewe People in Ghana'.

there was a commitment to representation of the different ethnic groups in Ghana on the Arts Council, but the practical issue of what constituted the national culture, particularly in a post-colonial setting, continued to exercise the minds of the members of Parliament. The minister was advised that: The first place he [the minister] should look for development of this [the arts] is the villages. Encourage young people in the villages because the villages are the true repositories of our cultural heritage. (ACG, column 306)[7]

This "nationalist" approach to arts was not just discussed in music and dance but extended to museums. Harcourt Fuller, in his exploration of the "nation" concept, reiterated the processes of engagement during the launch of the national museum of Ghana. He stated that "the national collection represented Nkrumah's desire for Janus—attempting to anchor the nation in a glorious historical past, while looking toward a bright future of national unity."[8] This thought pattern was also reflected in Nkrumah's African Genius speech, where he entreated the performance artists and scholars to treat the past with respect while realigning some elements from it for the future. To understand the past, we must engage its remnants in the present and future and understand how its general classification of "sacred and secular" influences specific conceptions and practices. Sacred dances are restricted music and dance forms performed only by initiated members, whereas secular dancers are open to participation by everyone based on gender and social hierarchy in the community. However, in practicalizing of these demarcations within the nationalist agenda, there were challenges in the formulation of the concept of "national art forms." This is because, for some reason, the secular forms are favored for national and international showing over the sacred within both religious and diplomatic contexts. I am yet to see a sacred dance from Ghana serving as a welcome performance for dignitaries, even if it has been altered and performed without rituals by the Ghana Dance Ensemble. I interpret this as a paradox and a challenge to national representation in that the secular needs the sacred to survive, and therefore highlighting one over the other for whatever reason without mentioning this interdependence makes their analysis a bit challenging within indigenous epistemology. Moreover, the other three categories, namely Professional, Academic, and

---

[7] Trevor Wiggins, 'Personal, Local, and National Identities in Ghanaian Performance Ensembles', in *Learning, Teaching, and Musical Identity: Voices Across Cultures* (Indiana University Press, 2011), 170–83.

[8] Fuller, 'Building a Nation: Symbolic Nationalism during the Kwame Nkrumah Era in the Gold Coast/Ghana'.

Amateur receive their artistic inspiration from the Traditional category with strong ties to history, structure, and performance ideals. The Professional, Academic, and Amateur categories are postindependence/colonial and Pan-Africanist mutations and/or appropriations of traditional dance structures. Their proliferation and expansion evolved after the creation of the Institute of African Studies in 1962. Since their creation can be traced to specific political, educational, cultural, and commercial roots, exploring a dance like Kete from a comparative analytical purview opens different discursive possibilities that are missing from Ghana dance analysis. It must also be highlighted that even within the Traditional categories, there are appropriations of the forms in ways that even challenges the very "traditional" tag they bears. Mitchell J. Greco's exploration of the term "traditional" from the perspectives of Gerhard Kubik and J. H. Nketiah traces its racist past and acknowledges that it has become a colonial legacy even into today's use of the term to describe most ethnic music and dance forms from Africa. He shares that

> [...] the use of traditional as a "euphemistic surrogate for primitive" was a result of the scientific paradigms that assumed the existence of set stages of cultural development that engrossed European thought prior to the 1960s. "Traditional" developed as a concept that "came from an ideology that saw Western influence as the major—and sometimes exclusive—agent for social and cultural change" in the African continent. However, there was contact, exchange and migrations of people within African societies as well as the Islamic and the Asian world well before European contact, which inherently caused changes in cultural and musical features. The Islamic Period of African history and other eras prior to European contact and colonization of the continent in the 1800s are commonly called Africa's "prehistory," which showcases the continued Euro-centric view.[9]

Although Awuah, like many other African researchers, has not interrogated the term within decolonial discourses, it needs attention. However, just like I have explained under dancing event, I align with Trevor Wiggins' description of the term, which falls within my dancing event exposition. Wiggins

---

9 Mitchell J. Greco, 'The Emic and Etic Teaching Perspectives of Traditional Ghanaian Dance-Drumming: A Comparative Study of Ghanaian and American Music Cognition and the Transmission Process', *ProQuest Dissertations and Theses* (Ann Arbor: Kent State University, 2014), https://login.ezproxy.library.ualberta.ca/login?url=https://www.proquest.com/dissertations-theses/emic-etic-teaching-perspectives-traditional/docview/1646474024/se-2?accountid=14474.

shares that in the traditional settings, "as the occasions for music and dance are part of rites of passage or for informal recreation decline, there has been an increase in the number of cultural festivals organized by individual towns. These typically involve a celebration of local culture before invited national representatives, together with a competition for performance groups."[10] This also provides an interesting point of departure in the analysis of "traditional dances" as it is evident from these "necessary appropriations" that dancing within villages has evolved. So, the question then becomes, if these contexts that necessitate and validate indigenous dances are no longer finding space within the life cycle, are these dances still considered "traditional dances"? In our interrogation of other categories, have we been unjust in pointing wrongly at the changes they go through without consciously admitting same processes that are obvious in the Traditional category? Are we unconsciously biased toward the Traditional category because of nostalgic sentiments?

## Language and the Shaping of Dance Identities in Ghana

The narratives about self, community, and nationhood are held together by language, which evolves as situations evolve. The African/Ghanaian resorts to two major mediums of communication that are oral and kinesthetic that situate their beliefs and ideologies in varied cultural contexts through performance. Therefore, traditional and, to an extent, neo-traditional dances cannot exist in most indigenous Ghanaian communities without oral language because it plays a key role in the labeling, identification, and documentation of dances just as much as the body, music, and sociocultural structures do. Through dancing, the Asantes, for example, can negotiate the politics of identity and develop a civic responsibility to the culture and the monarchy. Kete has since grown from Asante representation to becoming a form of Ghanaian cultural identifier in the diaspora.[11] Traditional/Indigenous dances are mediums for enculturation and bring meaning to the Asante people, which becomes passionately expressed through the body. What makes dance important to a community/society is not just the dancing but also the social structure that gives it meaning and relevance. So, the body, gestures, and music are only significant because of the social order they are performed within,

---

10 Wiggins, 'Personal, Local, and National Identities in Ghanaian Performance Ensembles', 2011.
11 https://youtu.be/vy8fuMuXgZE (This is a video of the Asante King paid a visit to Memphis in the USA where he was accompanied by the Palace Kete music and dance. This is symbolic because he is the custodian of the music and dance of the Asante people including Kete dance.

and herein lies the relevance of Williams' structural breakdown of culture and power in explaining the sociological makeup of dance in this work.

After Ghana attained independence in 1957, dance and music, including Kete, continued to remain an intrinsic and important element of the new Ghanaian state and, by extension, of Africa. To this day, most international dignitaries are welcomed by past and current governments with the Kete dance. For example, at the commemoration of the 400 years of slavery event in Ghana known as the "Year of return" in 2019, when African American descendants of enslaved people returned to the continent through Ghana, the Kete dance was used to welcome them from the airport and at national functions. Thus, the dancing body as an agency and conduit for expressing awareness of a geopolitical environment and knowledge of a people is and continues to be key to understanding any country's culture. Through the changing phases of Ghanaian and African politico-cultural histories, this truth has not been lost on its people.

Every political system has faced some disruption in its evolution, and therefore elements such as those identified by Williams as the Dominant, the Residual and the Emergent provide ways of discussing divergent aspects of culture. Williams explains that the "complexity of a culture is to be found not only in its variable processes and their social definitions—traditions, institutions, and formations—but also in the dynamic interrelations, at every point in the process, of historically varied and variable elements" (Williams 1977, 123). In the Ghanaian situation, the interrelations between traditional institutions like chieftaincy and rituals, modern political organizations such as the postcolonial nation, and Afrocentric ideologies need to be explored to better understand divergent cultural developments. It is evident from the number of stakeholders and the interactions that happen in the exchange of music and dance knowledge and/or transmission of dance-music forms from one category to another that it cannot just be simplified as a "mere" transfer. It has been evident thus far that in the transmission of dances from the palace (traditional category) to the academy, there are underlying tensions that are borne out of the problems of transitioning from independent ethnic groups to colonized nation and to postcolonial states. The "permission asking" process and the decisions that go on from the artistic director upon receiving the permission can be integrated into Williams' cultural theorization.

Raymond Williams' conception of culture as a malleable and interconnected category of a people's developmental practices posits the subcategory of the Dominant as ideological positions that shape a society, and which are held and accepted by the majority as truths and norms for living. These ideologies find their validation and power from the sociocultural creations of the majority and are mostly enshrined through language and performance mediums such as storytelling, music, and dancing (Williams 1977, 121). I see similar traits in each category, especially in the exchange between traditional institutions and professional and academic representatives. When the Professional receives knowledge from the traditions, the national interest of the state then shifts to creating a national identity rhetoric. So, from a rural context, the dances are transposed into national representation politics, not just ceasing to be a traditional dance but most importantly, assuming the identity of "Ghanaian dance." From this discovery, it becomes pertinent to understand the nuances within the transmission process from the palace to the academy through the professional dance ensemble as not just a simple handover process but, more importantly, as a canvas for painting fluid concepts of ownership, choreography, and representation. Herein lies the cogent part of my claim that the neo-traditional genre and the categories of the professional and academic are residual within Williams' theoretical analysis. Although it might seem contradictory to group these two categories and their output of neo-traditional dance-music together as a revival of a traditional form for the purposes of exhibition and analysis by the state and academy, we cannot overlook the strong influence of the chieftaincy institution in validating their performance. It is absolutely crucial not to forget that the neo-traditional renditions still maintain the names of the dances and are practiced by indigenes, so one dance like Kete has three different renditions through the Professional, Academic, and Amateur categories. Kete in the Manhyia palace serves a culturally specific purpose in ethnic politics, so its performance remains within specific contexts. Kete by the ensemble serves the nation-state through the theater, so whatever elements and semiotic additions, like adorning dancers with national colors rather than traditional clothing, are encouraged, and hence an allowance also is made for experimenting through choreography. The Kete of the academy further allows for experimentation within academic grounds, which lacks strong ties to ethnic and professional representation politics. It is purely for academic requirements to attain grades in class and toward graduation from a BA program or BFA program. My observations are not intended to be reductionist by limiting arts to economic freedom and education for grades. On the contrary, they go beyond these because they shape societies in ways that are not economic. By positioning the Professional and Academic Categories as residual elements, I refer to the fact that they were created and validated by the dominant Traditional category, which still influences how dances are performed.

## Traditional Dance Proliferation and the Postindependence Formulation of "National Identity"

From the foregoing discussion, the materialization of the "nationhood" pursued by the first republic of Ghana had to be explored through the integration of indigenous art forms representing the different ethnicities that made up Ghana.

Given the British colonial strategy of "indirect rule" that leveraged the authority of chiefs and paramountcies[12] for domination and economic exploitation in Ghana, the most effective means of fostering unity among the people was through traditional elements that held individual communities together, such as music and dance. Dr. Kwame Nkrumah, in his politico-cultural approach to nationhood, actively promoted traditional performing arts, including music, dance, and drama, as crucial components of Ghana's cultural identity and unity.[13] In the October 1963 speech aptly titled "The African Genius," he highlighted the relevance of locating the African self, relocating/repositioning that self in postcolonial politics, and highlighting the "black genius" inherent to reclaim authority. He stated that

> the personality of the African which was stunted in this process can only be retrieved from these ruins if we make a conscious effort to restore Africa's ancient glory. It is only in conditions of total freedom and independence from foreign rule and interferences that the aspirations of our people will see real fulfilment and the African genius finds its best expression.[14] The speech advocated that a rigorous and systematic exploration of indigenous/traditional knowledge be pursued and used as the springboard for future developments. In this way, the school

---

12 N. J. K. Brukum, *The Northern Territories of the Gold Coast under British Colonial Rule, 1897-1956, a Study in Political Change* (University of Toronto, 1997), https://tspace.library.utoronto.ca/handle/1807/11542?mode=full; N. J. K. Brukum, 'The Voices of the Elite in Northern Ghana, 1918-1938', *Transactions of the Historical Society of Ghana*, no. 7 (9 February 2003): 271–81.

13 Botwe-Asamoah, *Kwame Nkrumah's Politico-Cultural Thought and Policies: An African-Centered Paradigm for the Second Phase of the African Revolution*; J H K Nketia, *Ethnomusicology and African Music: Modes of Inquiry and Interpretation*, Ethnomusicology and African Music: Collected Papers (Afram Publications, 2005), https://books.google.ca/books?id=CaafAAAAMAAJ; Ofotsu Adinku, 'Cultural Education in Ghana: A Case Study of Dance Development in the University System', *Dance Chronicle*, 2004, https://doi.org/10.1081/DNC-120029926; Hagan, 'Dondology: Music, Mind and Matter'.

14 Nkrumah, 'The African Genius'.

of music and drama/dance were empirically justified to promote dance studies at the university.[15]

I propose that Nkrumah's concept of African Personality is a phenomenological construct rooted in African Indigenous Knowledge Systems—embodied, performed, and self-generative. Nkrumah employed this concept to draw the attention of colonially influenced Ghanaians and Africans to the stark realities of their disconnection from their cultural heritage. Through the lens of Nkrumaism, his political ideology, he advocated for three actionable tenets to guide a return to cultural roots and traditional knowledge systems.

Fuller posits that Nkrumah's political philosophy and ideology, evident in both theory and practice as a leader, aimed at political emancipation, African liberation, and socialism as a means to eliminate European imperialism[16] Within these three practical tenets, the arts were envisioned to serve a purpose in the broader context of "total emancipation." Ofotsu Adinku, a pioneer of Ghanaian dance education, clarifies that the School of Music and Drama was established to research Ghanaian and other African dance forms for theater and educational purposes. He emphasizes that "the national dance company (Ghana Dance Ensemble) and the dance section (of the School of Music and Drama) were established for the research and study into various aspects of Ghanaian and other African dance forms: movement activities, choreography elements, costume, make-up, and other dramatic expression, for the theater and for teaching in schools."[17] Nonetheless, despite the alignment of the arts with the overall objectives, the institutional establishment faced resistance from the academic community, much to the dismay of its pioneers. This resistance reflected a significant level of colonial influence and ignorance about the potency of traditional knowledge in Ghanaian/African identity formation, as well as its role in the industrial and economic revolution of the "new" Ghana. Sylvanus Kuwor pointed out that, despite Nkrumah's commendable efforts to institutionalize the study of traditional forms, many scholars and knowledgeable individuals opposed the idea and resisted it in various ways. As a result, studying dance at the university level in Ghana became unattractive, lacked respect, and was often considered by nondance students as a discipline without a future. The challenging situation could be linked to the perception that dance in Ghana is deemed sufficiently impor-

---

15 Nkrumah.
16 Fuller, 'Building a Nation: Symbolic Nationalism during the Kwame Nkrumah Era in the Gold Coast/Ghana'.
17 Adinku, *African Dance Education in Ghana: Curriculum and Instructional Materials for a Model Bachelor of Arts (Hons.) Dance in Society.*

tant in the everyday lives of people but not considered relevant in higher educational institutes like the University of Ghana (Kuwor 2013). Interestingly, the resistance to the study of dance in higher institutions seems to be a global phenomenon, extending to even so-called developed countries. Interestingly, the resistance to the study of dance in higher institutions seems to be a global phenomenon, extending to even so-called developed countries.[18] Despite the challenges dance has encountered as a scholarly discipline in academic institutions globally, it has consistently resisted attempts to label it as "irrelevant." The stereotype associated with dance and music being deemed irrelevant has been a common element in the ongoing struggle for its scientific validation in higher education, particularly since its breakthrough in Ghana in 1963. It's important to note that mass acceptance of dance as a scholarly pursuit was not widespread even before 1963, as the contexts for their performances and perpetuation differed. For more than four decades, the Ghana Dance Ensemble and the School of Performing Arts have conducted research and documented materials related to traditional music, dance, and tropes. While the Ghana Dance Ensemble is acknowledged for creating and widely disseminating the Neo-traditional dance genre through alternative structuring, I contend that the Department of Dance Studies has played a pivotal role in advancing the nationalist agenda beyond the achievements of the Ghana Dance Ensemble. Professors Nketia and Opoku shared the belief that training dance students in the music and dance forms of other ethnic groups, apart from their own, provided an opportunity to embody aspects of another group's history, aesthetic elements, and humanity. Nketiah, in an interview with Wiggins, reiterated the roadmap for realizing this vision in practicalizing national identity. He asserted that

> at the higher level of culture, we are Ghanaians, so that means that on the second level you will recognize the identity of ethnic groups, but each ethnic group then becomes a unit in a higher complex. So, anything that is good, from any ethnic group, can represent Ghana. We never really thought of Ghanaian national culture as an integrated one [...] even though it has emerged that we are using materials from here and there, but it was not to create one uniform culture but to have a common point of reference. So that, in a creative work, if you have a

---

18 Fiona Bannon, 'Dance: The Possibilities of a Discipline', *Research in Dance Education* 11, no. 1 (2010): 49–59.

little bit of that and that, it is Ghanaian. If it is one good thing from one area, it is still Ghanaian.[19]

In this way, the appreciation developed as a result made one capable of accepting that "we are all one and together as Ghanaians" than as separated ethnicities. Another added layer to this was the inclusion of other knowledge forms like economics, archaeology, history, political science, medicine, and anthropology, among others, into the dance and music modules. These programs, together with dance and music studies, would help shape a more rounded Ghanaian who is not only endowed with some traditional knowledge but, most importantly, a combination of others that would drive the economic reformation and independence of Ghana to come.

However, one area of the work of the academy that has seen very slow growth is scholarly publication on the black dancing body as an agency. Not much has been done to additionally situate the Ghanaian/African agency of dance as a concrete element of the cultural revitalization that happened in the 1960s and still happens now. The literature on dance from then had always stayed true to historical and ethnographic analysis of movement systems. These were done most of the time without further critical expositions of the educational legacy on the African genius and personality of the black dancing body and its reflection in postcolonial theorization. What the academy has no shortage of are the numerous practical performances within and outside the university. Neo-traditional dance creations abound in the repertoire of the Ghana Dance Ensemble and the Department of Dance Studies' repertoire. The data presented in this research augments existing research on curriculum, cultural revitalization and resistance, and the agency of indigenous dance knowledge as empirical knowledge that validates everyday experiences.

## Pedagogy, Curriculum Design, and Neo-Traditional Dancing in the Academy

The "academy" in this context, representing the University of Ghana, plays a crucial role in promoting the research, teaching, publication, and advancement of movement/dance knowledge systems through scholarly praxis. The university has been a pioneer in experimenting with traditional music and dance forms, especially in the context of proscenium stage variations in

---

19 Trevor Wiggins, 'Personal, Local, and National Identities in Ghanaian Performance Ensembles', in *Learning, Teaching, and Musical Identity: Voices Across Cultures*, 2011.

Ghana. Neo-traditional dance, as a rendition of traditional dances, is systematically adapted to various theater conventions, including the proscenium stage, end-stage, round stage, and thrust stage.

The choice of stage arrangement adds layers of structure, influences audience and performer positions, and impacts the overall performance. For instance, an African or Ghanaian drama piece incorporating music and dance in its narrative would be influenced by the type of stage it is performed on. Choreographers are aware of the specific challenges posed by each stage, and the setting, timing of actions, and corresponding lighting effects contribute to the visual perception of the dance, distinguishing it from traditional dances within their original contexts.

Despite the significance of the impact of different stages on neo-traditional dance renditions in the academy, there is a lack of specific literature addressing the effects of proscenium, end-stage, round stage, and thrust stage on these performances. In the instructional process, the Mawere Opoku Dancehall serves as a versatile space for teaching and demonstrations. The dance hall is rearranged for two primary purposes: first, for instructors and teaching assistants to demonstrate movements in a circle, especially with respect to the specific dance type, or in a formation on the proscenium stage within the same hall. Second, for student instructions, the "follow the leader" approach is often employed, with the instructor standing on the stage, back to the students, demonstrating movements, and allowing students to observe and replicate.

These two positions are what most graduates from the Ghanaian Academy use in movement instructions wherever they find themselves, especially in the diaspora. The teaching structure is mentally steered toward a "stage" and so pedagogy consciously or unconsciously leans toward it. This approach is pedagogically popular in the transmission of movements from its roots in the academy because of the political position of the University of Ghana, becoming the first African university to award an accredited certificate in dance studies. The dream of creating a traditional knowledge-inspired pedagogy from an academic program originated in 1952 within the National Theatre Movement[20] based on recommendations from the then Prime Minister, Dr. Kwame Nkrumah, during the build-up to Ghana's independence.[21]

---

20 Wiggins.
21 Kuwor, 'Transmission of Anlo-Ewe Dances in Ghana and in Britain: Investigating, Reconstructing and Disseminating Knowledge Embodied in the Music and Dance Traditions of Anlo-Ewe People in Ghana'.

The intersection of mainstream politics and culture introduced a fascinating dynamic to a model emphasizing the role of art in fostering solidarity. According to Kuwor, "it is interesting that the artistic somewhat precedes the political and, in a way, it emphasizes that the rallying together through the arts strengthened the political movement for liberation [in Ghana]."[22] This underscores the significance of the academy as a vital partner in the liberation of Ghana's academic knowledge production. By design, the academy serves as a conduit for decolonization, influencing the conscious Ghanaian—one equipped with the skills, knowledge, and empathy for their culture, and ready to leverage it for the development of their country and people. Nkrumah believed that education should have both an instrumentalist function and a motivational purpose. Its goals extended beyond producing skilled workers to forging a nationalist and socialist consciousness among all Ghanaians.[23] This educational philosophy, evident in Nkrumah's reforms, played a role in shaping the structure and setup of his cultural ideologies toward decolonization.

As a result, traditional music and dance forms were consciously and unconsciously integrated into the larger Pan-Africanist movement in the 1960s. Adinku notes that "the idea of the establishment of the (dance) company came from the first president, Dr Kwame Nkrumah, and it was in line with his concept of cultural emancipation of Ghana and Africa."[24] While this idea may have appeared inconsistent with the notion that traditions are separate from modern/urban life, the purpose for which performance arts were incorporated into the decolonization and Pan-Africanist framework was primarily to project a "unified" Ghanaian identity rather than ethnic segregation or differences. Adinku further emphasizes the potency of the academic program, stating that "since the diploma dance program at the University of Ghana was the first of its kind in Africa, it was designed to be on the same level as a Bachelor of Arts degree. The diploma was, therefore, accepted for graduate work in dance by international institutions."[25] The decision to teach elements of traditional culture in the university necessitated corresponding changes to contexts that legitimized the dances within traditional settings. Nkrumah supervised the creation of the Institute of African Studies (the flagship institute) at the University of Ghana in 1962, driven by his strong belief

---

22 Kuwor.
23 Ama Barbara Biney, *Kwame Nkrumah: An Intellectual Biography* (SOAS University of London, 2007).
24 Adinku, *African Dance Education in Ghana: Curriculum and Instructional Materials for a Model Bachelor of Arts (Hons.) Dance in Society.*
25 Adinku, 'Cultural Education in Ghana: A Case Study of Dance Development in the University System'.

in African knowledge systems as potent for African development. Kwame Botwe-Asamoah adds that

> Kwame Nkrumah's thoughts on colonialism lay the foundation of his political and cultural philosophy. He found colonialism crude and overt in terms of economic exploitation. Besides, it was also insidious as it dehumanized the cultural personality of the African. As noted by several writers [...], African culture and world view: epistemology, cosmology, aesthetics and axiology were severely attacked by the European Christian missionaries, tourists and anthropologists during colonialism. The nature of education and the body of literature produced during colonialism invented "the so-called inferior traits" of the African [...] This dehumanization campaign which, Diop points out, "finally deeply affected" the cultural personality of the African. Thus, through psychological, coercive and brutal methods, the Europeans effectively dislocated the African from his cultural center and "placed him on the margins of their cultural context."[26]

It is crucial to highlight that the academy/university was already grappling with identity and political issues within its administration. Therefore, it is not surprising that the African scholarship revolution would originate from within this contested space. Botwe-Asamoah contends that "in effect, the educational system was characterized by absurdities in the transportation of Eurocentric education into Africa." In the British colonies like the Gold Coast (now Ghana) and Nigeria, the school system trained the students to be inferior copies and caricatures of the Englishman. Being dislocated, the African students became "neither fish nor fowl, as they were denied" information about "their African past and told they had no present" (Botwe-Asamoah 2005). Nevertheless, it was within the African Genius speech that "Nkrumah insisted on the resuscitation of the glories and achievements of the African past, to inspire the new generation with a vision of a healthier future. The speech spelt out his cultural thought as a guiding principle for all the cultural institutions in Ghana" (Botwe-Asamoah 2005). It was through this ideology that the mandates of the schools of music and drama/dance were solidified to promote the foundations and studies of Neo-Traditional performance art forms at the university. The situation required solutions that would be generational, dynamic, and true to Africa in reclaiming its humanities.

---

26 Botwe-Asamoah, *Kwame Nkrumah's Politico-Cultural Thought and Policies: An African-Centered Paradigm for the Second Phase of the African Revolution.*

Frustrations with the colonized mindset influenced Nkrumah's political philosophy, Consciencism. Consciencism is,

> [...] as an African-centred paradigm for [...] the African revolution [...] [-]an attempt at fashioning out an African-centred socio-political philosophy to supplant the legacy of colonial social thought [...] Critical to Nkrumah's political philosophy was his cultural thought and policies, which were aimed at restoring African cultural heritage and integrating them into the new Africa. These policies were meant to bring a complete fusion between African culture and politics through which the African personality could find its highest expression. To this end, he saw theatre as an intellectual forum whereby the vital values in African heritage and African personality could be examined and recovered to influence the socioeconomic aspirations of the new Africa.[27]

The mediums of music and dance were seen as means to address the identity conundrum, drawing the "new" African/Ghanaian back from under colonial mindset and subjugation. Professors J. H. Nketia and Mawere Opoku were tasked by the government to find the best ways of using traditional dances for new artistic developments (Adinku 1994). This set the stage for the critical examination of dance within the academic setting. The influence and impact of the Academy, particularly through the Institute of African Studies and the Ghana Dance Ensemble, cannot be understated, especially in shaping current identity politics. Due to its peculiar position, the Academic category must strengthen its relationship with others and create avenues that provide sustainable and relevant data for our cultural evolution. In response to the effects of globalization and neo-colonial influence on the educational curriculum, including dance studies, over the years, it is argued that the time has come for a reformation rooted in a decolonial position. The proposal suggests a consensus among experts and policymakers to restructure and recalibrate the focus of the entire performing arts curriculum. This restructured curriculum should feature key indigenous knowledge concepts aligned with the African personality and the fundamentals of black artistic excellence. The suggested approach involves developing a "culturally inclusive pedagogy," which is sensitive to the nuances of each culture studied and borrowed from, fosters the development of students' abilities through their dancing bodies in space and time, and promotes awareness of an increasingly interconnected world. After 50 years, there is a need to further redefine the African personality to meet African needs.

---

27 Botwe-Asamoah.

## Exploring Neo-Traditional Dance Pedagogy Post-1992 Constitution of Ghana and Its Global Implication

The 1992 Constitution of Ghana marked the end of military intervention in the country's history, bringing about Democracy and prompting a comprehensive assessment of various aspects, including education. This section examines the dance curriculum from 1992 to 2020. The objective is not a comparative analysis of specific courses but rather to spotlight current courses, trace their historical roots, and assess their relevance to African/Ghanaian individuals in dance scholarship today. As established, art forms like dance, music, and drama have historically been and continue to be significant intellectual sources shaping the identity and developmental blueprints of African nations. However, performing arts as academic disciplines often face challenges and are among the first to be considered for budget cuts in times of financial constraints in education.

It is imperative to reevaluate and implement policies and dynamic pedagogies at tertiary and secondary educational levels that yield results directly tied to national development,[28] making them essential contributors to the overall progress of the nation. To delve deeper into the pedagogical framework in Ghana, an analysis of the academic foundation of dance studies is necessary to understand how curriculum development and an exploration of the body in space, including its politics, power relations, and social restrictions, contribute to the propagation of the African body and personality in economic development. The rationale for this analysis is supported by data from autoethnographic, historical, ethnographic, and scholarly sources[29] that have

---

[28] This is not to say existing policies are not fully developmentally focused with performance arts as partners, but rather their potential is not fully realized due to inability to fully explore their potentials.

[29] J. H. K. Nketia, 'Contextual Strategies of Inquiry and Systematization', *Ethnomusicology* 34, no. 1 (1990): 75, https://doi.org/10.2307/852357; Nketia, 'The Role of the Drummer in Akan Society'; Nketia, *Ethnomusicology and African Music: Modes of Inquiry and Interpretation*; J.H.K Nketia, 'African Music and Western Praxis: A Review of Western Perspectives on African Musicology', *Canadian Journal of African Studies / Revue Canadienne Des Études Africaines*, 1986, https://doi.org/10.1080/00083968.1986.10804143; J. H. K. Nketia, *Reinstating Traditional Music in Contemporary Contexts: Reminiscences of a Nonagenarian's Lifelong Encounters with the Musical Traditions of Africa* (Regnum Africa Publications, 2016), https://books.google.ca/books?id=dJY5swEACAAJ; Adinku, 'Cultural Education in Ghana: A Case Study of Dance Development in the University System'; Botwe-Asamoah, *Kwame Nkrumah's Politico-Cultural Thought and Policies: An African-Centered Paradigm for the Second Phase of the African Revolution*; Amegago, 'An Holistic Approach to African Performing Arts: Music and Dance Curriculum Development and Implementation'; Kuwor, 'Understanding African Dance in Context: Perspectives from Ghana'; Awuah, 'A Study of Amateur Groups' Re-Interpretation of Traditional Dances in Ghana: Role on Continuity and

been advocating for the development and expansion of the academic module at the University of Ghana linked to national developmental purposes.

A revised curriculum should emphasize the inclusivity of African knowledge, representing a fusion of cultural elements reflective of a "culturally responsive body." This body should be trained within an African-centered cultural paradigm capable of showcasing African values in performance and literature. An examination of the dance curriculum from the 1960s reveals a focus on the modus operandi of the Ghana Dance Ensemble, which promoted the performance of rearranged ethnically inspired dances without a thorough conceptual analysis of the dancing body within the academic space. The consequence of this omission is a repetition of dance structures that meet academic requirements for grades and graduation but lack critical analysis of body changes. This situation has led Ghanaian students, studying dance for over four decades, to neglect positioning their bodies as elements of philosophical thought capable of generating knowledge systems aligned with the evolving dynamics of urban and globalized life. Only a few scholars from

---

Safeguarding1'; Cudjoe, *The Contexts and Meaning in Asante Dance Performance: The Case of Kete*; Daniel K. Avorgbedor, 'Some Contributions of "halo" Music to Research Theory and Pragmatics in Ghana', *Bulletin of the International Committee on Urgent Anthropological and Ethnological Research*, 1991; Kofi Anyidoho and Richard Rive, 'Writing Black', *World Literature Today*, 1982, https://doi.org/10.2307/40137451; E. John Collins, 'Ghanaian Neo-Traditional Performance and "Development": Multiple Interfaces between Rural and Urban, Traditional and Modern' (Leiden, The Netherlands: Brill, 2019), 120–38, https://doi.org/10.1163/9789004392946_009; John Collins, 'Ghanaian Christianity and Popular Entertainment: Full Circle', *History in Africa* 31 (2004): 407–23, https://doi.org/10.1017/s0361541300003570; Midas Chawane, 'The Development of Afrocentricity: A Historical Survey', *Yesterday and Today*, no. 16 (2016), https://doi.org/10.17159/2223-0386/2016/n16a5; Birgit Meyer and Kwame Anthony Appiah, 'In My Father's House: Africa in the Philosophy of Culture', *Journal of Religion in Africa*, 1994, https://doi.org/10.2307/1581314; Daniel Avorgbedor and Kofi Agawu, 'African Rhythm, a Northern Ewe Perspective', *Yearbook for Traditional Music*, 1996, https://doi.org/10.2307/767817; Kuwor, 'Transmission of Anlo-Ewe Dances in Ghana and in Britain: Investigating, Reconstructing and Disseminating Knowledge Embodied in the Music and Dance Traditions of Anlo-Ewe People in Ghana'; Sylvanus Kwashie Kuwor, 'The Impact of Adzido on Black Dance and Crosscultural Education in British Schools', *Review of Human Factor Studies* 19, no. 1 (2013); Samuel Elikem Kwame Nyamuame, 'History, Religion and Performing Yeve: Ewe Dance-Drumming, Songs and Rituals at Ave-Dakpa, Ghana', *ProQuest Dissertations and Theses* (2013); Younge, *Music and Dance Traditions of Ghana: History, Performance and Teaching*; Kwakwa, 'Kwabena Nketia and the Creative Arts: The Genesis of the School of Music and Drama, and the Formation of the Ghana Dance Ensemble'; Hagan, 'Dondology: Music, Mind and Matter'; Paulding, 'Asante Kete Drumming: A Musical Analysis of Meter, Feel, and Phrasing'; George Sefa Dei and Marlon Simmons, 'Indigenous Knowledge and the Challenge for Rethinking Conventional Educational Philosophy: A Ghanaian Case Study', *Counterpoints* 352 (2011): 97–111.

the department, including Mawere Opoku, Ampofo Duodu, J. H. K. Nketia, Ofotsu Adinku, Patience Kwakwa, and Sylvanus Kuwor, among others, have consistently worked toward promoting Ghanaian body exploration from dance-musicking perspectives. The primary role of the academy is to train skilled labor to support national and global development. However, when the acquired skills don't perceive themselves as agents of change but rather as entities subject to others' influence, the African Genius loses its value.

The Department of Dance Studies administers two programs for students pursuing a Bachelor of Fine Arts (BFA) and a Bachelor of Arts (BA). The BFA program focuses exclusively on the study of music, dance, and drama within a four-year period, while the BA program combines performance arts courses with other humanities courses. Each academic year batch group typically includes around 800 students, showcasing substantial growth in the number of individuals opting for dance studies at the university. This increase is attributed to evolving course allocation policies within both the BFA and BA modules. The courses offered encompass a variety of subjects, such as dance technique, dance criticism, anatomy and physiology of the dancer, dance research methods, dance analysis, and labanotation, among others. While there have been changes in the course structure and syllabi, they still draw significant influence from the early certificate level structure established in 1962, progressing to the diploma level in 1975. Sylvanus Kuwor's critical analysis of the pedagogical structure in the earlier curricula sheds light on this historical relationship. He observes that "[...] courses in the final examination for the Certificate in Dance were divided into two groups namely, Written Papers and Practical Examination [...] the written papers [are]: Introduction to Movement Analysis and Notation, Studies in African Dance Forms and Theory of Music. The practical Examination consists of Exercises and Reading in Labanotation Texts, Studies in African Dance Forms and Composition of Dance based on Studies in African Movements [...] ."[30] Having been a student of the Dance Studies Department from 2009 to 2013, the syllabus I encountered profoundly shaped my perspectives on various aspects of my culture and fostered an appreciation for its role in the political development of Ghana. This enlightening knowledge, though seemingly apparent, still escapes the broader public and political elite in their quest for political and economic autonomy. I will now scrutinize the course syllabi for the years 2020, 2021, and 2022 to derive insights for analysis.

---

30 Kuwor, 'Transmission of Anlo-Ewe Dances in Ghana and in Britain: Investigating, Reconstructing and Disseminating Knowledge Embodied in the Music and Dance Traditions of Anlo-Ewe People in Ghana'.

## 2020/2021/2022 Curricula

The Department runs a four-year bachelor's program divided into Levels 100 to 400. These are grouped into two streams of "Conceptual Dance Knowledge (CDK) and Practical Dance (PD)." Below is the breakdown of the courses and their descriptions. The information in the description sections is my summarized analysis of the course based on my study of each individual course syllabus.

| Level 100—First Year/Course Code | Course Title | Description |
| --- | --- | --- |
| DANC 119 | Dance Forms of Africa | Course explores the historical and contextual tenets of selected dances from selected African countries. |
| DANC 113 | Introduction to Practical African Dance I | Course introduces students to beginner neo-traditional dancing. |
| DANC 116 | Introduction to Practical African Dance II | Course introduces students to intermediate neo-traditional dancing. |
| DANC 112 | Introduction to Traditional Dance | Course introduces students to beginner neo-traditional dancing. |

| Level 200—Second Year/Course Code | Course Title | Description |
| --- | --- | --- |
| DANC 229 | Traditional Dance I | Course explores second neo-traditional dancing. |
| DANC 227 | Dance Technique I | Course explores traditional dance technique. |
| DANC 225 | Practical | Neo-traditional performance. |
| DANC 223 | Orientation to Dance Theatre | Course introduces the history of neo-traditional dancing in Ghana postindependence. |
| DANC 221 | Introduction to Dance Cultures of the World | Students explore dance knowledge from selected countries around the world. |
| DANC 228 | Dance Technique II | Course explores intermediate traditional dance technique. |
| DANC 226 | Traditional Dance II | Course explores neo-traditional dance. |
| DANC 224 | Practical Dance II | Neo-traditional performance. |
| DANC 222 | Introduction to Movement Analysis/Notation | Laban Movement Analysis. |

| Level 300—Third Year/Course Code | Course Title | Description |
| --- | --- | --- |
| THEA 346 | Costume and Makeup | Introduction to dance theater costuming, costuming for dance, costuming for community engagement/performances. |
| DANC 352 | Theatre Management | Principles of theater Management as a dancer/performer. |
| DANC 346 | Intermediate Labanotation II | Laban Movement Analysis. |
| DANC 344 | Intermediate Dance Technique II | Contemporary African Dance technique. |
| DANC 342 | Traditional Songs II | Introduction to traditional song composition and performance for the stage. |
| THEA 341 | Stage Craft | Principles of stage craft. |
| DANC 348 | Traditional Drumming II | Introduction to drumming as a dancer. |
| DANC 345 | Lighting Design for Dance | Principles of lighting for dance |
| DANC 343 | Intermediate Labanotation I | Laban Movement Analysis. |

| Level 400—Fourth Year/Course Code | Course Title | Description |
| --- | --- | --- |
| THEA 466 | Costume Design and Construction Costume History | Final year costume explorations. |
| DANC 490 | Advanced Labanotation II | Laban Movement Analysis. |
| DANC 470 | Community Project | Principles of community engagement and problem solving. |
| DANC 452 | African Instrumental Music Performance and Songs | Principles of African Instrumental Music Performance and Songs |
| DANC 450 | Production Participation (yearlong) | Principles of theater production. |
| THEA 465 | Costume Design and Construction Costume History | Final year costume explorations. |
| DANC 480 | Special Dance Study | Principles of dance ethnography and fieldwork |
| DANC 460 | Choreography | Choreography fundamentals and performance |
| DANC 451 | Advanced African Traditional Songs I | Principles of African Instrumental Music Performance and Songs |
| DANC 449 | Dance Ritual and Art | Theoretical exploration of dance as or in ritual |

## Conceptual Dance Knowledge and Practical Dance Breakdown

| Conceptual Dance Knowledge (CDK) | Practical Dance (PD) |
|---|---|
| DANC 119—Dance Forms of Africa | DANC 113—Introduction to Practical African Dance I |
|  | DANC 116—Introduction To Practical African Dance II |
|  | DANC 112—Introduction to Traditional Dance |
|  | DANC 229—Traditional Dance I |
|  | DANC 227—Dance Technique I |
|  | DANC 225—Practical |
| DANC 223—Orientation to Dance Theatre | DANC 228—Dance Technique II |
| DANC 221—Introduction to Dance Cultures of the World | DANC 226—Traditional dance II |
|  | DANC 224—Traditional Dance II |
|  | DANC 222—Introduction to Movement Analysis/Notation* |
| THEA 346 Costume and Makeup | DANC 344—Intermediate Dance Technique II |
| DANC 352—Theatre Management | DANC 342—Traditional Songs II |
| DANC 346—Intermediate Labanotation II* | DANC 342—Traditional Songs II |
| DANC 345—Lighting Design for Dance* | THEA 341—Stage Craft* |
| DANC 343—Intermediate Labanotation I* | DANC 348—Traditional Drumming II |
| THEA 466—Costume Design and Construction Costume History | DANC 452—African Instrumental Music Performance and Songs |
| DANC 490—Advanced Labanotation II* | DANC 450—Production Participation (year-long) |
| DANC 470—Community Project* | DANC 460—Choreography* |
| THEA 465—Costume Design and Construction Costume History | DANC 451—Advanced African Traditional Songs I |
| DANC 480—Special Dance Study |  |
| DANC 449—Dance Ritual and Art |  |

The asterisk (*) connotes courses that have a combined practical and conceptual element.

## Addressing Curriculum "Issues"

The dance studies curriculum at the University of Ghana has undergone continuous development over the years. Despite critical scholarly analyses of pedagogy by individuals like Ofotsu Adinku, Sylvanus Kuwor, Pascal Younge, and Modesto Amegago, among others, the absence of video documentation on performance structures over the years has left limited reference points for critical comparisons. One notable issue with the curriculum is its failure to expand to include other dance cultures beyond the "overused" dance forms from specific ethnicities like Ewe, Akan, Ga, and Dagbani. This overreliance on dances from these cultures has hindered research interest in other minority cultures. This issue is perceived as a "political omission" when advertising a program that should represent all 16 regions of Ghana today. The curriculum's roots are deeply entrenched in nationalism, reflecting the political motivations behind the establishment of institutes for music and dance research and performance in Ghana. Two predominant streams of pedagogical methods have been identified at the University of Ghana from 1963 to the present: "Nationalist Pedagogy" and "Contemporary Pedagogy."

The "Nationalist Pedagogy" aimed to counter colonial influence postindependence and emphasize the value of indigenous knowledge systems in shaping Ghanaian identity. This was evident in the setup of the Institute of African Studies and the Ghana Dance Ensemble. The inclusion of international scholars, especially those of African descent, in the curriculum brought an evolution to accommodate diaspora knowledge and eventually integrate "contemporary iterations."

On the other hand, "Contemporary Pedagogy" marked an epistemological shift toward academic dance theater. This signaled the expansion of dance theater in Ghana, championed by both Academic and Professional dance categories. It gave rise to neo-traditional dance research and performance elements, becoming a focal point of dance research from the 1960s to the present.

To contribute critically to the discourse on the transmission and embodiment of dance at the University of Ghana today, one must master the nuances of these historical timelines. Awuah's categorization emphasizes that performers in each category contribute to its nuanced structure. Therefore, constant amendments to Ghanaian dance pedagogy are necessary to include elements of "progressive thinking" and Afrocentric perspectives, fostering arguments for the genius of black dancing bodies.

## Summary

This chapter delved into the foundational aspects of traditional dancing in Ghana, providing insights into traditional dance categories and their postindependence variations. The discussion encompassed traditional dance-musicking, shedding light on the proliferation of traditional dance and its role in the formulation of national identity in the postindependence era. The chapter emphasized the need to address the impact of colonial influences on Ghanaians and Africans, urging a return to cultural roots through traditional knowledge systems. Additionally, the exploration extended to post-1992 neo-traditional dance pedagogy and institutional curriculum design. It highlighted the necessity for immediate expansion to accommodate emerging categories with distinct characteristics in their performance structures. This recognition points to the evolving nature of dance in Ghana and the ongoing efforts to adapt pedagogical approaches to reflect the dynamism of traditional and neo-traditional dance forms.

The journey through the historical and contemporary dimensions of traditional and neo-traditional dancing in Ghana sets the stage for further discussions on the cultural, educational, and political implications of these dance forms. As the exploration continues, it is essential to consider the nuanced nature of dance in shaping identities, fostering national pride, and contributing to the ever-evolving cultural landscape of Ghana.

# Chapter 5

# FROM PALACE TO ACADEMY: AN EMBODIED JOURNEY

This chapter details an autoethnographic account of my embodiment in my father's palace and a suburb in Kumasi known as Fante New Town. These settings influenced my learning of Kete and the acquired realities as a royal turned commoner. I employ autoethnography toward "finding new ways to write about social life and, to better understand our society, and to promote self-reflective and critical research. Therefore, primary-bodily data are of utmost importance [and] autoethnographic research includes methodological implications and raises the question of situating the body about knowledge construction, "evidence and the evidence of knowledge."[1] I position my embodied recollections concerning the absorption and dissemination of Kete within various contexts of my identity—first as a royal, then as a "commoner," entertainer, and artist-student-dancer. These corporeal memories are rooted in diverse experiences, encompassing my personal Kete dance training and performances during my childhood. These memories extend through significant phases, including the period before, during, and after my father's installation as a sub-chief in our rural town in Ghana known as *Mpohor*. They also encompass my active involvement with amateur groups, professional companies, and my time as a student at the University of Ghana's academy. This narrative delves into the intricacies of learning and practicing Kete in Kumasi, incorporating personal anecdotes. Furthermore, it sheds light on the circumstances that led to my transition from royalty to commoner, navigating the performance of identical variations under different identities and locations. This exploration aims to offer a foundation for understanding the dynamics of transmission and assimilation, highlighting the nuanced knowledge acquired within distinct social classes.

---

1 Grit Kirstin Koeltzsch, 'The Body as Site of Academic Consciousness. A Methodological Approach for Embodied (Auto)Ethnography', *Academia Letters* (2021): 1–5, https://doi.org/10.20935/al3104.

This autoethnographic narrative examines my assimilation of the Kete dance within the framework of three categories as outlined by Grit Koeltzsch: (i) self-observation and reflexivity, (ii) bodily perceptions and experiences across time and space, and (iii) past and present (Koeltzsch 2021).

**Fieldwork in Ghana**

The fieldwork for this research adopted a multisited approach to data collection, focusing on two regional capitals in Ghana: Kumasi, the capital of the Ashanti Region, where the Kete dance originates, and Accra, serving as the capital of the Greater Accra Region and the national capital of Ghana. In Kumasi, I engaged in data gathering, participant observation, and video recording among the master drummers and dancers at the Asante Monarch's palace, known as the Manhyia palace, as well as at other venues such as funerals and parties.

In Accra, field data collection took place at the University of Ghana and among selected amateur groups within the city. Although the official data collection period for my PhD was between May and September 2021, the autoethnographic perspective suggests that it began when I first started learning Kete dance steps and movements in my father's house/palace. My involvement deepened as I took on roles such as drum carver, supporting drum player, and eventually, dancer. This engagement was further influenced by my observation of master/virtuoso performers before me. Primary data collection occurred in various suburbs, including Manhyia, Fante Newtown, Ashtown in Kumasi, and Madina, Legon Campus, and Maamobi-Nima in Accra. Audio-visual performances were recorded to aid in the analysis.

Interview questions were meticulously designed to delve into experiential narratives that illuminate dance as a human phenomenon. The primary focus of the interviews was on traditional dancers and musicians, particularly those associated with the Kete dance form. Additionally, I conducted interviews with university dance students and performers with knowledge of Kete, instructors, selected members of the Ghana Dance Ensemble, and Mrs. Judith Opoku-Boateng, the head archivist of the J. H. Kwabena Nketia Archive. It is essential to note that, during the course of this research, the Kete dance form was not actively taught at the Department of Dance Studies. This was primarily due to the absence of faculty with the requisite training to teach Kete. Nevertheless, the dance ecosystem at the University of Ghana, featuring entities like the Ghana Dance Ensemble, Abibigromma Theatre Company, and the Department of Dance Studies in close proximity, facilitated informal learning opportunities. For instance, the Ghana Dance Ensemble and Abibigromma Theatre Company occasionally recruited students for specific events, training them in various Kete variations as needed. Consequently, students were informally taught outside the formal curriculum. The interviews conducted varied in formality, depending on the participant's preference, and encompassed an exploration of Asante and Kete dance vocabulary, as well as their transmission within both traditional and academic contexts. Notable interviewees included dance researchers such as Eric Awuah, Sylvanus Kuwor (PhD), Dr. Kofi Anthonio, Senyo Okyere, and master drummers at the Department of Dance Studies, including Prosper Ablordey, Seth Gati, Kwadwo Boakye, and Lenny Asharku.

## Revisiting Manhyia: Transitioning from Nostalgia to Reverence, Embracing Dance Knowledge as a Researcher

Manhyia, in the Akan language, consists of two separate words, "Oman"—meaning a people or a nation—and "hyia"—signifying a gathering or meeting of a people. Therefore, the combination of these words denotes a place where the nation or people meet. In this context, it refers to the house or palace of the king, known as the Asantehene (literal translation: Asante king) of Asanteman (literal translation: Asante people or nation). Manhyia is situated in Kumasi, the capital of the Ashanti Kingdom and the Ashanti Region, and it holds personal significance for me as it is within walking distance from where I was born and grew up. I have visited the palace on numerous occasions, both independently and with my first amateur Kete group, during festive occasions for performances and educational trips. The palace serves as the residence of the current king and the Asantehemaa (Asante Queen Mother), as well as housing the Manhyia Archives (affiliated with the University of Ghana Archives) and the Manhyia Museum. The surrounding area also features various institutions, such as the local branch of the Ghana Prisons Service, a police station, a hospital, a fire service station, a radio station, and the office of the Lands Secretariat.

During my return to Manhyia for data gathering as a researcher, I adopted a more observant and analytical perspective than during my previous roles as a performer and school pupil. Before my visit, I had established connections with the palace performance group through the assistance of Mrs. Judith Opoku-Boateng, the head archivist of the J. H. Kwabena Nketia Archive at the University of Ghana. She played a crucial role as my gatekeeper in reaching Nana Kwadwo Boateng, the Asante Kete Chief, at the Manhyia Palace. Nana Kwadwo Boateng is a highly regarded Kete performer and indigenous archivist, dedicating his entire life, from childhood to Kete music and dance performance in the palace. His historical perspectives on the form and personal narratives, having served two monarchs, are invaluable in understanding his mastery of the art. Before my departure to Kumasi, Judith connected me with another PhD student who had recently returned from fieldwork at the Manhyia Palace. Since it was my first time entering the palace as a researcher, I sought guidance on how to conduct myself appropriately. Despite being familiar with palace etiquette, I appreciated the coaching and took notes for reference.

On August 5, 2021, my field support team and I were scheduled for an interview with the Asante Kete Chief, Nana Kwadwo Boateng, at the Manhyia Palace. Concerned about potential changes in the schedule, I attempted to confirm the appointment by making several calls. However, my calls went unanswered, leading to some apprehension as Nana Kwadwo Boateng's busy schedule could entail unexpected official duties. In response to this uncertainty, I consulted my hired linguist, Mr. Frank Owusu, for guidance. He reassured me that things would proceed as planned.

Engaging the services of a linguist/spokesperson was crucial when communicating with a sub-chief or king, as palace communication involves intricacies. Despite being an indigenous person, I lacked expertise in palace oratory and politics. Additionally, my status as a "commoner" in Manhyia restricted direct communication with any chief, except in specific circumstances where the chief waives official communication protocols. Taking precautions was essential to avoid any inadvertent breaches of protocol or misunderstandings.

Anticipating a lengthy meeting during our first encounter with the Kete Chief, I took precautions to ensure that my team, including Nana Twumasi-Ntiamoah (audio-visual support) and Joshua Benumanson (audio-visual support), could stay beyond the initially planned 5 hours. I made arrangements for three meals throughout the day and extended the rental of audio-visual equipment. The scheduled appointment with the Kete Chief was deemed crucial, and I was not willing to take any risks, as it represented a significant opportunity to access unpublished embodied historical data relevant to Ghanaian dance, absent from any existing theses or journals.

Upon our arrival at the entrance of the Manhyia Palace, I was surprised to find the chief informant waiting. After exchanging pleasantries, we proceeded to the palace compound. The strong security presence at the entrance was navigated smoothly with the assistance of our informant. As we walked from the outer court to the inner court, we encountered numerous elders and young people who greeted our lead informant with hand gestures and appellations. Some inquired about our identity in proverbial language, making it clear that we were considered "outsiders." I had decided beforehand to keep my royal lineage out of the conversation, recognizing its potential to steer discussions in directions that might not align with my research goals. The chief took the lead in the conversation.

**Image 3** Walking into Manhyia Palace. Source: Photo by Joshua Benumanson (2021) showing myself with Mr. Frank on the right leading me to the second gate.

Initially, our informant intended to use the court of the Asantehemaa (Asante Queen mother) for the interview, but we discovered that it was occupied for court deliberations on stool allocation in a neighboring town. Consequently, our informant directed us to an older, unused courtyard, where we eventually settled for the interview.

Prior to commencing the questioning, my informant inquired about my origin, catching me off guard. I realized that my responses would likely prompt a genealogical inquiry to confirm my connection to the Asante kingdom. As I sat down to set up my recorder, he asked, "Young man, where are you from?" After providing my place of residence, he repeated the question, making it clear that he was interested in my hometown and family lineage.

**Image 4** With Nana Boakye (ketehene). Source: Photo by Twumasi Ntiamoah (2021).

Subsequently, he inquired about my clan affiliation and clan totem. These ethnically probing questions allowed the informant to assess my responses carefully before acknowledging them.

Even though these questions typically should have been directed through my hired linguist, the informant addressed them to me directly, deviating from the norm. This established a hermeneutic approach to questioning and adopted a semi-structured interview style. He specifically requested that I communicate with him directly, rendering my linguist redundant.

### Fieldwork in the United States and Canada (Virtual)

In Philadelphia, I conducted interviews over Zoom and, at times, through phone calls with Asante Kete dancers and musicians. I capitalized on my

**Image 5** Interviewing Nana Boakye. Kete chief seated on the right. Source: Photo by Twumasi Ntiamoah (2021).

established relationships with most of the informants and performers with whom I had collaborated in Ghana for many years, seeking their insights for my research. While I initially intended to visit three of my informants as part of an extensive research endeavor, financial constraints and pandemic-related restrictions led me to resort to virtual interactions. Additionally, I undertook archival research at the Temple University Library and explored online resources. During these virtual sessions, I engaged in extensive conversations with key scholarly informants, including Professor Molefi Asante Kete, who generously shared his knowledge and guided my exploration of Afrocentricity. I also consulted with my supervisor, Professor Karen Bond, who assisted me in exploring a phenomenological analysis of the Kete dance

**Image 6** Touring Manhyia Palace with Nana Boakye. Source: Photo by Joshua Benumanson (2021).

form. Furthermore, Professor Whitney Hunter consistently encouraged me to delve deeper into Kete dance epistemologies.

## Navigating Identity through Dance: An Autoethnographic Exploration

Growing up, I often found myself pondering questions, and instead of verbal responses, I received answers through actions and bodily expressions. It was not that my respondents were unwilling to speak; rather, they encouraged me to learn through observation and imitation. This questioning process evolved throughout my life, eventually becoming the focus of my master's and PhD inquiries. During my fieldwork in Ghana, my mother would routinely bring up a repeated question I used to ask when she took me to witness dance performances in our village. I would inquire, "Maa, what are you doing moving like that?" At the time, her responses seemed puzzling, but as I delved into the study of dance as a performer and emerging scholar, these responses became revelations. Her answer, "wo be nyini abɜto!" (lit. you will grow up to meet these same things), marked a crucial turning point in my fascination with dance studies. Having a mother who is a dancer provided my initial influence. This indigenous approach to knowledge assimilation involved children consciously and unconsciously developing keen observation skills crucial to their embodied learning within the community. Unbeknownst to me, I was inquiring about the movement system of the body I emerged from—how it came to know itself and confidently express itself through dance within a community that engaged in similar movements to the same music.

Later on, I realized that this movement system, deeply rooted, lived, and respected over centuries among my people, became a significant element in shaping my understanding of myself and my identity. The term "identity" itself, as a word and concept, only scratches the surface of these complex realities. Anthropologist Edward Hall aptly notes, "Culture hides much more than it reveals, and strangely enough what it hides, it hides most effectively from its participants." Years of study convinced him that the real task is not merely to understand foreign cultures but to comprehend our own. This perspective allowed me to reflect on my childhood experiences, helping me conceptualize the transient body in diverse social, cultural, and political contexts within my ethnic group. As the child of a sub-chief in Wassa Mpohor, my transition into a higher status and validation as royalty mandated me to dance during my father's ascension to the stool. I recount how the selected dance and its movements transformed and influenced my understanding of Akan linguistic patterning and its power to affirmi individual identities. My official dance training commenced at the age of six, involving specific movement patterns distinct from those I observed outside my father's house.

My initiation into singing and dancing occurred at a tender age under the guidance of my mother, an accomplished dancer. In the rich tapestry of traditional Ghanaian societies, women, particularly mothers, play pivotal roles in the preservation and propagation of folktales. My mother, like many rural women, would often express her joy through spontaneous dance movements, setting the stage for my earliest lessons. In my 2017 master's research in Togo, I delved into the significant roles women play in transmitting music and dance, emphasizing their instrumental contribution to preserving intangible cultural heritage. My mother's influence on my early understanding of expressive movement was profound. Initially, I observed her spontaneous fits of dance to convey her mood, but it was through her physical guidance that I began to attach movements to my emotional states within various contexts.

My traditional music and dance education took shape under the guidance of two individuals from distinct social classes—my mother and father. While my mother held the status of a commoner in my father's house, her lineage traced back to Asante Mampong, endowing her with royal status in her paternal family. On the other hand, my father hailed from Wassa Mpohor and held royal standing within his community. Both ethnicities, part of the broader Akan group, introduced me to slight sociocultural variations, particularly in language dialects. This early exposure to diverse cultural elements became pivotal to my identity, shaping my ability to navigate social roles in my future dance career, especially as I transitioned between royal and commoner duties. The negotiation of these dual identities through dance provided a foundation for my understanding of expressive movement within the intricate web of sociocultural dynamics.

## Navigating Royal Etiquette through Dance: Lessons from Chieftaincy

My training as a royal extended beyond the dance arena, encompassing various facets of royal etiquette. Instructed to "walk as a royal," I learned specific salutations and cues appropriate to my royal status. The meticulous guidance covered a spectrum of behaviors, including sitting, eating in public, drinking from a cup, maintaining posture, and adopting a distinctive gait.

A notable aspect of my training involved synchronizing movements with my father, who actively participated in dance practice. His engagement in the same movement patterns conveyed a profound lesson about the unity of our roles and identities. Throughout our practices, he would impart wisdom through emphatic phrases such as "a royal does not sweat on the dance floor," "you are the son of great ancestors," and "wisdom and dancing abilities are in your blood." In these moments, the interplay of specific hand and foot movements became a ritualistic validation of my identity—a process where I understood myself exclusively through the language of dance. The profound declarations, combined with the prescribed movement patterns, instilled a sense of purpose and legacy in my dance journey. My father's exhortations, including visionary statements like "you will dance with me, your father, in glory," and "the stool and the music are yours alone to take after I am gone," fortified my understanding of the weight carried by the royal mantle.

Crucially, the authority of the chieftaincy institution, deeply rooted in Ghanaian tradition and predating European colonialism, provided a formal validation for my learning and eventual public performance of specific movements. This connection between royal etiquette, dance, and the chieftaincy institution underscored the intricate interplay between tradition, identity, and performance in the Ghanaian cultural landscape. George Bob-Milliar explains chieftaincy as a resilient indigenous governance system that incorporates executive, judicial, and legislative powers; has withstood the challenges of British imperialism and various postindependence regimes; and today plays a crucial role in settling disputes and promoting socioeconomic development.[2]

Embedded within the fabric of Ghanaian and African societies, chieftaincy stands as the pinnacle of indigenous governance, shaping the enforcement of customary rules and the evolution of social, political, and environmental knowledge. This venerable institution holds a paramount position, serving as the central nexus around which traditional societal organizations revolve.

Chieftaincy's influence extends far and wide, permeating various aspects of life and culture. It is the bedrock upon which social classes are not only delineated but also enacted, negotiated, and performed. Within this framework, traditional festivals, social performances, and rituals find validation and support. Chieftaincy institutions, therefore, play a pivotal role in the propagation and legitimization of cultural identity, contributing to the preservation and continuity of indigenous heritage. Napoleon Bamfo shares that Chiefs in Ghana and other parts of Africa are widely recognized due to their various religious, social, administrative, and judicial roles. Although they may appear to live a luxurious and privileged life, chiefs must navigate complex structures and adhere to local traditions and moral standards to avoid being removed from their positions.[3]

The subtle but powerful dynamics of chieftaincy were ingrained in my upbringing through my father's unconscious demonstrations, particularly during public outings. His interactions with community members, his demeanor while walking about the community, and, significantly, his dance performances at various events served as living expressions of the authority vested in the chieftaincy institution. Following his enstoolment as chief, the palace became a hub of activity, attracting individuals from diverse backgrounds for meetings and discussions. On specific occasions, my father would summon me to greet these visitors. Later revelations from my mother unveiled the deeper meaning behind these orchestrated appearances—a declaration to all present that he, my father, had a son who could potentially succeed him in the

---

2 George M. Bob-Milliar, 'Chieftaincy, Diaspora, and Development: The Institution of Nksuohene in Ghana', *African Affairs* 108, no. 433 (1 October 2009): 541–58, https://doi.org/10.1093/afraf/adp045.

3 Napoleon Bamfo, 'The Hidden Elements of Democracy among Akyem Chieftaincy: Enstoolment, Destoolment, and Other Limitations of Power', *Journal of Black Studies* 31, no. 2 (11 February 2000): 149–73.

**Image 7** Author performing at a durbar, 2016. Source: Photo by Twumasi Ntiamoah.

future. In hindsight, I understand that I was akin to an "insurance policy" for my father's lineage, perhaps even receiving special favor among my siblings. This practice of showcasing a designated "heir" aligns with prevalent norms in patriarchal societies, where men in elevated political and cultural roles, such as chiefs, often prioritize the continuity of their lineage.

In the period leading up to my father's anticipated ascension to the chieftaincy role, I found myself unintentionally thrust into a rigorous training regimen. As one of six male siblings in line to succeed him, my enrollment in this intensive program was unique. Unlike my elder brothers, who were spared such intense preparation, I became part of this specialized training because of the pressing urgency and imminent prospect of my father assuming the mantle of chief elect.

While my siblings underwent some form of training based on their royal status, the gravity of the training I received was distinct. The urgency stemmed from the fact that, unlike during my brothers' time, our father was now the chosen chief-elect of his clan. It is an unspoken understanding within royal families that any of the chief's sons could potentially be chosen as his successor in the event of his demise. This practice is not uncommon among royal families and dynasties, as highlighted by George Ayittey, who notes that succession is not always automatic and competition within the royal clan may determine the final choice[4] During these training sessions, which delved into

---

4 G. Ayittey, *Indigenous African Institutions* (Brill, 2006), https://books.google.ca/books?id=sW-wCQAAQBAJ.

royal dance etiquettes, my father revealed that he, too, had received similar instructions during his childhood. The additional lessons he underwent were designed to accentuate his status among his people and prepare him for the weighty responsibilities that lay ahead. It's important to note that proficiency in dancing is a crucial prerequisite for enstoolment, and any prospective chief within the Akan ethnic group, which comprises myriad subgroups, must demonstrate these skills to avoid rejection.

From a young age, I quickly grasped the profound respect and elevated status accorded to cultural bearers of indigenous knowledge within royal lineages. However, I soon realized that the social privileges associated with this esteemed position were predominantly experienced beyond the confines of the palace. While I received teachings pertaining to the people, these instructions imposed certain limitations on my actions, particularly in the realm of dancing and my public interactions within the broader landscape of cultural politics. During my training periods, I was initiated into specific knowledge and belief systems deemed sacred and esoteric. A cardinal rule accompanied this exposure: absolute discretion. I was sternly instructed never to divulge these secrets unless my father granted permission. This initiation into the dichotomy of "for them" and "for us" mirrored Koeltzsch's exploration of mental and physical barriers affecting performances, particularly in her analysis of skating (Koeltzsch 2021). Esotericism emerged as a pivotal element of my royal identity, permeating not only my engagements in dance and music performances but also influencing my everyday actions in public spaces. These cultural dogmas became integral to my physical responses, shaping my interactions with both space and matter.

In delving deeper into the labyrinth of esoteric knowledge, I encountered the metaphysical dimensions of Akan cosmology. This exploration profoundly informed my tripartite conception of self, unraveling layers of significance within the Akan cultural framework. The Akan people's unwavering emphasis on kingship ties and the pivotal role of spiritual "understanding" underscored the importance of esotericism in delineating boundaries within families and societies. Esotericism, while not always overt in character, wielded considerable influence in shaping the distinctions between the public and private domains and delineating the differences between a noble and a commoner. This intricate tapestry of metaphysical insights provided a nuanced understanding of the cultural intricacies that underscored my identity, intertwining the seen and unseen realms within the rich fabric of Akan cosmology. The importance of esoterism in my indigenous knowledge accumulation is influenced by Akyeampong and Obeng, who aver that "the Asante [Akan] universe [is] suffused with power. *Onyame* (the Supreme Being) had created a universe impregnated with his power. Power was thus rooted in the Asante cosmology, and individuals and groups that successfully tapped into this power source translated this access into authority if they controlled social institutions. Authority (political power) could be monopolized, but access to power (Twi: *tumi:*, "the ability to bring about change") was available to anyone who knew how to make use of Onyame's powerful universe for good or evil."[5] In the realm of royalty, I discovered that "power and authority" were not just abstract concepts but were deeply embodied and expressed through the art of dance. For me, dance became a profound medium, serving as a sacred bridge to the past and a powerful means of affirming my identity as both an indigene of Wassa Mpohor and Asante Mampong. During my rigorous Kete dance training sessions, my father assumed the role of a discerning spectator, carefully observing my every move. In these transformative moments, my father adopted a unique instructional approach, addressing me in the third person during dance lessons. I would hear phrases like, "A Chief's son must dance with pride," "a chief's son should be the center of attention, performing masterfully with understanding," and "a chief's son must carry his traditional music in his heart, mind, and spirit." This unconventional method initially created a distinct separation between the father-son relationship on the dance floor. However, as I reflect on these teachings now, I understand that they were deliberate efforts to instill in me the profound responsibilities that come with royal lineage.

My mother later revealed that these instructions were designed to impress upon me that a Chief's reign is finite and the title must be carried forward to ensure the survival of the lineage. My father emphasized that the transition from prince to chief is inevitable, and one must be prepared to shoulder the responsibilities more earnestly than the title itself. Dance, in this context, served as the sacred language through which these teachings were transmitted, preparing me for the vital role I would one day assume. In this sacred journey of learning, I was also introduced to three symbolic elements of communication: iconographic symbols, dance movements, and costume patterns, each contributing to the rich tapestry of royal expression.

A spectacle deeply ingrained in the fabric of traditional Ghanaian events is the grandeur of a durbar, or gathering featuring a chief or king. Among the iconic elements that define such occasions are the resonant beats of drums, vast crowds, and the presence of a palanquin carrying dignitaries—typically the chief or king and a young companion. The palanquin, symbolic of elevated status, signifies a position of honor and distinction within a specific geopolitical context. In the preparations leading up to my father's enstoolment, the palanquin played a pivotal role in the dance rehearsals. Housed within the palace, they practiced dancing within the mid-air confines of the

---

5 Akyeampong and Obeng, 'Spirituality, Gender, and Power in Asante History'.

palanquin. Skilled carriers, usually men from the palace, lifted the chief aloft. In this elevated position, my father would execute dance movements while seated, and I, his son, would replicate these movements while standing. The mid-air rehearsals within the palanquin became a ritualistic and symbolic precursor to the grand coronation day. As the momentous day approached, a series of events unfolded. First, my father underwent solitary rituals at the ancestral shrine, marking a sacred connection to the lineage and traditions. Upon his return, the ceremonial activities commenced, starting from his private residence, progressing through the village square in a regal procession, and culminating at the palace, where he would undertake the solemn oath of office. This intricate choreography of rituals and performances encapsulated the essence of traditional enthronement, with dance serving as a central element in expressing and embodying the elevated royal identity.

**Image 8** Author's father, Nana Amponsah Cudjoe, at his coronation in the year 1999.

**Image 9** Emmanuel Cudjoe at his father's coronation ceremony in the year 1999.

In the lead-up to my father's enstoolment, the palanquin emerged as a central stage for a regal dance performance that transcended the ordinary. Together, my father partook in a ceremonial dance within the confines of the palanquin, a symbolic representation of elevated status and honor. Positioned side by side, he would sit, adorned with the state swords, while I stood, mirroring every movement with precision and grace. One particular routine, the "Dwannyini mienu shia a, nayehu bɛɛma," held a distinct significance. This choreographed sequence conveyed a powerful message to onlookers, signaling my father's strength and triumph over adversaries. As we danced, the air resonated with exclamations from the crowd, expressing admiration and acknowledgment: "You look good dancing, our chief," "You are the son of great ancestors," and "Wisdom and dancing abilities are in your blood," among other accolades. These affirmations, coupled with the rhythmic hand and foot movements, became a reaffirmation of my identity and responsibility. The cheers and praises from the community resonated with a shared sense of pride, acknowledging our role as custodians of tradition and the embodiment of a legacy passed down through generations. In the dance of royalty within the palanquin, a harmonious connection was forged between the past, the present, and the collective spirit of the people.

The untimely passing of my father, a mere three years after his coronation, marked the beginning of a profound shift in my life's trajectory. Departing from my father's hometown and the structured confines of royal life, I found myself in the vibrant and eclectic atmosphere of Fante New Town in Kumasi. Here, the meticulous traits cultivated through the disciplined Kete dance training began to yield to the unassuming norms of commoner life. In this new milieu, the intricacies of how one drank from a cup or carried oneself held little significance. It was a realm where distinctions of royalty faded, and the mantra became "we are all the same." Adapting to this altered reality, I embraced a new set of traits to seamlessly assimilate into my surroundings. Fante New Town became the backdrop for my educational journey, encompassing primary and secondary schooling.

It was in this dynamic suburb that I rekindled my connection with Kete, albeit in a different context. Engaging with amateur groups that traversed Kumasi and beyond to perform at funerals, I delved into a more fluid and adaptable version of the dance. Here, the movements were crafted to resonate with the solemnity and context of funeral ceremonies. Beyond dance, I expanded my skill set to include drum playing, a pursuit restricted in my father's palace due to my royal status. I immersed myself in the art of carving drum shells, stretching animal skins over meticulously carved wood, and tuning the drums to achieve their distinct pitches. This chapter marked not only a transition in social status but also a profound journey of acquiring diverse skills and experiences that would shape my identity in the years to come.

## Exploring the Phenomenological Essence of Self

My engagement with phenomenology in my PhD years sparked a profound realization and prompted a deep exploration of my childhood curiosity and the perplexity surrounding gestures. I became enthralled by the epistemological significance of my bodily memories and their experiences, which would significantly shape my analysis of Kete movement analysis. Drawing from my own childhood experience is paramount to my position as a student, performer, and expert of the dance form. This is important because, as Karen Bond contends, a "phenomenological inquiry into children's meaning-making as a source of theoretical and practical knowledge remains limited"[6]—a

---

6 Karen Bond, '"Me, a Tree" – Young Children as Natural Phenomenologists', in *Back to the Dance Itself: Phenomenologies of the Body in Performance* (Urbana, IL: University of Illinois Press, 2018), 205–32.

sentiment with which I concur. Had my experiences been extrapolated earlier in my studies of movement and dance, it is conceivable that I would have contributed more extensively to the literature on Ghanaian experiences. I agree with Bond's perspective that these critical limitations have the potential to restrict our understanding of children's embodied abilities in dance. It is intriguing to observe how our children, often designated as future leaders, encounter obstacles in pursuing the study and exploration of dance in Ghanaian schools. While cultural beliefs contribute to this phenomenon, it does not negate the fact that, even after 50 years of dance development in Ghana, negative perceptions toward dance persist and are passed on to children early in life, perpetuating a detrimental cycle. Similar to Bond, I align with her position that she is "not looking for resolutions in theory [but rather] [...] consider how children's lived experience drawings and utterances about dancing might strengthen a collection of empirical and philosophical ideas from literature" (Bond 2018).

By incorporating a deliberate focus on "systematic introspection and memory documentation" (Koeltzsch 2021) into dance curriculum development in Ghanaian primary schools, there is an opportunity to capture children's lived experiences not merely as ordinary but as a conduit to enhance our understanding of bodily assimilation processes in Ghana, an area currently lacking scholarly data.

I employ the "Experience Inquiry" approach, placing lived experience at the core of empirical analysis and understanding. First, I must add that my self-realization is made up of cultural and religious interconnections. I believe in the tripartite conception of man as body, soul, and spirit. This conception of the self and my experience as a dancer, cultural ambassador, and Christian were pivotal in how they influenced my conception of tangible and intangible realities. As a dance arranger/composer/choreographer, I have often, aside from my obvious culturally accumulated knowledge, found it difficult to express in words my creative drive and abilities. Given that some tenets of academia have had their foundations in scientism and have not given much support to embodied or phenomenological inquiries and inputs, I found the empirical exploration of my experiences in this class theoretically viable for explaining my own experiences. Hence, my experiences as recounted in this work form part of my "self-theory"—that which allows my understanding, and especially my confusion, to drive my inquiry into phenomena through autoethnography. As Nick Crossley averred, "doing embodied (auto) ethnography means using the body as a research tool recognizing subjective experiences and reflexive embodiment" (Koeltzsch 2021). The critical discussion related to "reality" in the embodied experience gave me the opportunity to explore my transition between classes. What intrinsic value in Kete dance makes one "realize" and accept their class hierarchy? I ask this because there

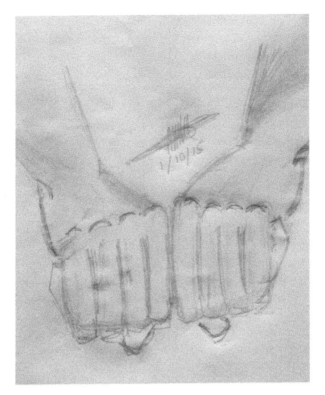

**Image 10** Dwannyinimienushia. Cudjoe, *The Contexts and Meaning in Asante Dance Performance: The Case of Kete.*

were some movements I was taught as a royal and that when I was a "royal," I performed.

However, I performed the same Kete variation after my transition, and so it is the same body, the same "royal blood" flowing inside me, but the reality of the meaning affirmed the reality of my acquired status in Fante New Town-Kumasi. For example, I researched selected Kete movements like "*Dwannyinimienushia a, nayehu bɛɛma.*" See photo below:

> This movement [motif] translates into "when two rams clashes, the stronger emerges." *Dwannyini* literally means an adult Ram (in this context with horns); *mienu* literally means the number two; *shia* literally means to clash; *nayehubɛɛma* literally translates to we see the stronger man. Movement-wise, this is exhibited by the adjacent hitting of the two clenched arms. This symbolizes competitiveness or war and further goes on to add that in the face of confrontation, only the strong will survive.[7]

---

7 Cudjoe.

Now, as a royal, I was taught this movement to represent my authority over others. It allowed me to leverage my bloodline and attribute the valiancy and exploits of my forefathers, even though I was a little boy. As such, I was accorded the "royal meaning" whenever I performed this with my father. It was, metaphorically, a challenge to anyone who was also heir to the throne because I had brothers, and then to the common folk. However, in Fante New Town, I could not perform this in that royal capacity because first, the land was not my father's land, and I was a "commoner." Also, I was not competing for a throne, and as such, my performance in the movement was devoid of that rhetoric. For an exercise we did in one of my dance classes, we were encouraged to spend up to one hour in a familiar place, record our experiences in the space as if it were the first time, employ all our sensory channels, respond to the space with body movement, close our eyes for part of the time, and then finish the entry by writing about the experience. This was a sensory exercise that allowed me to conceptualize space outside of social class. In this sense, the space became the defining element of my outward conceptualization of self to the point that I employed my sensory abilities to facilitate my transition from my old reality to the emerging reality of a new space. Learning and performing Kete in Fante New Town was a process of engaging reality from space, senses, and the conscious and unconscious selves.

## Kete as "Artifact"—the Palace as a Museum of Ancestral Legacies

The concept of a museum, from a Western perspective, typically refers to a physical architectural structure, either privately owned or public, that houses artifacts and elements of ancient or immediate civilizations. According to the International Council for Museums, a museum is a nonprofit, permanent institution in the service of society and its development, open to the public. It acquires, conserves, researches, communicates, and exhibits the tangible and intangible heritage of humanity and its environment for purposes of education, study, and enjoyment[8] Museums are valuable resources for learning about heritage, although they tend to emphasize tangible heritage more than intangible forms. In this context, I situate my father's palace within the discourse of museology and propose that traditional palaces across Ghana can be considered museums.

The key distinction between the Western Museum and the traditional one I propose lies in the latter consciously including intangible elements such as

---

8 ICOM, 'Museum Definition', ICOM Resources, 2007, https://icom.museum/en/resources/standards-guidelines/museum-definition/.

dance, sound, rituals, and living human interactions daily. Therefore, it represents a mixture of tangible and intangible heritage elements within a given culture. "Museums and galleries are arguably the most significant facilities for housing tangible heritage materials and, in doing so, allowing people to make connections to the past" (Awuah 2016). I consider my father's palace a museum of ancestral legacies because, within traditional beliefs, an empty physical space doesn't equate to the absence of ancestors. Although physically deceased, their spirits are believed to be very much alive, influencing daily life, and even dictating the name and title a king/chief answers to through the stool he chooses to sit on during his lifetime. According to my mother, the souls of the ancestors are constantly present, making the space sacred. Any music played for the living, especially for dancing, is considered the same for the spirits. My father's house adorned its walls with photos of his forebears, along with artifacts such as bows and arrows, animal skulls, fabric materials, and antiques dating back centuries. Similar to conventional museums, each of these items carried specific meanings, but more importantly, they were woven into the folklore of our community. The knowledge embodied in these artifacts served as creative impulses for the creation of dance movements and musical accompaniments.

My father's palace walls had selected Adinkra symbols painted on them and made deliberately visible for all to see. Adinkra symbols are peculiar to the Akan ethnic group, and their uses are symbolic. According to Cynthia Mawuli, Adinkra symbols comprise a rich and intricate system that conveys narratives about ritual, tradition, and beliefs. These symbols, found on various crafts and fabrics, are worn to reflect one's mood, ethnicity, group affiliation, status, and influence within the Akan social context, thereby endorsing and accentuating an individual's status and mood with symbolic content deeply rooted in historical, social, philosophical, and political values.[9]

The ubiquity of these symbols is so extensive in Ghana that they are featured on every currency denomination and government building. Some of these symbols are

*Akofena* depicts two crossed traditional swords meaning "Sword of War" and symbolizes courage, valor, and heroism.[10]

---

9 Cynthia Adjovi Mawuli, *Transmission and Embodiment of Heritage: An Analysis of Adinkra Symbology on Traditional Clothing in Ghana* (Central European University, 2019).

10 (See) Mawuli, Cynthia Adjovi. "Transmission and Embodiment of Heritage: An Analysis of Adinkra Symbology on Traditional Clothing in Ghana" (2019).

*Dwennimmen*, literally meaning "ram's horns," deriving from the geometric shape of two rams' horns, symbolizes strength (in mind, body, and spirit), humility, wisdom, and learning.[11]

*Nyame Dua, meaning* God's tree symbolizes God's presence or protection.[12]

The three highlighted symbols, among the myriad of Adinkra symbols employed by the Akan ethnic group, adorned the inner walls of my father's palace. During his swearing-in ceremony, he wielded two traditional state swords known as Akofena, a symbol of authority (depicted above). The wall behind his stool in the palace was adorned with the same symbol, conveying his authority to guests. The other two symbols adorned opposite walls within the palace. I observed these symbols on the official palace's traditional drums and some of my father's garments. Acquiring knowledge about these symbols has deepened my understanding, allowing me to establish meaningful connections between the tangible and intangible elements inherent in my Kete dance, where each movement holds a relationship with these symbols and their nuanced meanings. Within this confined space, a unique curatorial politics played out in plain sight, visible only to the trained eye. The negotiation of spatial elements, including space, matter, artifacts, and philosophical components such as music, dance, and body movements, formed an intricate dance of preservation within the palace. If we consider Marie Mauze's notion that museums aim to inform the public about the culture and history of a group of people for a better understanding of their community's past and present,[13] then the palace serves as a preserver of indigenous culture, heritage, and language for future generations. Unseen curatorial politics, consciously or unconsciously managed, orchestrated the exhibition of all resources in the palace, allowing generations of Wassa Mpohor indigenes to connect with their past and present.

---

11 (See) Mawuli, Cynthia Adjovi. "Transmission and Embodiment of Heritage: An Analysis of Adinkra Symbology on Traditional Clothing in Ghana" (2019).

12 (See) Mawuli, Cynthia Adjovi. "Transmission and Embodiment of Heritage: An Analysis of Adinkra Symbology on Traditional Clothing in Ghana" (2019).

13 Marie Mauzé, 'Two Kwakwaka'wakw Museums: Heritage and Politics', *Ethnohistory* 50, no. 3 (Summer 2003): 503–22, https://doi.org/10.1215/00141801-50-3-503.

Reflecting on my childhood and political affiliation leads me to the conclusion that I was "curated" for exhibitions within the palace "museum," not only as a representation of royal dispensation but as a cultural constituent essential for the continuity of the political system. As a dancer performing Kete before my father's guests, I validated these positions. If a curator is a custodian and organizer, then individuals in royal lineages, like me, have always been "exhibitions," continually "represented" to the outside world through bodily actions, including dance. Given our oral heritage, I argue that information about our identities and roles in the cultural ecosystem is imprinted on our bodies through costumes, props used in ritual performances, music and dance, and our public interactions. As Awuah notes, "museum curatorial practices promote re-interpretation, re-structuring, re-coordination, and re-assessment of ownership and authority," crucial talking points in anthropology and sociology (Awuah 2016). The symbols, seating arrangements, adherence to rituals, acknowledgment of the supernatural (ancestral presence), music, dance performances, and the "exhibition" of people and skills were all integral components of a traditional museum exhibition.

Reflecting on my childhood learning process and my political affiliation, I realize that I was "curated" and subsequently put on "display" to the outside world through dancing. Life in my father's palace has become one of the most remarkable lived experiences of my life. The stories of my forebears, embodied through traditional dancing, will be passed on to future generations, just as they were done for me. I learned early on, from my father, mother, and Kete dance tutors, that formal education needed the balance of "home knowledge" or Indigenous knowledge systems.

Examining the factors and parameters that influence one's education in Kete dance from the palace and the traditional setting versus that of the academy, I cannot understate the role my father played in my learning and appreciation of Kete dance. Although he is not here to witness the man I have become, I take this opportunity to express my gratitude to him. I believe in the notion that destiny makes no mistake in giving us families and affinities. Despite being a prince and a potential chief, life's experiences have taught me that my relevance is intertwined with my lived experiences and how they translate into my relationships today.

I see myself as a reproducer and regenerator of the "truth" of indigenous knowledge that my father, his people, and his life bestowed upon me. For example, in my earlier years, I did not fully understand the cacophony of musical instruments playing simultaneously, producing different but correlated sounds. Now, I interpret it as a codependent relationship and acceptance of different tones, tunes, sounds, and opinions that collectively shape who we are and will become. Music from these traditional instruments, along with accompanying dance movements, symbols, proverbs, and language, among others, validates my identity. My experiences thus far constitute my "truths," and these lived experiences will become the experiences of my unborn children to live, negotiate, and carry on.

**Image 11** Author performing with Abibigromma Theatre Company 2013.

**Images 12** (Right) Performing with Abibigromma Theatre Company.

**Image 13** Author performing at the University of Ghana 2013.

## Conceptualizing My Bodily Perceptions within the Urban Political System of Fante New Town-Kumasi

*Asuo twa okwan.*
*okwan twa asuo*
*Opanin ne wana*
*Yebo kwan no ko to asuo no*
*asuo no firi tete*
*asuo no firi tete odumanko*
*Odomanko Odomanko asuo no firi tete*

*(Twi language translated into English)*

*The river crosses the road*
*The road crosses the river*
*Who existed first?*
*The road was constructed to meet the river*
*The river began from the ancient times*
*The river began from the ancient times*
*God, God, the river comes from ancient days*

The above extract is from a song I learned as a child from my maternal grandmother's hometown, Asante Mampong. This stanza metaphorically represents the origin and historicity of the Akan/Asante beginning. It alludes to authenticity from the Akan's philosophical knowledge of Odomankoma (God), whom no man on earth knows the beginning or end of. By referencing the paradox of what came first, the water or the path, the stanza demonstrates the futility of investigating things that are too "big" to understand. I chose this stanza because my conception of self as an Akan/Asante is encapsulated in this song/poem. Without the need for scientific validation, my ancestors created the artistic ability to claim identity metaphysically, aesthetically, and physically through dancing. Therefore, whenever a Kete dancer points to the sky or spreads both arms open toward the sky during a Kete performance, they are alluding to their source of identity.

I was relocated from the palace to be with my mother and other maternal siblings. My father's hometown and chiefdom of Wassa Mpohor in the Western Region of Ghana gave me the opportunity to succeed. On my mother's side, from Asante Mampong in the Asante Region, I did not need to fight for any stool if I wanted one, as there were many available, although they were foreign to me since I did not grow up there. These two sociocultural positions have become influential in my journey to understanding the social and political order of my kindred and their use of movement systems in negotiating these positions. My ethnic connections to Wassa and Asante helped me understand how my body assimilated dance information. Both geographical positions and histories informed the transmission of Kete in peculiar ways that influence nuanced execution. However, it was only when I arrived in Fante New Town, a suburb within the suburb of Kumasi, that my training and understanding of Kete would take shape. Fante New Town is a place where Ghanaians of many ethnicities reside, creating a mixture of identities and traits that make the area identifiable with common ethnic stereotypes. Here, most people learned to understand Asante's knowledge through dance-musicking. Once a person learned to perform any of the popular Asante suites, like Kete and Adowa, well, questions about their ethnicities and origins disappeared. Through dancing, one represented the interest of the Asante through its culture. The performance of "Asante identity" through dance like Kete was already an epistemological indication of concepts of "nationhood" before Asante dances were even added to the national repertoire. Hence, the Traditional category as the source of dance and music knowledge, exemplified by cosmopolitan Kumasi, made it possible for figures like Nketia, Nkrumah, and Opoku to think of promoting a mainstream nationalistic agenda for decolonization. This success was evident in Kete performances in places like Fante New Town and other popular Kumasi suburbs.

My experiences as a learner and performer in Fante New Town allowed me to phenomenologically interrogate my dance learning experience at the University of Ghana. The Dance Department at the University, like a suburb, is comprised of individuals from different ethnicities who converge to learn neo-traditional music and dance forms. Similar to my training in Kumasi, this environment was historically modeled to promote a national and continental approach to decolonization through the performance of art forms. Unconsciously, like in my earlier environment and without strict ethnic genealogical requirements, I was able to align my body with a history that was progressive toward defining the contemporary or "new self," reflecting Ghana's identity after independence. My point here is that, regardless of kinship ties and their biological validity, dancing serves as a means of connecting to the evolving knowledge of one's environment, allowing for a progressive understanding of the body in dance scholarship in Ghana. Unfortunately, in my experience, I have found that people feel "lost" even when performing neo-traditional dances at the University of Ghana. This phenomenon should be explored further to better understand the challenges and complexities associated with the performance of neo-traditional dances in an academic setting.

**Image 14** Author with Akuaffo Hall chief, the University of Ghana 2015.

## Transitioning from Royal to Amateur to Academic Kete

After my father's death, his extended family, my mother and I, relocated due to family issues with my father's family. This twist of fate, or rather, a calculated move against me, led to my distance from the family. The trauma of this experience impacted my affinity for Kete, and even when we moved to Kumasi, I did not immediately turn to dancing Kete as a form of therapy. Growing up with these memories was challenging, but I overcame them with the help of my devout Christian mother. She consistently encouraged me in her Christian faith, saying, "Son, Jesus Christ is up to something strange in my life. The drums are calling. Go dance." I found solace in her words and returned to dancing, Kete. Fortuitously, our new settlement was just opposite one of the Asante king's sub-chief's palaces. I would often go there to witness beautiful Asante dances and music, reminiscent of what my mother taught me during my childhood. My interest in Kete and other dances intensified, and I devoted my full attention to both school and the dance group I joined. During my junior high school years, I was recruited into the school choir and the cultural group. I ascended through the ranks to become the lead dancer of the dance group in Fante New Town, the school choir conductor, and a compound overseer in my school. I had to relinquish my passion for football to dedicate myself to teaching newcomers and choreographing dances for performances.

My school, affiliated with the Anglican Missionary Church, organized music, dance, and drama competitions during "Ash" Wednesdays. I led my school singlehandedly to various competitions, gaining popularity in both my school and the Fante New Town suburb.

**Image 15** Author performing with the Dance Department, University of Ghana, 2016.

During my senior high school years at the Adventist Senior High School in Kumasi, financial difficulties arose for my mother. Although I was initially admitted to study science after passing my Junior High School Common Entrance exam, my passion for dance led me to switch to Arts. However, the prospect of paying fees seemed bleak, and the strong connection to dance kept growing. Fortunately, one of my paternal sisters from my father's side came to our rescue.

Now, my focus shifted to studying to become a medical doctor, adhering to the mantra that "passion determines direction and sacrifice ensures results." However, after calculating the cost of medical education in Ghana and realizing that my mother lacked the financial means to support this dream, I returned to my first passion—dance. To dance and raise money for the subsistence of my family became my weekly job. The decision to pursue dance in academia, however, is not always an easy one for most families in Ghana to accept.

When I chose to pursue dance in university after completing senior high school, it created a rift in my family. It is important to note that within traditional Ghanaian societies, career decisions are typically seen as a parental right rather than the children's. Although this situation has improved over the years, there is still more work to be done. This perspective is rooted in the Akan philosophy that all elders are considered knowledgeable and better positioned to make future decisions for their children. However, this notion is not entirely true.

Despite the family rift, I remained resolute, even though the risk of not being able to attend school due to a lack of financial support was probable. I resorted to baking bread, working at a book publishing shop, and dancing Kete at funerals to save for my education at the University of Ghana's School of Performing Arts. I enrolled as a performer in the Ahenemaa Kete Group in Kumasi, where I became a mentee to the leader, known as Chairman Paakwo, who remains a mentor to me. As a policy of the group, I was required to rise through the ranks, starting with no dance experience. Consequently, I began my training as a musician and drummer. This reorientation provided me with the opportunity to learn more than I initially knew, and the fact that I felt at home with the group helped shape me into one of the best dancers to come out of the group to date. The group was one of the most popular in Kumasi, and we were booked for performances every weekend, sometimes up to six months in advance. This allowed me to raise enough money to assist my mother with bills and save for my university education.

Along the way, I also acquired bamboo flute playing skills to complement my Kete dancing, which further heightened my popularity. I learned traditional funeral songs on the flute, and when dancing services were not needed,

I was employed to play the flute. Weekends in Kumasi are busy with funerals, so in a day, I could perform at about five funeral occasions either as a flutist or a Kete dancer. I managed to balance all these commitments while still attending school and dedicating time to my studies, ultimately securing admission to study at the University of Ghana.

**Rediscovering Myself**

In the Amateur category, I consciously set aside my title as a prince, relinquishing the associated embodied qualities to evolve into a dancer available for hire. The pivotal moment prompting this decision occurred when we performed for other royals in Kumasi, and I was instructed not to direct certain movements toward myself but rather to venerate the audience members. This political shift signaled to me that my transition was underway, and I was nearing the transformation into a student ready to learn anew. My mentor and teacher emphasized that I was training to be a performer and entertainer, catering to the enjoyment and pleasure of others. In this role, I was addressed as a performer/entertainer at funerals, parties, and weddings and, on occasion, faced harsh criticism from dissatisfied customers who viewed us through the lens of our roles. These encounters helped me understand the distinct perspectives people held regarding my dancing as a royal compared to that of an entertainer. Throughout my elementary, junior high, and senior high school years, I performed as an amateur traditional dance performer within indigenous communities. However, upon entering the University of Ghana as a performing arts student, I began aligning myself with my academic identity as a student performer. The additional skills and knowledge gained from the university provided me with the opportunity to redefine my identity and performance skills on international stages in the United States of America, London, Hungary, Norway, and France, among other places. In all these capacities, I did not perform as a royal. In fact, in most instances, no Ghanaian audience could discern my royal status from my movements. Instead, my performances focused on displaying the aesthetic qualities of Kete to diverse audiences. Internally, I recognized that my bloodline and experiences thus far underscored the undeniable fact that dancing is inherently political. It goes far deeper, constituting a real and integral aspect of my existence as a Ghanaian first and as a global citizen, where I derive meaning through interactions and performances.

At the School of Performing Arts, I pursued studies across three streams: Theater Arts, Music, and Dance Studies. In my first year at the university, I was a nominee for two prestigious awards—the "Discovery of the Year Award" and the "Most Talented Student of the Year." My proficiency in

Kete became highly valued within the school, leading to my selection in my second year to represent the School of Performing Arts on a national television dance competition program called the "Heritage Africa Reality Show." Participating in the show, I competed against my seniors and professional dancers with expertise in the full repertoire of the Ghana Dance Ensemble, encompassing over 60 dances. Despite my relative disadvantage, as my skills were primarily focused on the Asante dance suite, especially Kete, I enrolled in part-time dance lessons to broaden my capabilities for the competition. Although I reached the semi-final stage and was eventually evicted, the experience provided valuable knowledge and growth. Following this, I was nominated by the Students Representative Council of the University of Ghana for the "Most Outstanding Student of the Year in 2010" during their end-of-year review. Nominated for this award marked a historic achievement as the first and only dance student recipient to date. In 2010, I was chosen by my school, through the African Youth Exchange Program, to represent its interests by teaching dance and music to American children and youth during the summer. While at Camp Hale in New Hampshire, I was recognized as the best camp counselor. The following year, in 2011, I returned to camp duties as a counselor in Massachusetts, where I worked in heritage parks, conducting regular performances. My proficiency in Kete dance has presented unique opportunities, including performing before presidents and diplomatic dignitaries. One notable performance took place at Ghana's national 59th Independence Day celebration, where I participated in a private function at the Ghana National Theatre for the First Lady and the summit of 20 Western and Eastern African First Ladies.

Even before completing my undergraduate studies, I received an invitation from the Abibigromma Theatre Company, the resident professional theater company of the University of Ghana. I joined as a guest performer and later served as a national service personnel, assisting in teaching Kete dance and dramatic arts to undergraduate students and junior high schools outside the university. Following the successful completion of my undergraduate studies with a First-Class Honours degree, my unwavering goal was established—to delve into the study of safeguarding intangible cultural heritage forms, particularly Kete. This decision came effortlessly, as my profound passion and primary driving force in life centered around Kete dance music. I chose to pursue the MA African Studies program, considering it the home where dance studies, research, and performance originated. Upon enrollment, I was promptly appointed as a Graduate Assistant, responsible for teaching dance and music to undergraduate students at the institute. This marked a significant step in my journey, blending academia with my lifelong dedication to Kete.

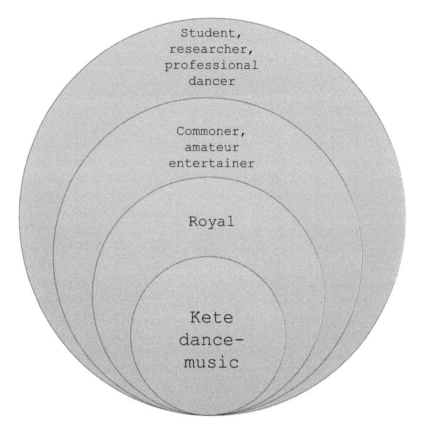

**Figure 2** My embodied journey as a dancer-scholar since 1992.

My journey from a royal to an amateur, a student, and eventually a professional dancer-scholar would not have been conceivable without the foresight of Nkrumah, Nketia, and Opoku in establishing the institute to promote dance. Following their visionary initiative, I've traced my development as a Kete dancer and performer, exploring my embodied learning through the frameworks they established, as identified by Awuah (2014, 2015). The image encapsulates my transformative path and the indelible connection to Kete, where indigenous knowledge was transmitted to me through movements. Kete has been the guiding force that brought me to this point.

## Summary

This chapter has presented an autoethnographic narrative detailing my childhood experiences in my father's palace and the Fante New Town suburb of Kumasi. The chapter elucidates how these environments shaped my learning of Kete and the subsequent transformation from a royal to a commoner. In doing so, the autoethnographic account positions my assimilation of Kete dance within the three categories delineated by Grit Koeltzsch (Koeltzsch 2021). The chapter delves into my Kete learning experiences in both the palace and Kumasi, highlighting the circumstances that facilitated my transition from royalty to commoner and showcasing the performance of identical variations under different identities and locations. This sets the stage for the exploration of transmission, assimilation dynamics, and the nuanced information acquired within distinct social classes. Chapter 6 will examine foundational gender concepts within Kete dancing, exploring the competencies essential for the performance of gendered movements by male and female dancers. It will unravel the gendered messages contributing to the aesthetic presentation of movements in the Kete dance form.

# Chapter 6

# GENDERED AESTHETIC APPRECIATION AND EVALUATION WITHIN ASANTE KETE DANCE

Whether considered as a personal movement practice or a cultural phenomenon, Kete has much to say about the people who perform it. Whatever symbolic messages the Kete dance form carries can become a subject of interpretation by choreographers, scholars, teachers, writers, and audience. In this section, I explore the foundational cultural gender concepts embedded within Kete music and dancing. The discussion delves into the specific competencies essential for the performance of gendered movements by both male and female dancers. Additionally, I highlight the gendered messages conveyed through these movements, contributing to the overall aesthetic presentation within the Kete dance form. This exploration aims to shed light on the intricate interplay of gender dynamics within the rich cultural tapestry of Kete, offering insights into how gender is embodied and expressed through this traditional Ghanaian dance form.

The embodiment and expression of gender within the traditional Ghanaian dance form of Kete are deeply intertwined with the concept of Africanist aesthetics. Dance ethnologists such as Kariamu Welsh-Asante and Ofotsu Adinku[1] have contributed significantly to the understanding of Africanist aesthetics, which has found relevance in Ghanaian dance scholarship. This aesthetic perspective extends not only to the four dance categories identified by Awuah (2015) but also encompasses African diasporic dance performances. Modesto Amegago emphasizes the necessity of grasping African philosophy to comprehend African aesthetics fully.[2] In agreement

---

1 K. Welsh-Asante, 'African and African-American Dance, Music, and Theatre', *Journal of Black Studies* 15, no. 4 (1985): 381–403; Adinku, *African Dance Education in Ghana: Curriculum and Instructional Materials for a Model Bachelor of Arts (Hons.) Dance in Society*.
2 Amegago, 'An Holistic Approach to African Performing Arts: Music and Dance Curriculum Development and Implementation'.

with Amegago, I acknowledge that African aesthetics in Kete are shaped by a complex interplay of biological/physical, social, economic, political, religious, and ethical values. These values find expression through the bodies of performers, the perceptions of spectators, and the custodianship of the dance form in diverse contexts. This holistic understanding illuminates the rich tapestry of gendered expressions within the cultural framework of Kete, offering insights into the intricate relationship between aesthetics and the broader philosophical foundations of African dance.

Within the broader exploration of a generalized African aesthetic, the distinct elements of style and character play a crucial role in defining gender roles and cultural stereotypes. These elements not only serve as aesthetic markers but also contribute to gendered interpretations of societal norms and issues through performance. In the context of Kete, these aesthetic nuances become embodied expressions that reflect and communicate the intricate dynamics of gender within the cultural and social fabric of Ghana. As dancers engage with the traditional movements and gestures of Kete, they bring to life a visual and embodied narrative that encapsulates the essence of gender roles and the societal expectations placed upon them. This dynamic interplay between aesthetics and cultural symbolism further deepens the understanding of how Kete serves as a vessel for expressing and challenging gender norms within the broader African context. The gendered expectations within Kete are intricately connected to Asante spirituality, where belief systems encompass the realities of ancestral spirits, the importance of male and female fertility for procreation, and the traditional institution of marriage. The performance of Kete, with its specific movements and expressions, serves as a tangible affirmation of one's belief in and respect for cultural roles, religious principles, and social hierarchy within the Asante community. In this way, Kete becomes not only a dance form but a sacred and symbolic enactment that reinforces the spiritual and cultural values associated with gender, fostering a deeper connection between the physical movements of the dance and the spiritual and social dimensions of Asante life.

The aesthetics of African dance, particularly within the context of Kete, is deeply rooted in communal narratives rather than individual expressions. This communal spirit is reflected in the philosophy, norms, values, customs, and material culture of the Akan society, forming the foundational aesthetics of music and dance practices. An analysis of Kete dance through a gendered lens reveals how Akan society culturally comprehends gender disparities and crafts vocabulary, gestures, and movements through male and female bodies to maintain a harmonious balance between opposites. The lack of emphasis on gendered aesthetics in Ghanaian dance scholarship is attributed to the continued reliance on Western concepts of the self. Despite Nkrumah's politico-cultural agenda, which aimed to reshape cultural narratives through institutions like the Institute of African Studies, the Ghana Dance Ensemble, and the School of Music and Dance, the ideological influence did not permeate secondary and primary institutions thoroughly. The struggle to shift away from colonial concepts and influences was predominantly fought at the higher educational level, leaving lower school levels still entrenched in colonial ideas. Kwadwo Okrah explained that, after gaining independence, Ghana expanded its educational system, inherited from colonial powers, due to political expediency. Unfortunately, the neglect of traditional aspects of education in favor of a Western-oriented approach led to the alienation of students from their own culture, resulting in social disintegration, dysfunctional family life, and a rise in delinquency and crime. This phenomenon is rooted in the fact that rural children are being prepared for a world that does not yet exist, rendering their education unfit for integration into their own society, causing a cultural confusion and moral purposelessness.[3]

In the exploration of gender within African/Asante epistemology, the concept transcends the classification of male and female as opposites but rather emphasizes their role as complementary partners. This understanding of complementarity serves as the foundational framework for analyzing the aesthetic elements of Kete dance. The Afrocentric thought, as articulated by Asante and Mazama,[4] differs from Western conceptions and is deeply embedded in the social and cultural fabric of the Asante people, evident in their various dance forms, including Kete. Within the Asante society's leadership structure, political power is distributed between the king/chief and queen mother/queen, operating in a complementary fashion with shared responsibilities. This structure reflects Asante philosophy, where gender identity and equality are intrinsic values. Emmanuel Akyemang and Pashington Obeng emphasize the crucial role of women in Asante culture, particularly as queen mothers who play a co-ruling role in state affairs, challenging the perception of women as subordinate in non-African cultures. They highlight the importance of women in preserving family, lineage, and state, noting their critical roles as biological, economic, and societal producers (Akyemang & Obeng, 1995). Historically, during wars, while men engaged in frontline battles, Asante women contributed by chanting spiritual songs believed to possess protective elements for the men. Additionally, women engaged in symbolic acts, such as pounding empty mortars with pestles, as a form of spiritual

---

3 Okrah, *Nyansapo (the Wisdom Knot): Toward an African Philosophy of Education.*
4 Asante, *Afrocentricity*; Mazama, 'The Afrocentri Paradigm: Contours and Definitions'; Asante, *Afrocentricity, the Theory of Social Change.*

torture against Asante enemies (Akyemang & Obeng, 1995). This holistic understanding of gender within Asante culture forms the basis for interpreting the gendered dynamics within the Kete dance tradition.

Akan societies, including the Asante, exhibit predominantly matriarchal characteristics. In such societies, certain philosophical perspectives about womanhood contribute to validating gender disparities. The significance of various activities is often weighted, with certain roles and responsibilities traditionally considered more important for women, while others may be associated with men. For instance, active participation in political discussions or taking leadership roles in matters like marriage politics might be less common for women. This perspective aligns with the views of Afrocentric scholar Nah Dove, who avers that the concept of matriarchy emphasizes the contemporary aspect of the female-male relationship, where both genders work together in all areas of social organization, with women being revered for their roles as mothers, conduits for spiritual regeneration, bearers of culture, and centers of social organization (Dove in Mazama 2001). The ability of an Akan woman to bear children is considered central to her identity, especially in the context of her role as a queen or queen mother within the community.[5] In Akan societies, gender roles and activities are reinforced through dance movements, such as those seen in the Kete dance. Men are expected to display more "open" and powerful movements, reflecting their traditional role as protectors of their families and communities. Women, on the other hand, are encouraged to express gracefulness, using dance to convey modesty and demureness in alignment with their gender identity. Furthermore, there is a strong emphasis on showing respect to mothers and women within Akan culture. During Kete dance performances, men are reminded through songs, proverbs, aphorisms, and wise sayings to demonstrate respect for women and mothers. Disrespectful behavior toward women is seen as a serious offense, carrying potential consequences not only for the individual but also for their extended families (Personal interview with Chairman Paakwoh, 2021). The corporeal expressions among the Asante people, as detailed by Duodu (1972), emphasize a distinct way of holding the body in different situations. Notably, kings and queen mothers are portrayed sitting erect on royal stools, showcasing movements with competence and fluidity, a contrast to the postures of commoners. Gendered movement requirements further manifest in specific variations designed for kings, queen mothers, and sub-chiefs. In the Akan society, where only males can hold the position of main chiefs, certain

---

[5] Janice Pearl Ewurama De-Whyte, '(In)Fertility in the Akan Culture', in *Wom(b)an: A Cultural-Narrative Reading of the Hebrew Bible Barrenness Narratives* (Brill, 2018), 53–75, https://doi.org/10.1163/9789004366305_004.

gestural variations, like "Dwannyinimienushia a, nayehu bɛɛma," are exclusively reserved for men due to their traditional role in warfare.

Another movement variation symbolizing the chief or king's authority involves pointing to the left and right, rolling hands a few inches from the chest in a counter-clockwise direction, and crossing both hands in an X-shaped form over the chest. This signifies the king or chief's custodianship of all stool lands, asserting political power through structured and functional movements to music. In a similar vein, a queen mother can demonstrate the same movements when leading that society. These gendered movement distinctions contribute to a nuanced understanding of how both male and female dancing bodies operate within the context of Kete performance and communication. The example provided illustrates the social construction of meaning-making within the context of Kete dance. Analyzing Kete dance through the epistemological lens of the "social construction of knowledge," as expounded by Okrah (2012) and aligned with the pedagogic philosophy of John Dewey, sheds light on the idea that education is a dynamic process inherent in the lived experiences of individuals. Dewey's perspective emphasizes that education should reflect present life, being as real and vital to the learner as the experiences encountered in their immediate surroundings. In the case of Kete dance, the embodied knowledge and gendered movements serve as forms of life that are worth living for their intrinsic value. This underscores the significance of Kete dance as a form of education that is deeply rooted in the authentic realities of Asante culture, contributing to a holistic understanding of life for those engaged in its practice. In exploring aesthetics within the indigenous elements of semiotics, linguistic structuring through gestures, and contexts, this contribution delves into the socio-politico-cultural role of kinaesthetic communication in Akan societies, specifically through the Kete dance. The focus is on understanding how the sociolinguistic structure of Kete dance can be examined within the framework of traditional African philosophies. Awuah's perspective highlights several key points: first, traditional African philosophies are integral to African cultures; second, dances emerge from within these cultures; and third, the dance materializes the meaning of metaphors through aesthetic bodily movement expressions embedded in choreographic structures/forms within society. The critical question then arises: how does the dancing body, encompassing both male and female, effectively transmit meaning to foster socio-political cohesion? Awuah's inquiry underscores the intricate connection between Kete dance, cultural identity, and the communication of profound sociopolitical meanings within Akan societies.[6]

---

6 Awuah, 'A Study of Amateur Groups' Re-Interpretation of Traditional Dances in Ghana: Role on Continuity and Safeguarding'.

## Clarifying "Traditional and Neo-Traditional Kete" Dance Renditions Today

As a practitioner who has engaged in all four categories of traditional dance at various points in my life, I can affirm that each category provides distinct opportunities for movement analysis. Additionally, each category exhibits fundamental and recognizable characteristics that set them apart, encompassing performance styles, costumes, and other defining elements. It's noteworthy that, with the exception of the Traditional category, which maintains "ownership" of tradition-based and contextually functional movement systems, the other categories predominantly present neo-traditional interpretations of traditional dances. Kariamu Welsh and Elizabeth Hanley's definition of neo-traditional dances, described as creations resembling traditional dances but not strictly adhering to all the aesthetics and cultural rules of the society,[7] is particularly relevant for examining aesthetics in the context of dance. This definition effectively distinguishes between the aesthetic expectations of what is considered traditional and what falls under the category of neo-traditional. The fluid movement of dancers across different categories over time has significantly impacted the performative and politico-cultural aspects of many traditional and indigenous dances in Ghana. It's crucial to emphasize that this migratory phenomenon is also observed in the performance and teaching of the Kete dance form. Practitioners from the Asante region, which is recognized as the home region of the Asante Kete dance, often travel to other parts of the country to teach Kete. This highlights the concept of "neo-traditional" dance, emphasizing its flexibility across geo-historical and political boundaries. However, it is essential to recognize that when Kete is taught to individuals from different areas or ethnic groups, aesthetic requirements for their performance, including gendered dress codes, may undergo changes. Consequently, the continual perpetuation of the dances without consideration for elements such as gendered aesthetics can lead to a potential loss of traditional meanings during transmission and translation.

In the Ghanaian context, tracing the proliferation of the Kete dance form and its influence on varied sociocultural contexts can be challenging, particularly in professional groups like the Ghana Dance Ensemble in Accra. The concept of aesthetics in this context is viewed as an evaluative range within which variations in movement are assessed for their suitability in social, political, and cultural contexts. It's crucial to grasp the diacritic

---

7 K. Welsh-Asante and E. A. Hanley, *African Dance*, World of Dance (Infobase Publishing, 2010), https://books.google.ps/books?id=uMcPuAEACAAJ.

element specific to Asante dance forms, as articulated by Albert Mawere Opoku. He characterizes Asante dance with intricate and subtle manipulations of hands, arms, and legs, body sways and tilts in polyrhythmic combinations, expressive miming with rich symbolic undertones, and the typical Asante hauteur (Opoku 1987). This description highlights the nuanced and distinctive features that set Asante dance apart, emphasizing its complex and symbolic nature. The description of Asante dance, particularly the Kete dance form, places it within a specific aesthetic framework that dictates how performances should unfold. This framework demands an understanding of nuanced communicative expectations for both male and female bodies. The elements of intricacy, subtlety, body sways, and expressions are all gendered, emphasizing that performances should adhere to cultural standards that dictate how these elements are manifested differently for men and women. This reinforces the importance of gendered aesthetics in Kete dance, where the form becomes a vehicle for cultural expression with specific expectations for each gender. I posit these nuances as "hard" and "soft" movement variations. There is a tacit concept of how male and female bodies may be perceived culturally among the Asante. Although this concept might not be perpetuated by other ethnic groups in Ghana within the "hard and soft" categorization, I situate this concept empirically within Asante linguistics. Statements like "sa mmb3ma mu" (dance like men), "ma wo ko kó nny3 duru s3 b33ma" (lit. let your heart be as strong as a valiant man), "nanti s3 obaasima" (lit. walk like a virtuous woman), "ahoɔf3 dua" (lit. beauty tree), "m3ny3 gidigidi s3 b33ma" (lit. do not do your things roughly like men do), promote the argument that there are clear expectations for the actions of male and female in Asante societies.

The cultural belief that specific gestures and mannerisms are reserved for certain individuals and genders in Kete dance reflects the importance placed on maintaining traditional norms and expectations. If a man is observed "to dance like a woman" or vice versa, it may be perceived as a "gendered anomaly," suggesting a deviation from established cultural norms and potentially challenging the traditional gender roles within the dance form. This underscores the significance of adhering to prescribed movement variations that align with culturally defined gender expectations. Albert Mawere Opoku's insight highlights the significance of gestures in Kete dance, emphasizing that certain gestures are reserved for individuals of specific ranks, particularly senior rulers, who are mostly men. The example of placing the right fist atop the left fist carries symbolic meaning, indicating a higher chieftaincy rank. Opoku emphasizes that expertise in dance alone is not sufficient for a chief; familiarity with the traditional language of gesture is equally crucial. Failure to adhere to these cultural protocols may result in censure, reprimand, and potentially heavy fines, underscoring the importance of understanding and respecting the nuanced language of movement in Kete dance.[8]

Stuart Hall's concept of representation[9] becomes crucial here in understanding the significance of codified movements in Asante aesthetics, particularly in the context of Kete dance. The codified movements in Kete serve as a diacritic representation of the people's structured belief systems and opinions, offering insight into their way of life. Hall's notion of representation as the intentional selection of meanings, shaped by a people's culture and experiences, aligns with the understanding that Kete dance is a form of language that conveys meaning through intentional and culturally informed movements. This perspective underscores the cultural richness embedded in the gendered movements and aesthetics of Kete dance, highlighting the importance of decoding these representations to grasp the deeper cultural meanings they convey.

**Asante Aesthetics as an Evaluative System**

Asante movement systems, symbology, music, costumes, and gender roles form the aesthetic foundations upon which Asante societies evolve. Here, aesthetics is a "communal evaluation process"[10] that shapes the qualitative presentation of certain elements of the culture. Given its importance to ethnic identity and survival, aesthetics extends into collective rendering of characteristics, meaning-making processes, and everyday phenomena. Albert Mawere Opoku's definition of dance as a language or mode of expression, utilizing movements and gestures rooted in everyday activities to convey both special and ordinary experiences, emphasizes the deeply ingrained connection between dance and cultural expression (Opoku 1964). This definition aligns with the perspectives of other renowned dance scholars like J. H. Kwabena Nketia and Modesto Amegago, highlighting the necessity of delving into the broader life and culture of African people to truly comprehend African dance aesthetics (Kuwor, 2017). Opoku's notion that individual expressions, even those expressing sorrow, are contingent on communal acceptability underscores the communal

---

8 Opoku, 'Asante Dance Art and the Court'.
9 Stuart Hall, *Representation: Cultural Representations and Signifying Practices.*, Culture, Media and Identities (SAGE, 1997), https://login.ezproxy.library.ualberta.ca/login?url=https://search.ebscohost.com/login.aspx?direct=true&db=cat03710a&AN=alb.1932763&site=eds-live&scope=site.
10 Amegago, 'An Holistic Approach to African Performing Arts: Music and Dance Curriculum Development and Implementation'; Kuwor, 'Understanding African Dance in Context: Perspectives from Ghana'.

nature of African dance. The collective cultural context shapes and influences the vocabulary of movements and gestures used in dance. This perspective resonates with the understanding that African dance is not merely a physical activity but a profound means of cultural expression, embodying the rich tapestry of experiences, values, and traditions within the community. By acknowledging dance as a language, Opoku elevates its status beyond mere physical movement, emphasizing its role as a dynamic form of communication deeply rooted in the cultural fabric of African societies. This holistic approach to understanding dance aesthetics calls for an appreciation of the interconnectedness between dance, life, and culture, affirming its significance as a living expression of African heritage. By acknowledging dance as a language and mode of expression deeply rooted in everyday activities, Albert Mawere Opoku underscores its dynamic role in conveying both special and ordinary experiences within a cultural context. This perspective aligns with the views of other notable dance scholars, such as J. H. Kwabena Nketia and Modesto Amegago, emphasizing the need to explore the broader life and culture of African people to fully grasp African dance aesthetics (Kuwor, 2017).

In the context of this comprehensive understanding, the concept of beauty, within the broader framework of aesthetics, emerges as a platform for unraveling a society's qualitative affinities and artistic influences. Beauty, as expressed through dance, becomes a lens through which one can discern the values, preferences, and cultural nuances embedded in a community's artistic expressions. This multifaceted exploration not only deepens the appreciation of dance as a vibrant form of cultural communication but also reveals the intricate connections between aesthetic choices, societal values, and artistic traditions within African heritage. Thomas DeFrantz posits that "amid continuous overarching questions around what the terms of "beauty" may be and who may name them, I contend that "beauty" might be recuperated effectively as a critical paradigm when deployed within a particular, culturally explicit frame of performance analysis"[11]. However, amidst the complexities of "beauty" that DeFrantz observes in African American dance performances and its resistance against racial tenets of judgment, the concept of African aesthetics is crucial to reclaiming African epistemological foundations in contemporary dance scholarship because it is one of the core principles of African dance. For example, in Kete dance performances, appreciations and evaluations are tied to beauty. As such, certain required cultural values and symbols are demonstrated to that effect ranging from the chief/queen,

---

11 Thomas F. DeFrantz, 'African American Dance – Philosophy, Aesthetics, and "Beauty"', *Topoi* 24, no. 1 (2005), https://doi.org/10.1007/s11245-004-4165-7.

onlookers, and commoners to the performers themselves. To the Asante's, the Kete dancer who dances "beautifully" may receive the following appreciations: onlookers fixing coins on the forehead of the dancer, throwing money on the dancer, and toward the drummers, wiping the face of the dancer with cloth, putting cloth around the neck of the dancer, using cloth to fan the dancer, drummer circling one of the supporting drums around the dancer, nodding of the head, and many times you see raising the right hand with the middle and the forefinger together, pointed at the dancer. It is important to note that under normal circumstances, a wrong use of the above-mentioned signs and symbols of appreciation may lead one into trouble and may face the moral law of the people, but there is an exception to "strangers" when they violate "the law." Inasmuch as appreciation is expressed or even performed, you may also encounter some registration of dissatisfaction/displeasure with the Kete performance which may lead to an instant stoppage of the dance performance. Such actions include, but are not limited to, wrongful execution of gestures, playing rhythms wrongly and off the bell pattern, dancing with left hand toward a chief, dancing seductively toward a chief/queen, and so on.

Building on the premise of the complexity of Asante culture, the discussion now delves into Kete as a catalyst for the conceptual formulation and definition of Kete aesthetics. Aesthetics, within this context, is viewed as an evaluation system grounded in three key principles: gender group, linguistic organization, and competence. In the performance of Kete, these three elements serve as departure points to assess a performer's dancing and music in relation to the contextual standard. The concept of competence, as an Akan aesthetic element, is intricately woven into both the material and immaterial cultures of the Asante people. Dissecting Kete as an intangible element in isolation from its material connections would be to strip it of its rich cultural context. Modesto Amegago aptly refers to these connections as "interwoven biological/physical, social, economic, political, religious, and ethical values" (M. Amegago 2000). From this interwoven knowledge system, aesthetics emerges as a "mutual" agreement between the environmental, cosmological, and philosophical facets of culture and the modes of specifications (Kuwor 2013). This perspective underscores the holistic nature of Kete aesthetics, emphasizing the need to consider the broader cultural, social, and philosophical dimensions that contribute to the evaluation and appreciation of Kete performances. The interplay of gender dynamics, linguistic organization, and competence forms a dynamic tapestry that shapes the aesthetic principles inherent in the vibrant tradition of Kete dance. This perspective finds resonance with Robert Farris Thompson, who describes African aesthetics as a "mode of intellectual energy that only exists when in operation; in other words, art must have a function within the society to have value."[12] In these two positions, there is a coexistence and validation of aesthetic elements as conduits for manifesting the African truth of reality and intelligence.

Within the broader conception of aesthetics, Akan/Asante dance elements play a foundational role in the analysis of visual, musical, and multisensory modalities of Akan life. Akan aesthetics is intuitive, communal, and evaluative. This aligns with the perspective of dance ethnologist Kariamu Welsh-Asante, who elucidates that African aesthetics is intuitive in nature. This intuitive quality emphasizes a deep connection between aesthetics and the lived experiences, values, and communal expressions within the Akan/Asante culture, highlighting how Kete dance serves as a dynamic and meaningful form of cultural expression. The African aesthetics is characterized by empathetic qualities, which are intuitive and infused with emotions, and does not have a neural form; every movement, word, and gesture in African aesthetics reflects the cultural values of the society, enabling the recall of history and culture through signs and symbols, thereby empowering the community.[13] Kariamu's statement resonates closely within the context of Asante Kete dance philosophy. During a Kete performance, specific gestures have the power to evoke communal feelings and convey deep messages. For instance, when a Kete dancer runs into the arms of an elderly person while dancing, it symbolizes a message of dependence and support, with the gesture suggesting, "You are my support; I depend on you." This act triggers emotions, and, according to custom and tradition, the elderly person is expected to ensure the well-being of the dancer in a supportive manner. This gesture takes on nuanced meanings in various contexts, such as when widows perform it during funerals. In this case, the gesture symbolizes that the widow, or widows collectively, have lost their primary support (the husband), and they now need emotional assistance to navigate life in the absence of their spouse. Therefore, emotions in indigenous dances, like Kete, are intricately connected to specific events and not isolated from the dance itself. Kete dance serves not only as a means of expressing emotions but also as a conduit for addressing the emotional needs of the community at a given time.

---

12 Robert Farris Thompson, 'An Aesthetic of the Cool', *African Arts* 7, no. 1 (12 February 1973): 41–91, https://doi.org/10.2307/3334749.

13 K. Welsh-Asante, *African Dance: An Artistic, Historical, and Philosophical Inquiry* (Trenton, NJ: Africa World Press, 1996).

## Improvisation in Kete Dance-Music

Improvisation in the Kete dance may not be immediately apparent to the untrained eye due to the repetitive nature of themes and gestures in the performance. However, it's important to correct the assumption that there is little to no possibility of introducing "new" or different elements in the dance. Improvisation in Kete dance is indeed present, but it operates within the framework of established themes and movements. Skilled Kete dancers have the ability to infuse creativity and spontaneity into their performances while adhering to the fundamental elements of the dance. This improvisation might involve subtle variations in movement execution, emphasis on specific gestures, or nuanced interpretations of traditional themes. The mastery of improvisation in Kete dance requires a deep understanding of the dance form, its cultural significance, and the ability to seamlessly integrate new elements without disrupting the overall aesthetic and symbolic integrity of the performance.

In Kete dancing, improvisation plays a crucial role and is closely scrutinized. Creativity within Kete dance involves the introduction of new movements that complement existing ones. It is important to emphasize that creativity in Kete dance is only considered appropriate and acceptable when it aligns with the cultural parameters of the Akan people. For the Akans, creativity is viewed as a material manifestation of the spirit, serving both the community and the individual. Consequently, creative expressions are recognized and acknowledged collectively rather than individually.

Drawing from my own experiences of over 25 years of performing Kete dance, I have, at times, spontaneously demonstrated gestures during performances that were not explicitly taught to me. Later, I discovered these movements in old archives I had not seen before. Surprisingly, my mentor and teacher revealed that these variations were thought to have become extinct, and I had unknowingly revived them. This realization led me to understand that, as a Kete dancer, there is a depth of knowledge beyond what can be verbally expressed, and my attunement to cosmic powers allows for a "sympathetic understanding" of the dance form. I contend that within Akan community dance practices, there is a tacit understanding that no individual owns a dance form or can be credited as the sole "choreographer." This perspective suggests that creative inspiration stems from one's belonging to the community and being creatively influenced by it.I argue that the communal narrative of creativity and ownership in Ghanaian/African dance is centered on the interplay of "individual creation," "group mediation," and "social acceptance."[14] This should be recognized as a genuine marker of

---

14 Emmanuel Cudjoe, 'Exploring Female Voices through the Togo-Atchan Dance as a Communicative Tool for Community Development in Togo-West Africa' (Choreomundus International Master Consortium, 2018).

group aesthetic representation and identity. The epistemological foundations of Akan dance practices are rooted in the social, political, spiritual, and cosmological worldview of the Akan ethnic group, with the Asante constituting a predominant demographic within this cultural context.

## Gendered Drums

From a gendered perspective, Kete drums or instrumentation feature both male and female drums, signifying the importance of gender within Akan ethnicity. This intentional inclusion highlights the significance of gender in the cultural fabric of the Akan people. Welsh-Asante (1985) emphasizes the importance of rhythms in African dance, stressing the need to recognize the combination of male and female patterns that constitute musical sound.

In Kete, the male drum is known as Kwadum, depicted as the largest drum in Image 1. Adjacent to it is the female drum known as the Apentemma. The collaboration of sounds from both the male and female drums is crucial for a complete and culturally authentic performance. The master or male drum, Kwadum, produces a deep or bass-like sound, symbolizing the male surrogate voice. This is complemented by the female drum, Apentemma, which has a higher tone, representing the female surrogate voice. The harmony between these male and female elements is integral to the integrity of the drumming and dancing in Kete, and their absence is considered a deviation from cultural norms and ethics.[15]

In addition to the gendered drums, singing during Kete dance serves as another foundation of Asante musical aesthetics. This aesthetic principle is based on the cultivation of smooth and melodic voices as well as the virtuosic transition of music to suit various occasions. The combination of both male and female voices is valued for producing harmonious music that enhances the overall auditory experience for listeners. Therefore, it is considered artistically standard to have representation from both genders in singing during Kete dance performances. The arrangement within the performance space is also gendered. Typically, the Kete drummers are positioned in the front, while the female dancers and singers stand behind them. This arrangement is deeply rooted in Asante epistemology, reflecting the cultural expectation that men are obliged to defend and protect their women regardless of the circumstances. It's important to note that this arrangement does not imply control or suggest weakness on the part of Asante women; rather, it aligns with specific cultural norms and values.

---

15 https://omeka-s.grinnell.edu/s/MusicalInstruments/page/kete

**Image 16** Kete drums in their red and black colors.

**Image 17** Kete drums as used by amateur groups. Source: Photo by Twumasi.

## Kete Dance as Indigenous Epistemological Expression of the Asante People

While serving as a social and court dance form, Kete also holds a connection to the supernatural. According to a historical account from hunters, who are considered the creators or discoverers, its origin is linked to "spirit; and first considered a hunting (Abɔfoɔ) dance." According to Pascal Younge, "the Abɔfoɔ [Abɔfo agorɔ [...] is performed by the chief as an acknowledgement of his attributes as a hunter. These special qualities include bravery, fearlessness, being a courageous leader, intelligence, and, above all, being a spiritual person."[16] Therefore, the performance and choreographic structure of Kete dance serve as reflections of the Asante belief in the supernatural, where the physical realm intertwines with the realm of the deceased. An examination of the dance's structures reveals numerous elements that seamlessly blend beliefs with movement, creativity, and performativity. Structurally, Kete is organized into stanzas accompanied by music. The salutation phase holds particular significance in the performance of Kete, reflecting the deep-rooted importance Asante/Akan people place on the act and art of greeting. This cultural value is embedded not only in their oral communication but also in their musical and dance traditions. Demonstrating proficiency in the politics of greeting is highly esteemed in the community, judged by specific performance and aesthetic conventions. In both social gatherings and the context of Kete dance, adhering to geometric and directional rules during greetings is essential. The customary greeting involves a handshake or a wave, following a counterclockwise to clockwise direction (right to left). The aesthetics of greeting within the Kete dance demand competence and skill. Children, for instance, are expected to look downward or place their left hand behind them while performing a greeting. Additionally, in the dancing context, the acknowledgment of status follows a hierarchical order, starting from veneration to God above, then to the king/queen or chief, and finally to the rest of the people, all within the boundaries of aesthetic allowances. Each movement variation within Kete encapsulates multiple layers of meanings that, to date, have not been thoroughly examined by any Ghanaian dance scholar. Drawing on Kuwor's categorization, Kete, akin to many other indigenous dances, unfolds three levels of meaning: literal, metaphorical, and philosophical (personal interview, 2021). For instance, in the literal interpretation of the Kete performance, a waving gesture signifies greetings or salutations. Metaphorically, the act of waving from the right to the left symbolizes moving

---

16 Younge, *Music and Dance Traditions of Ghana: History, Performance and Teaching.*

toward life, extending to waving to address the living souls present, thereby carrying deeper layers of significance within the cultural and philosophical framework of the dance. The act of waving within the Kete dance not only conveys literal and metaphorical meanings but also encapsulates a profound philosophical understanding of order, veneration, and cultural competence. This interpretation aligns with the epistemological principles of salutations within the Akans/Asantes' daily lives. In the broader context of Akan/Asante culture, greetings are considered expressive speech acts intricately linked to sociocultural norms. The performative verb "kyea" ("greet") triggers a sequence of interactional performances encompassing both verbal and non-verbal elements. This complex interplay of greetings in Akan/Asante society serves as a medium for conveying social meanings, as highlighted by Kofi Agyekum.[17] Conceptual explorations by Welsh-Asante (1985) have identified seven aesthetic senses that form the foundational principles of African dance aesthetics. These senses include polyrhythm, polycentrism, curvilinear, dimensionality, epic memory, repetition, and holism. In the context of this study, I will delve into three of these principles, elucidating their relevance and incorporation into the aesthetics of the Kete dance.

***Polyrhythm:*** The multiple rhythmic structure of the musical ensemble is the propulsive power that initially moves one to the performance space. Welsh-Asante observed that "the deeper you travel, [the more you hear and] the more you feel,"[18] and the simultaneous overlay of rhythms as well as movements is a mainstay in Kete dance. Dancers are captured in space and time due to their continuous interaction, mediation, and deep engagement with the music. Each second or minute spent in the performance space of Kete dance accentuates intricate and subtle manipulation of hands, arms, and legs and the raising and lowering of the shoulders into various polycentric variations. For example, a Kete movement variation performed with a sword and musket in both hands as props ties together the aesthetic requirements of the male dancer's gender, social status, and context in emphasizing the meaning of his gestures and dance movements. As per Asante/Akan tradition, commoners are typically prohibited from performing with a sword. However, the mimetic representation of the action and ideas encapsulated in the polycentric variation might share similarities between the dancer and the king/queen, albeit within an alternative context. While their performances are

---

17 Kofi Agyekum, 'The Pragmatics of Akan Greetings', 2008, https://doi.org/10.1177/1461445608091884.

18 Welsh-Asante, 'African and African-American Dance, Music, and Theatre'; Welsh-Asante, *African Dance: An Artistic, Historical, and Philosophical Inquiry.*

both representations, differences in factors such as the degree of arm bending or flexing, dynamic levels (low, medium, and high) of the entire body or the arms, intensity in gestural depiction, energy, and subtlety can exist. The basic understanding, however, revolves around the initiation and conclusion of the motif. To further illustrate this perspective, let's consider another example. A king or queen is expected not to perspire or display high levels of athleticism while dancing, given their royal status. Their movements are meant to be elegant, subtle, graceful, and somewhat restrained. Conversely, a commoner is allowed to showcase virtuosity and athleticism in their performance, suggesting that their movements may appear as an exaggeration compared to those of the king. These polyrhythmic and polycentric variations are executed in full costume by the king, whereas the commoner performs with their cloth lowered and tied around the waist, exposing the upper torso. This symbolic act signifies the relational difference in power and identity. Similarly, the combination of various drums in the Kete ensemble, each producing distinct sounds, conveys the concept of communalism and the acceptance of different voices at different contextual levels.

***Epic memory:*** The principle of epic memory in African dance aesthetics, particularly within the context of Kete, delves into the historical, emotional, and multi-sensory dimensions embedded in the cultural fabric of the people through expressive movements. While Kete operates within the social framework of power and identity, its perpetuation and effectiveness in society are sustained through the conduit of heritage and epic memory. In this context, the meanings conveyed through various gestures encapsulate the histories and cosmological beliefs passed down by generations. A notable illustration of epic memory can be observed in a greeting motif during a durbar or funeral. A proficient Kete dance performer adheres to a specific order of greeting, first directing salutations to the highest-ranking member(s) of the society, such as the chief/king or queen mother, followed by the elders, and then the musicians. The dancer employs a specific hand gesture, placing the right palm facing upward in the left and extending them away from the chest toward the intended recipient. In this seemingly simple act, the communication process unfolds, with the dancer serving as the sender of the message through the movement motif. The positioning of the sender and receiver, in conjunction with the directional aspect, conveys to the entire congregation that communication has commenced, grounded in etiquette and a shared understanding of order. These lived experiences, embodied in gestures within Kete and other Asante dance suites, serve as a manifestation of memories showcasing the restoration of heritage, its ongoing relevance, and the purpose behind the continuity of these dances. Traditional philosophies within the Akan framework do not compartmentalize the past from the present; rather, they view life as dynamic and not static. The Asante construction of their living realities, as manifested in the Kete dance, is informed by the spirit of their culture, propelling their concept of aesthetics rooted in epic memory.

**Repetition:** Welsh-Asante purports that "a dance that is performed only once is cold, impotent, unable to elicit praise or criticism because of the incompleteness of the dance"[19] . Praise and criticism are essential features of aesthetic appraisal. Repetition in Asante culture means emphasis and acceptance of order, and enforces identity, ideologies, philosophies, and Asante worldviews. In a similar vein, Amegago "opines that repetition enables the performers and spectators to absorb and retain the performance components and as such requires the necessary skills and meaning."[20] The specific Kete variation in which a dancer of royal lineage gestures or points to the sky and then to his chest carries profound significance within the societal order. This gesture symbolizes the acknowledgment that only God is positioned above him in the hierarchical structure. The repetition of this particular gestural variation serves as a continuous affirmation of the dancer's esteemed position. It is a ritualistic act that underscores and reinforces the indigenous epistemology of order within Asante society. Welsh-Asante's perspective on repetition in African aesthetics, emphasizing its role as the intensification of movements rather than a mere chorus, provides a valuable lens through which elements in the Kete dance can be understood. In Kete, repetition serves a crucial purpose, not as a monotonous refrain but as a means of communicating cultural knowledge systems that are deeply rooted in the past and actively lived in the present. This repetitive nature becomes a significant educational medium, contributing to the preservation and transmission of indigenous knowledge. The theoretical framework of African aesthetics, as articulated by Welsh-Asante, sheds light on the philosophical underpinnings of Asante Kete. The movement variations within Kete are intricately connected to specific social contexts, serving to elicit and affirm structures of social order within Asante society. Mawere Opoku's assertion that dance is a reflection of life expressed through dramatic terms resonates within the Ghanaian/African perspective. The act of dancing, symbolizing vitality, contrasts with stillness, which is associated with death. This broader understanding underscores the pivotal role that movements, especially in dance, play in cultural embodiment and the transmission of cultural heritage.

---

19 Welsh-Asante, 'African and African-American Dance, Music, and Theatre'.
20 M. M. K. Amegago, *An African Music and Dance Curriculum Model: Performing Arts in Education*, Carolina Academic Press African World Series (Carolina Academic Press, 2011), https://books.google.ca/books?id=zI0DtwAACAAJ.

## Kete Performativity

Performances in dance serve as powerful symbols of identity, representing an ongoing process of conceiving and reconceiving both self and society. They act as conduits for affirming, resisting, and sustaining culture, embodying the dynamic interplay between individual and collective identities within a cultural context (Cudjoe, 2015). Judith Hamera emphasizes the significance of analyzing movement systems within the framework of performance. She suggests that performance serves as a heuristic tool for exploring various aspects of everyday life, history, the economy, the law, material culture, and other cultural forms that may not traditionally be viewed as performance. The goal is to delve into their aesthetic, theatrical, spectacular, and audience-directed qualities and, subsequently, to elucidate how these qualities contribute to cultural and political dynamics.[21] In alignment with Judith Hamera's perspective, I concur with the assertion that Kete dance performance functions as more than just a display of cultural elements. Firstly, it serves as a platform to unveil the implicit ideals embedded in the dance, drum languages, customs, and visual images. It acts as a poignant reminder to the Asante people of the battles and sacrifices made by their ancestors to preserve their customs and traditions. Secondly, the performance of Kete dance not only presents the richness of Asante tradition but also acts as a vehicle for the revival of philosophical foundations and belief systems. Through shared common experiences, Kete performances at festivals, marriage ceremonies, funerals, and wars contribute to the relearning of cultural values. Julia Davidson's concept of dance as a means of cultural production resonates here, emphasizing that dance, as a form of cultural performance, has the interpretability to reinforce cultural ideas and values. In this way, Kete dance constitutes a double form of "performance"—it is both an entertaining performing art and a medium theorized "as performance" within the broader cultural consciousness and the dance genre itself.[22] The comprehensive understanding of Kete performativity involves the thorough interpretation and analysis of all aspects of a performer or group's competence, encompassing sounds, move-

---

21 Judith Hamera, 'Performance Studies in Critical Communication Studies', in *Oxford Research Encyclopedia of Communication*, 2018, https://doi.org/10.1093/acrefore/9780190228613.013.640.
22 Julia R. F. Davidson, 'Listening to the Dancing Body: Understanding the Dancing Body as Performative Agent within the Choreographic Process Thesis Submitted in Partial Fulfillment Of the Requirements for the Degree of Master of Arts in Dance Mills College Spring 2016 By' (2016), https://pqdtopen.proquest.com/doc/1781226761.html?FMT=ABS#:~:text=The performativity of dance relies,body (Franko%2C 2012).

ments, and gestures produced during the performance.[23] In a traditional setting, a performer who deviates from the gestural rules in Kete dance may be perceived as a poor representation of the community. This deviation can even extend to being considered a stain on the performer's family legacy. Therefore, the art of dancing Kete necessitates a profound grasp of the linguistic routines that facilitate effective communication with the music and the community.

Awuah, drawing on the Speech Act theory, contends that dance acquires meaning through the specific arrangement of movements to music, beliefs, and contexts. The expression in dance is intricately tied to the meanings derived from routines under performatives and speech acts, performed in alignment with the sociocultural norms and networks of society. This argument aligns with Kofi Agyekum's definition of linguistic routines, which encompasses sequential organizations beyond the sentence, involving activities of individuals or the interaction of two or more. These routines include gestures, paralinguistic features, topics, and rituals in everyday interaction (Awuah, 2014; Agyekum, as cited in Awuah, 2016, 2014[24]). Hence, competence in the performance of Kete is synonymous with aesthetic awareness based on communal acceptance.

The Kete dance not only physically replicates the people's understanding and interpretation of their histories and environment but also serves as a medium for expressing the transcendental elements of religious belief through dance.[25] The Asante people's Kete dance, rooted in cultural life, skillfully employs ordinary everyday movements in a structured communicative pattern to reflect and affirm belief systems. In this context, Asante dance scholarship must draw on the diverse movements and socio-politico-cultural structures as both parallels and opposites to enhance understanding through various levels of knowing. The Kete dance of the Asante people serves as a descriptive expression of their philosophical viewpoints, particularly through gendered movement variations. Opoku emphasizes that the distinguishing characteristics of Asante dance include intricate and subtle manipulations of hands, arms, and legs, body sways and tilts in polyrhythmic combinations, expressive miming with rich symbolic undertones, and typical Asante hauteur (Opoku 1987). Analyzing Kete through a performative lens

---

23 Margaret Kartomi, 'Concepts, Terminology and Methodology in Music Performativity Research', *Musicology Australia* 36, no. 2 (3 July 2014): 189–208, https://doi.org/10.1080/08145857.2014.958268.
24 This is from an unpublished presentation by Awuah.
25 Nketia and Merriam, 'Drumming in Akan Communities of Ghana'.

**Image 18** Kete dancer showcasing his total dependance on the community. Source: Photo by Joshua Borah.

provides an opportunity to unravel and discuss the acceptable parameters of gendered movements in various contexts of Kete dance. As Kete dance is a form of communicative behavior, aligning with J. L. Austin's perspective that in performative speech, the issuing of the utterance is the performing of an action when the requisite conditions of authority are met[26] is appropriate. Butler further elaborates that the repeated stylization of the body becomes a set of repeated acts within a highly rigid regulatory frame that congeals over time to produce the appearance of substance, of a natural sort of being (Hamera 2018).

Victor Turner's definition of performance as a constitutive process, emphasizing the act of "making, not faking" social life and cultural continuity, resonates with the essence of Kete dance (Hamera 2018). Ampofo Duodu's assertion that "philosophical utterances and ideas which are difficult to express or risky to proclaim verbally are embodied in symbolic dance movement" (Duodu 1972) provides a valuable framework for understanding the performativity embedded within Kete dance scholarship. I argue that within Asante society, contexts, meanings, and aesthetics find validation through potent kinesthetic arrangements, such as the described greeting in the Kete dance form. The communication of meaning, facilitated by aesthetic rules

---

26 J. L. Austin et al., *How to Do Things with Words: Second Edition*, Harvard Paperback (Harvard University Press, 1975), https://books.google.ca/books?id=V43VS07TGEMC.

and movement expressions, is intricately linked to all facets of belief within the culture. Moreover, the performance of these movements is politically supported by philosophical norms. Anca Giurchescu, a Romanian folk-dance scholar, reinforces this perspective by stating that "the structure of dance may be considered as a culturally determined 'program' where social, historical, and environmental factors interlock with the physical, psychological, and mental features to produce meaning."[27] Laszlo Felfoldi also underscores the importance of viewing dance as a complex phenomenon deeply embedded in its sociocultural context, inseparable from its creators, and representing a culturally patterned, grammatically structured, meaningfully kinetic sign system used and performed in a community by its members.[28] The significance of performing a "proper" greeting in Asante culture is highlighted, emphasizing that dance cannot be isolated but should be understood as an integral part of a community's cultural expression.

## Issues on Kete Dance Aesthetics within the Academy

The evolution of dance over centuries reflects the dynamic nature of movement systems, which continuously adapt to changing cultural contexts. The Akan Kete dance, as part of the expressive heritage of its people, plays a role in shaping collective meanings and identities. Albert Mawere Opoku, recognizing the evolving nature of traditions, sought to strike a balance between respecting cultural heritage and providing opportunities for future generations to engage with these art forms. In this context, the competence of a teacher in transmitting the dance's essence can be evaluated using the "theory of concept and realization" proposed by Bakka and Karoblis. This theory likely assesses how effectively a teacher conveys both the theoretical understanding and practical realization of the dance form. The "theory of concept and realization" proposed by Bakka and Karoblis emphasizes the importance of both the conceptual understanding and the practical execution of a dance. The "realization" involves the actual performance of the dance, while the "concept" encompasses the potential skills, understanding, and knowledge that enable individuals or a dance community to engage with and comprehend the dance. In the context of teaching Kete dance, this

---

27 Anca Giurchescu, 'The Power of Dance and Its Social and Political Uses', *Yearbook for Traditional Music* 33 (18 February 2001): 109–21, https://doi.org/10.2307/1519635.
28 Laszlo Felfoldi, 'Connections between Dance and Dance Music: Summary of Hungarian Research', *Yearbook for Traditional Music* 33 (1 January 2001): 159, https://doi.org/10.2307/1519640.

**Image 19** Kete Male and Female dancers executing the symbol of preparedness for any eventualities. Source: Photo by Joshua Borah.

theory becomes crucial in evaluating the competence of the teacher in the transmission process. As a teacher, you've highlighted the challenge of adapting complex movement sequences in Kete variations to ensure that students can comprehend and execute them effectively. This adaptation may involve simplifying certain sections of the dance to match the students' comfort levels and abilities. This decision, however, can have implications for both the music and the overall structure of the dance. Teaching Kete dance to students in different parts of the world introduces additional challenges, such as time constraints, available resources for music production, and the need to make adjustments for effective learning. In essence, the competence level of a teacher in transmitting Kete dance goes beyond just demonstrating the movements. It involves the ability to convey conceptual understanding, adapt to the needs and capabilities of the students, and make informed decisions regarding music assimilation and structural modifications. This holistic approach is essential for ensuring that the essence of Kete dance is effectively communicated and preserved across diverse contexts. "For example, dancing with the Ahenema,[29] which is not permitted to commoners in the Traditional setting is very prevalent at certain observed performances during varied

---

29 This is the name of a traditional slipper in the Akan language.

social occasions in Accra the capital city of Ghana during data gathering for instance." Mawere Opoku states that "for the ordinary citizen the situation can be more taxing; [when dancing] he must remember to show respect for the royal drums by baring his shoulders and wearing his Ntama,[30] or togas,[31] between his armpit and his waist. He must be more circumspect in his use of gestures than he would be in freer, informal, recreational dances."[32] Thus, the proficiency of a dancer within an academic setting significantly relies on their comprehension of the context in which they are learning the dance and the specific purpose(s) for which they might be called upon to perform. Egil Bakka articulates that "dance competence is defined as a combination of motor ability, knowledge, and understanding that empowers a dancer to execute a particular dance in accordance with the norms of a group."[33]

As mentioned earlier, to analyze the gendered aesthetics of the Kete dance form in Ghana, it is crucial to scrutinize Kete performativity in all four dance categories—traditional, professional, academic, and amateur. Only through this comprehensive examination can we clarify the performative differences across these contexts and understand the nature of changes in the Kete dance form since its transition "from palace to academy." In the academy, for instance, traditional gender requirements are often set aside as both men and women perform movements for academic assessments and examinations. The visible alterations that occur when the dances change location and context will be discussed next, drawing insights from Patience Kwakwa, a trailblazer in the development of professional dance in Ghana since 1963. These are:

**Rhythmic foundations.** The foundation for neo-traditional dances rests on understanding their rhythmic structures from the perspectives of the traditional people, the body, and the percussion instruments. In this realm of knowledge, the body functions as both a musical instrument and a responsive entity. According to Patience Kwakwa, the reciprocal relations between music and dance stem primarily from their shared temporal and rhythmic foundations. Dance movements, including motor beats, specific steps, and phrasing, articulate structures similar to those found in music. From the dancer's perspective, African music with its strict timing can be perceived as movements set to music, given its dance implications. A discerning dancer would not only

---

30  This is the name for traditional cloth worn by both men and women.
31  This is the name for traditional shorts worn under the cloth.
32  Opoku, 'Asante Dance Art and the Court'.
33  Judith Lynne Hanna and Theresa J. Buckland, 'Dance in the Field: Theory, Methods and Issues in Dance Ethnography', *Ethnomusicology*, 1999, https://doi.org/10.2307/852643.

hear but also feel the dance within the rhythms of the music, responding to and interpreting these rhythms in the fundamental movements, steps, and gestures of the dance rather than focusing on the melodic line. This principle holds true for dance songs as well, as their underlying motor beats and rhythms must be inherently danceable.[34] Within the neo-traditional setting of the academy, there isn't a stringent insistence, for instance, on the instruments necessary for producing the music. The Kete ensemble traditionally comprises five specific drums, each with distinct sounds and tones when played together as a cohesive unit. However, in the academy, certain drums might be included for convenience, potentially compromising the dance's musical foundations. The students' ability to replicate movement structures relies heavily on their musical discernment. Achieving a high level of proficiency in Kete necessitates training dancers to understand and synchronize their movements with the intricate rhythms imbued with cultural significance. Changes in tunes and tones can significantly impact students' assimilation of the music. Effective communication between the dancer and the master drummer is crucial, as traditional music forms often dictate movements in performances, encompassing numerous symbolic gestures. Failing to grasp this concept through technical training and the incorporation of drum patterns as course modules can result in the development of what might be considered a "subpar dancer." Students must be adept at listening to the master drummer to synchronize their movements, playing a pivotal role in preserving traditional dances within the academic setting. Despite the emphasis on maintaining authenticity, there may be situations that warrant the inclusion of additional drums in the ensemble.

***Teaching "improvisation, team, and solo dancing":*** These elements of traditional dancing are crucial to a student's understanding of movement systems. Improvisation is encouraged when the movements conform to or are rooted in the dance studied. Limits to the improvisation depend on the competence level of the teacher and the student's flexibility and adaptability to the dance Kwakwa explained,

> The technique of presentation is one in which an individual or a group of dancers follow the rhythms of the drums very closely but are given ample latitude for improvisation or elaboration on the basic step patterns at specific points during the performance. In Asante societies this elaboration takes place when an instrument in the Kete musical

---

34 Patience Abenaa Kwakwa, 'Dance and African Women', *Sage (Atlanta, Ga.)* 8 (1994): 10–15.

ensemble, such as the master drum, thus the *Kwadum* drum or a horn, calls a person in the language of the drum or horn to do so. In this kind of dance situation, dancers do not have to be given specific cues for changes in the various movement sequences. Changes are spontaneous, and the dancer may pick up any focal point in the musics as cue for making the change.[35]

In the academic context, separate technique classes, including both beginner and advanced levels, are employed to facilitate the analysis and learning of Kete movements. Unlike traditional settings, the academic environment does not strictly mandate the replication of indigenous movements, primarily due to time constraints and limited resources available for teaching the dance during the semester. Moreover, while team dancing is a prevalent traditional practice, it is not as prominent within the Kete dance form. Kwakwa refers to these team dances as

> dances whose step patterns and sequences are fixed and identified with particular rhythms in the music. Such step patterns and sequences, therefore, have their corresponding musical rhythms so that each time a rhythm is played by the musicians, dancers must execute the corresponding steps, movement patterns and sequences or gesture [...] They can be described as team dances because all the dancers usually of the same age group, wear a uniform, and execute the same movements or steps at the same time [...] In such dances, cues for changes in dance sequences may be given to the dancers by the drummer (particularly the master drummer) through a signal he plays on his drum. The lead dancer picks this up and signals simultaneously, using his cow tail switch, to the other dancers who act as directed. Alternatively, the lead dancer may signal the master drummer to indicate that dancers wish to change their dance sequence. In this case, the master drummer receives the signal and acts accordingly.[36]

This concept is not the same in the academy, as students are taught sequences to perform during exams rather than focusing on the individual solo dancing Kete is known for. Now, because of the influence of the academy, many students and amateur dancers perform in groups and in unison.

---

35 Kwakwa.
36 Patience A. Kwakwa, 'Dance in Communal Life', *The Garland Handbook of African Music*, 2008, 54–62; Kwakwa, 'Dance and African Women'.

**Image 20** Kete dancers display equality gesture. Source: Photo by Joshua Borah.

***Teaching "dances with flute and song preludes":*** The Ghana Dance Ensemble, wanting to stay as close and "respectful" to the tradition as possible, explored all the elements of traditional dance performances, including traditional songs. Songs are crucial to the meaning of the dances, as they provide valuable meanings and contexts for their propagation. Kwakwa states that "a song sung before a dance sequence indicates by association what the movements of that sequence should be. Accordingly, whenever the dancers (who are also the singers) raise a new song, they follow it up immediately with the right dance as the instrumentalists similarly respond with the appropriate rhythms."[37] As such, any traditional/neo-traditional dance class that ignores this component in the transmission process does harm to the propagation of the form. However, this component has not been a vital focus in the transmission of traditional dancing in the bachelor program of the dance department at the University of Ghana. Concentration is placed on performing dance sequences rather than attempting a holistic embodiment process.

As identified by Ethnomusicologist Kwabena Nketia in his earlier works regarding Asante musical types, he noticed the full musical instruments used in the Asante Kete dance, which are now omitted from the current Kete drumming as the dance left the Asante palace, especially the flute musical

---

37 Kwakwa, 'Dance and African Women'.

component. In his work, he avers that "it is important to note the decline of the singing of vocal preludes and flutes for Kete, which had once been sung to help listeners understand the meaning embedded in the drumming" (Nketia and Merriam 1965). This assertion by Nketia was further confirmed by the work of Rattray, who listed the three musical components of Kete as drumming, singing, and reed pipes in his research.[38]

## Summary

In this comprehensive discussion, I have explored the intricate relationship between Asante culture and the Kete dance, emphasizing its role as a conceptual framework that extends to various aspects of Asante life. Through an examination of Akan/Asante motifs, I've illustrated how Kete serves as a catalyst for understanding broader cultural phenomena, including language, visual elements, and musical components. The gender dynamics within Kete dance were scrutinized, revealing a complementary rather than oppositional relationship between male and female bodies, particularly evident in the drum music. This analysis underscores Kete's significance as a repository of Asante epistemology, shaping and reflecting the cultural, social, and philosophical dimensions of the community. Furthermore, the discussion delves into the performative nature of Kete, highlighting its role in the preservation and transmission of Asante heritage, both within traditional settings and academic contexts. The examination of Kete dance aesthetics within the academy sheds light on the challenges and changes that arise when traditional forms intersect with contemporary educational practices. Overall, Kete dance emerges as a dynamic and multifaceted cultural phenomenon, embodying and transmitting the essence of Asante identity, aesthetics, and philosophy.

---

38 Catherine Meredith Hale, *Asante Stools and the Matrilineage* (Harvard University, 2013), https://dash.harvard.edu/handle/1/11004913?show=full.

# Chapter 7

# ANALYSIS AND INTERPRETATION OF KETE FROM A HOLISTIC POSITION

In this research, the data from fieldwork is categorized into four main groups: "Personal Experience," "Revelatory Incident," "Realization and Concept," and "Performance and Propagation." I employed a "Pheno-choreological" approach, combining "Pheno," representing the phenomenology of experience, and "Choreology," signifying the study of movement structure. This approach aligns with John Dewey's theoretical framework on the "social construction of knowledge," as elucidated by John Okrah in his exploration of African Philosophy of Education (Okrah 2012). The argument posits that if a people's culture comprises nuanced elements specific to their self-identification and their interaction with the environment, then the collective knowledge facilitating such assimilation through individual experiences becomes integral to their social reality. Conducting a pheno-choreological analysis involves examining the implicit and explicit personal and collective experiences of musicians and dancers involved in Kete to generate interpretations consistent with their realization and concept of the dance form, as articulated by Bakka and Karoblis (2010).

The embodied realities mentioned above significantly shape the categorization systems of a community, impacting the creation of phenomena and their contextual understanding. When an individual assimilates social knowledge, such as Kete dance-music, they become an agent within a cultural network encompassing art, communication, and the generation of meaning through performance for subsequent generations. To interpret this interconnected data, I will utilize Kuwor's indigenous holistic approach to dances from Africa (Kuwor 2017).

In this chapter, I delve into the analysis of specific elements of Kete based on the data recorded during my fieldwork in Ghana. The data is categorized under the codes of "Personal History," "Revelatory Incident," "Realization and Concept," and "Performance and Propagation." These categories were derived from recurrent themes found in responses from my informants and discussions with experts during recording sessions. These themes are then situated within Kuwor's concept of "Ghanaian/African Holistic Nature." This approach is justified by the phenomenological nature of the research, exploring the transmission of Kete dance in both palace/traditional and academic settings. I argue that understanding the transmission of dance-music in Ghanaian villages or rural communities requires an exploration of their total cultural makeup and the parameters that shape their way of life. Through constant practice, elements embedded in their philosophical and cosmological worldviews are embodied, and to comprehend the artistic foundations, one must explore the personal journeys of individuals in the process, recording nuances and similarities and drawing on feedback to explain the phenomenon of Kete dance. For context, I define the coding categories to situate the analysis.

a) <u>Personal Experience:</u> This records the respondents ethnic and rural affiliation to the dance form. It includes his/her relationship to either the music or dance of Kete, whether they belonging to a family of performers or are part of a rural Kete performance group, and the number of years they have performed or been involved with Kete dance music. This is necessary to validate the person's knowledge of the form.

b) <u>Revelatory Incident:</u> This records the circumstances/incidents that necessitated a devotion to the Kete music-dance form and some unpublished information about Kete that is unknown to me as a performer-researcher. Moreover, these incidents act as impulses for even nonindigenous people to learn the dance, as is seen performed mostly by amateur groups in Accra and elsewhere in Ghana. It should be noted that such happenings had profound influence on the informants so much that after many years, they still speak fondly of such encounters and how, to this day, they continue to enjoy engaging in the dance form as either teachers, musicians, or consultants.

c) <u>Realization and Concept:</u> This details the depth of the informant's understanding of the elements that make up Kete as a conceptual basis for good practical performances. Each participant, when speaking about movement variations, most of the time provided background stories of such and how that influenced them in their performance.

d) <u>Performance and Propagation:</u> This details respondent's personal or communal take on the parameters of performance, propagation, and safeguarding of the dance form. It also highlights their "frustrations" about what they think is "wrong" with these things and some ideas on how to "make things better."

## Personal Experience

The four participants who consented to having their names and responses published all hail from a palace in the Asante Region. This holds significance for the research titled "From Palace to the Academy," as it delves into palace performance and transmission structures, representing the Traditional category. These participants provided nuanced details about movement structures that are not commonly explored in academic or professional/amateur dance settings. The responses from the participants revealed two key elements within palace performance. Firstly, there is a nuanced understanding of the "royal commoner" relationship on a social basis. Secondly, there is a comprehension of the range of gestures employed by royals and the political implications of these gestures in relation to the thrones they occupy and the administration of authority within the palace. Nana Boakye, a Kete master drummer with over 20 years of performance experience, specifically made it a point to situate himself in the political hierarchy of his family as well as his hometown. He averred that his

> father was also a well-known drummer for a band in Kumasi called *Akwasikra* and after school in 1999 I decided to pursue my talent with drumming because my family is known for drumming. During that period, I formed a group in Kumasi called *Amokom* and we usually represented at events such as funerals. Through the elders in our palace we were able to gain the best exposure in public because we always accompanied them with the drums from the palace to many events such as funerals because Kete is mainly played at these events.[1]

This statement elucidates the fundamental indigenous transmission approach to learning drumming within the palace. The process is primarily embodied, emphasizing that one does not need to attend a formal classroom to learn. It can be inferred that family roles within indigenous communities play a crucial role in sustaining heritage forms such as music. Consequently, a drummer attains a level of knowledge comparable to that of the king, who dances to the rhythms provided by the drummer. The training period for the master drummer and royal family members, particularly the queen and king, involves extensive education. The history conveyed through stories and the philosophical meanings behind them are familiar to the drummer. This shared knowledge enables both the drummer and the royals to establish a profound connection to history, and their performances serve to validate these stories.

---

1 Boakye, *Kete with Nana Boakye*.

For young palace drummers and dancers, the assimilation process involves accompanying the royals to special functions where they observe and learn the protocols of public performance. This exposure allows them to witness seasoned dancers performing for the public, mentally preparing them to envision their own future performances. Apprentices may attend such public performances for many years before being granted the opportunity to perform publicly. Following each public performance accompanying royals to social functions, there is an evaluation process. Any technical or gestural mistakes, whether conscious or unconscious, are discussed, and corrections are made as needed. This feedback loop ensures continuous improvement and adherence to the standards set by the royal tradition. Nana Boakye highlighted that the significance of corrections varies, with more emphasis placed on experienced dancers compared to newcomers. In cases where the mistakes are deemed serious, more severe penalties, such as suspension from performing as court dancers for a designated period, may be implemented. This strict approach aims to ensure that gestural and technical mistakes are not repeated, upholding the high standards expected in court performances. Nana Boakye recalls a specific incident that significantly influenced his self-critique and his perception of those who perform for chiefs and queen mothers. He narrates, "At a particular function, my team of drummers played a 'wrong' rhythm than the Ohene (chief) requested, and our mentors quickly reprimanded us. So, we changed to the right rhythm. Shortly after that, they took over the drumming, and we sat behind them" (Boakye 2021). This incident highlights the strict expectations and immediate corrections within the context of performing for royalty, emphasizing the importance of precision in drumming for such esteemed occasions. This incident held significant importance for two primary reasons. Firstly, the drummers could have portrayed the chief as an incompetent dancer by playing the wrong rhythm, potentially causing him to perform incorrect movements. Such a situation would have been a considerable disgrace for the king, leading to a loss of trust from his subjects. Given the role of the king as the custodian of music and dance, it was crucial to avoid any perception of his mistakes. Secondly, the young drummers could have faced punishment, impacting their confidence and learning process. The mentors' decision to swiftly correct the rhythm aimed to prevent these potential consequences. Boakye reflects that, following this incident, he understood its implications and took it upon himself to ensure that such a mistake was never repeated. The training process for newcomers is not rushed. Nana Boakye shared that he learned various Kete musical variations and styles from numerous master drummers, including one from the Kumasi Cultural Centre, at a certain point in his life. His teachers at the palace would select other seasoned and highly respected Kete master drummers and dancers in his community and send him to understudy. Apart from musician/drumming families serving as court musical suppliers, palaces have strategies in place for recruiting drumming talents not connected to known families or even linked to palaces. Nana Boakye remembered what motivated him to learn Kete drumming and shared that

> I come from a palace in the Ashanti Region called *Asante Asokore* with [chieftaincy] seats in Koforidua and that was where the desire grew. I started dancing at the age of 14 and I can boldly say that many in my family know how to dance the Kete because of our royal foundation. When I was encouraged to drum by my fathers, I was very excited, because the first time I played it felt good and how I played made we realize that I could later become a genius at it. I would have stopped if I was not fruitful the first time but that experience motivated me to keep learning and even pursue it as a career.[2]

After many years of training and performance as a Kete master drummer and dancer, Nana Boakye was selected to be a sub-chief in his community for his exemplary service to the Asante kingdom. He stated that

> Manhyia [as a suburb in Kumasi and as the palace of the Asantehene] is my home because we [family] also inherit a sub-chief throne from there. For the past three months, I have been negotiating the possibility of occupying a vacant seat in the palace due to my lineage and experience in royal affairs and especially with regards to my experience as a court drummer who has worked with many chiefs and kings from childhood. The king makers deemed it fit for me to take the position due to these credentials and above all to represent them at the Manhyia palace. I had planned to accept the offer but after careful consideration I cannot see myself in that capacity because I will not be able to continue as a musician/drummer and because chiefs are not permitted to drum in public. I have informed them that I will not be able to occupy the seat because it comes with a lot of limitations especially with my work. The demands of the position and the constant kingdom meetings and deliberations at the kings palace will not allow one the room to pursue other passions because being a royal demands a lot of appearances and work.(Transliterated from Twi to English)[3]

---

2 Boakye.
3 Boakye.

Due to his unique position as a master drummer and dancer in a palace, as well as an independent group leader, Boakye's experience was invaluable in helping me understand the political power play that influences the transmission process of Kete. This is because there are restrictions on practicing the form if one should be promoted, and given that most court drummers are also likely sub-chiefs, the "lineage-based-drumming families may not have many people to pass on the knowledge of Kete to the newer generations." The monarchy also plays a key role in the spotting and training of dancing and drumming talents in the Asante Kingdom. The Kete-hene (Kete Chief) of the Manhyia palace at the time of this research recounted how he was spotted by the Asantehemaa (Queen Mother) and was urged to study the drumming. He recounts that

> We were taught how to play the Kete drums in the year 1981. It was here in the Manhyia palace I first saw and learnt the Kete drum music. Initially, I complained of the difficulty in learning how to play the Kete at the early stage and then Otumfour Nana Opoku Ware II who reigned in that era urged me to learn how to play and encouraged me constantly personally. I have accomplished a lot in my life by learning the Kete including travelling to many international destinations and performing Asante music. I often wonder what would have happened if I had listened to those who first told me not to learn the indigenous knowledge of my ancestors because they considered it "devilish." Through this same Kete study and eventual performances, I have also been able to support many people especially in my family by helping them to also find opportunities outside of Ghana as performers each time I returned from international duties. (Transliterated from Twi to English)[4]

This incident was preceded by an encounter with the Asantehemaa herself when *Ketehene* recounted what led to him taking up the sticks for drumming. He did not recollect what the queen mother saw in him to ask him to play the drum because he personally did not come from a family of musicians, but in hindsight, he believes that this was done in order to continue the preservation of Asante historicity and identity through the music and dance forms. He rose through the ranks quickly and now serves as the *KeteHene* for the Asantehemaa. The Asantehene also has his own Ketehene. He recollects that during his childhood, he lived with the Asantehemaa, and while assisting her with household chores like fanning the fire, she mentioned they were seeking someone to learn drumming. Intrigued, he expressed interest, and when

---

4 Boateng, *Kete with KeteHene of Manhyia Palace*.

I played a rehearsed rhythm on the master drum, everyone was surprised. Despite his grandmother's initial disapproval due to her Christian beliefs, the Asantehemaa admitted him to her court as a musician, personally supporting his learning of Kete drumming and dancing. As an eager learner, he followed seniors to events and practiced in the palace. Unbeknownst to him, the Asantehemaa supported his participation in outdoor events, motivating him and deepening his understanding of the culture. Boateng shares that he owes everything to the Asantehemaa for providing this unique opportunity for his cultural immersion (Transliterated from Twi to English).[5]

The narratives provided by Nana Boakye and Nana Ketehene underscore the significance of recruiting young children into Kete music and dancing for the sake of cultural continuity. Moreover, they highlight the personal interest and investment made by even the most powerful individuals in the Asante kingdom in this process. This underscores the seriousness with which the palace/Traditional category approaches the preservation of their music and dance forms, and how the transmission of the "concept and realization" of Kete is carefully curated in the training and performance stages. These accounts were further validated through inquiries about gestural variations between royalty and the common folk. Earning the title of a master drummer or dancer in Kete requires consistent and excellent performance as demanded by the role. Another significant indicator of achieving the "master" status is when families approach an individual to take on apprentices for their children. Nana Boakye, who leads his own Kete group and performs in Kumasi and Accra, mentioned that he frequently receives offers from young individuals and family heads seeking apprenticeship in Kete. In his own words, "I cannot keep the knowledge alone, so I am always happy to receive apprentice. I however only work with those who are very serious."[6] The recruitment process for palace musicians, who are primarily from drumming and music families, follows a distinctive approach. Becoming a court dancer or drummer involves gaining access to specific information and being exposed to unique narratives that contribute to the formation of one's dance concept. This specialized knowledge influences the performance of court performers in a significant way.

The third master drummer/dancer, Nana Kwame Kyei Baffour, shared experiences similar to those of Nana Boakye and Nana Ketehene, affirming the role of palaces as custodians of indigenous music and dance. Kyei Baffour learned his drumming and dancing in Kumasi Ankaasi, growing up in a

---

5 Boateng.
6 Boakye, *Kete with Nana Boakye*.

palace environment. His initiation into the art was prompted by elders, and he became dedicated to preserving the legacy of those who had passed on, contributing to the continuity of Asante dance music heritage. The consistency in these accounts across different individuals and locations underscores the significant role of palaces in the transmission of indigenous music and dance. Additionally, colleagues and apprentices of the respondents supported these narratives, highlighting the respect and recognition they accorded to their leaders in the field.

## Revelatory Incident(s)

During the interview sessions, my respondents highlighted certain revelations that have not been explored in scholarly publications on Kete dance thus far. These incidents are revelatory in the sense that the informants acknowledge their rarity in the public performance structure of Kete today to the point that they are afraid these elements could disappear if not explored. The first revelatory element of the Kete dance from the Manhyia palace and other smaller palaces has to do with the inclusion of spirits/ancestors in the performance through the pouring of libations before the playing of Kete drums. Nana Ketehene shares that he knew of this element of the dance from a young age and was taught that "every place [venue of performance be it palaces or event centres] has its systems and rules of engagement both spiritually and physically and when a drink libation is poured it gives clearance for the quest to undertake a planned activity like playing Kete music and dancing. After the pouring of libation at a particular place, even the president will not be able to park his convoy there or even use that space for anything. To move the drums from the place of libation to another for whatever reason, new bottles of Schnapps brand of alcohol will have to be brought to start a new process before the drums can be moved" (transliterated from Twi to English).[7] The intriguing aspect of this account is that it challenges my preconceived notion that libations were only performed during specific religious rituals. Learning that this practice is still observed in the palaces of Asante chiefs highlights the significance of libations in validating the spiritual dimensions of Kete music and dance.[8] Nana Ketehene also shared that because they believe that spirits inhabit drums, before they are played in ceremonial capacity, libations of

---

7 Boateng, *Kete with KeteHene of Manhyia Palace*.
8 Joseph S Kaminski, 'Sound Barrage: Threshold to Asante Sacred Experience through Music', *International Review of the Aesthetics and Sociology of Music* 45, no. 2 (1 December 2014): 345–71.

alcohol have to be poured. He states that "with the first 4 drums which are the *kwabunu, apentema, apetea and aburukua*, one will have to give 'them' alcohol/schnapps to drink as customs demand. This gives way for the drummers to perform but failure to do this means there would not be any peace among the instruments. You need the drums to be at peace to produce the required music for the occasion they are called for."[9]

The revelation that Kete still grapples with the interplay between spirituality and performance etiquettes brings attention to the question of whether women are permitted to play drums, especially master drums, due to the presence of menstrual blood. Menstruation holds a dual significance as both an indicator of fertility and a marker of bad omens. In Asante culture, where blood is considered sacred and drums are believed to be inhabited by spirits, there is a reluctance to mix the two because it is believed that spirits disdain such contact with menstrual blood. Ketehene shared that

> in previous times, during Akwasidae when some of the sub chiefs would come to the Manhyia palace, women in the menstrual periods are expected to sit in a designated space and in a particular posture. They would typically be draped in *Dansinkran* cloth with shea butter smeared on their bodies. From time-to-time certain chiefs would look among the ladies and select the one(s) they prefer as stool wives—*Hweneye*.[10]

Nana Boakye corroborates the historical perspective that women were not allowed to sit behind or play a Kete drum. This restriction stemmed from the belief that if a woman, during her menstrual period, touched the drum, it would result in her inability to give birth.[11] The contemporary assessment and explorations of Kete in the other three categories—professional, academic, and amateur—do not emphasize issues related to blood as observed in the traditional context. In these categories, there is more flexibility to bypass certain dance requirements, such as pouring libation and checking for menstrual cycles of female dancers. The differentiation in treatment of blood-related issues is attributed to the symbolic representation of blood on the Kete drums. The red and black cloth that drapes Kete drums symbolizes the blood of enemies and fallen warriors during wars. While the Asante people, as warriors, honor and commemorate blood in this context, the categorical classification and the role of elemental spirits in traditional practices make blood-related

---

9 Boateng, *Kete with KeteHene of Manhyia Palace*.
10 Boateng.
11 Boakye, *Kete with Nana Boakye*.

issues significant. Pashington and Obeng's exploration of blood within the matrilineal system of Asantes is crucial to their survival state and that

> Asante thought on matriliny, blood (*mogya*), and the belief that only women can transmit blood to their offspring is more complex than the stock explanation of female infidelity. The visibility of menstrual blood, and its implications for fertility and failed fertilization, the valuable role of women as biological reproducers of Asante society, and Asante (especially male) esteem and awe of childbirth promoted the notion that only women could transmit blood. As one queen mother told Rattray[12]: "If my sex die in the clan then that very clan becomes extinct."[13]

The traditional stance on women drumming in the context of Kete music has evolved over the years, witnessing a shift towards greater inclusion. While palace performances of Kete music may still adhere to conventional gender patterns, the other three categories—professional, academic, and amateur—have seen increased participation of women in various roles, from singing to playing instruments like the bell and supporting drums. Nana Ketehene suggests that the rise of women drummers, despite the historical spiritual implications associated with menstrual blood, drums, and spirits, is driven more by sociological and reactionary factors than a simple embrace of contemporary changes. This shift reflects broader societal changes and challenges traditional gender norms within the realm of Asante percussion music. He avers that

> the truth is that in those days, women did not play Kete because their role in the space was to dance. What caused the changed over time with women playing Kete drums is that at some points in the history of Asante kingdom expansion, constant wars saw men, including court musicians called to the battlefield and so the remainder of people necessitated the role reversal. Another reason for the introduction of women was a direct decision of the men who when they receive performance assignments, delegate duties to some women with the skill. To me,

---

[12] Rattray is a renowned British anthropologist who studied the Asante for the most part of his career on behalf of the British monarchy. A. W. C. and R. S. Rattray, 'The Tribes of the Ashanti Hinterland', *The Geographical Journal*, 1933, https://doi.org/10.2307/1784589; Melville J. Herskovits and R. S. Rattray, 'Akan-Ashanti Folk-Tales', *The Journal of American Folklore*, 1931, https://doi.org/10.2307/535628; R. S. Rattray, 'The Tribes of the Ashanti Hinterland', *African Affairs*, 1931, https://doi.org/10.1093/oxfordjournals.afraf.a101640.

[13] Akyeampong and Obeng, 'Spirituality, Gender, and Power in Asante History'.

this is a distortion and the fact that it is allowed does not make it true. (Transliterated from Twi to English)[14]

The historical reluctance to allow women to play Kete drums was rooted in traditional gender roles, where women were primarily assigned the role of dancing in the space. However, shifts in this tradition occurred due to historical circumstances, such as constant wars leading to the absence of men, including court musicians, who were called to the battlefield. This necessitated a role reversal, with women taking on drumming duties. Additionally, men in leadership positions within the Traditional category made direct decisions to include women in drumming roles, either due to their skills or as a response to specific performance assignments. This change, while providing opportunities for women to participate in Kete drumming, is seen by some as a distortion of traditional norms. The paradox lies in the fact that the Traditional category, which advocates for the consistency of indigenous structures in Kete music, also takes liberties with the rules and informs major changes. This ongoing development raises questions about the evolving gender dynamics within Kete dance-music performance, especially as it proliferates rapidly in other categories. It suggests that more women may challenge traditional gender norms within the drumming aspect of Kete, leveraging the evolving landscape of neo-traditional dance for greater inclusivity.

**Kete and "deformity"**

The most intriguing aspect of my research on Kete pertained to the exploration of the body and deformity. According to the Merriam-Webster dictionary, deformity is defined as "bodily disfigurement."[15] In the context of Asante traditional standards, any form of bodily disfigurement is regarded as such. Nana Ketehene disclosed that there is a facet of Kete performance kept private, exclusively meant for the entertainment of the Asantehene. Intriguingly, these performers are individuals with hunched backs, and their role is to amuse the king. This raises questions about who trains individuals with hunchbacks to perform Kete. The fact that their performance is not made public prompts inquiries into the general attitude of the Asante people towards deformity—does it signify an attempt to downplay or ignore its existence? This leads to contemplation on whether there is a prevailing sense of shame or indifference regarding deformity. These questions, emerging from

---

14 Boateng, *Kete with KeteHene of Manhyia Palace*.
15 Merriam-Webster, 'Deformity Definition & Meaning', 2022, https://www.merriam-webster.com/dictionary/deformity.

my data analysis, are areas I aspire to delve into in future research, though concerns linger about the secrecy surrounding this performance and potential reluctance from the palace to divulge comprehensive details for research purposes. He shares the details of the hunchback Kete performance.

> We had an *Atsatsa*[16] group who danced for the Asantehene. When they dance, the few people in attendance are forbidden to laugh except the king because movements are for his amusement. If anyone was caught in the act they were fined heavily. They performed in a special costume known as *Granyo* which also featured the symbolic colours of red and black and also wore a hat[17] called *Nseneakyɜ*. Their role was to make the king laugh and in a sort of funny wager, they would bet money to make him laugh and when he did because of their dance antics, they would receive money. The most recent dead of this group of special dancers was called Opanin CK. They were only requested to perform when there was a funeral occasion and they would be required to cheer the king up especially if the deceased was a family member or sub-chief, or importance acquaintance. They also dance on Mondays and Thursdays for the king and queen mother in the *mmadɜ* court and no other persons except drummers and *Ndehemaa* are allowed in that space.[18]

The peculiarity of this group of performers opens many possibilities for analysis into aspects of "deformed" or nondeformed Akan dancing body in the communicative process of dancing. There are questions to be asked about the history of the deformed body in Asante performance practices, how that contributes to the indigenous concept of health and wholeness, and how those influence gestures and meanings through a performer. How has the academy not picked up on this opportunity to interrogate specific body types in indigenous dancing and how such communities navigate meaning making? Perhaps it could be that only performing for the king in secrecy is an affirmation of their relevance even as court jesters at a time of sorrow. Second, it could be that they possess or are trained in specific modes of "dance comedy" that are not public but important enough to have their own rhythms and audience with two (2) of the most powerful and important people of the land—the king and queen mother. On the extreme end of the spectrum, any drummer who made musical mistakes at the performance of these unique people faced grace

---

16 This stands for hunchback in the Twi language.
17 On record, they seem to be the only group of people who are allowed to wear hats especially because of their jester roles.
18 Boateng, *Kete with KeteHene of Manhyia Palace*.

consequences. This is because specific musical variations are created for a specific class of people within the kingdom for good reason. Nana Ketehene explains that "the hunchback performers have a specific rhythm they dance to and when on the dance floor, they request such a variation called *adabayɜ afunu* which is performed." In the past, a drummer's inability to respond by switching to the requested could lead to a beheading.[19]

## The necessity of Kete Transmission from Manhyia to the University of Ghana

The transmission of Kete of the Asante has a rich and complex history. The journey from the traditional setting of Manhyia, the palace of the Asantehene, to the University of Ghana reflects a dynamic process influenced by cultural shifts, educational institutions, and evolving societal norms. This transmission involves a meticulous passing down of knowledge, skills, and cultural significance, with key custodians like Nana Boakye and Nana Ketehene playing pivotal roles. The transmission extends beyond the palace to the academy, where the dynamics of Kete change. In the academic setting, traditional gender requirements are often relaxed, allowing both men and women to perform movements for academic assessments.

In 1963, Patience Kwakwa reported that Kete was officially "given to" Professors Mawere Opoku and J. H. Nkekia upon official request to study and experiment with the pioneering work of the Ghana Ensemble.[20] There is no official record of how many musical variations of Kete were allowed to transition from the palace to the academy and officially set of a proliferation of the form on a national and international scale. This account was personally corroborated by my informant Nana Ketehene, who happened to know of a special delegation of performers sent to the University by then Asante monarch Otumfuɔ Nana Osei Tutu Agyeman Prempeh II at the time to perform it for the first time on university soil. He confirmed the existing relationship between the Traditional category represented by the palace and the Ghana Dance Ensemble by corroborating how there has been a constant exchange of researchers to Kumasi and delegation of master drummers and dancers to Accra continuously. The Ensemble had a practice of inviting traditional master drummers and dancers from Kumasi from time to time to teach students at the school of music and drama. He recounted that

---

19 Boateng.
20 Kwakwa, 'Kwabena Nketia and the Creative Arts: The Genesis of the School of Music and Drama, and the Formation of the Ghana Dance Ensemble'.

> my first ever Kete dance performance in public was at the University of Ghana, Legon during the time of Professor Mawere Opoku as leader of the performance section. It was during the 1979 coup d'état regime of the late President Jerry John Rawlings, and it was difficult navigating performances and spaces due to strict rules and protocols against public gatherings. The occasion was a competition where different regions would showcase their dances at the university for jury to select the best. I think the Ashanti Region won that competition in that year. (Transliterated from Twi to English)[21]

This anecdote validates the role of the university in dance proliferation and its influence on the state of dance research and performance practices today. Nana Ketehene's authority in the field of Kete performance is validated by his position at the Manhyia Palace as an officially enstooled chief of Kete music and dance performance and propagation since 1982. He recounts his development of the palace systems and details his predecessors' role in maintaining Kete structures.

> When the palace Kete group was reconvened as is often the case from time to time, the reigning King Otumfuɔ Nana Opoku Ware II ordered a man called *Yamensa* to lead. He was the Ketehene in 1982. Since there are two separate Kete performance groups in the palace belonging to the king and Queen mother, I was also enstooled as Ketehene (Kete Chief) in 1982, to serve the Queen mother stool. was very young at the time when I became the Ketehene. After my inauguration, I was then formally introduced to the Otumfuo at that time who had a great sense of humor and joked with me by asking "Nana Ketehene are you enjoying the throne of a Kete Hene?" (Transliterated from Twi to English)[22]

Professors Opoku and Nketia after a while also requested for the Asante war dance Fontomfrom and the social dance Adowa to be taught at the University, and these were again granted. Opoku then selected specific movements from Kete and Fontomfrom and created a fusion called "Akan Ceremonial Suite." Due to the nationalist approach to dance studies at the time, it was perhaps apt to represent a larger Akan ethnic group instead of just the Asante in order to create equal representation for all the other Akan peoples who perform variations of Adowa, Kete, and Fontomfrom, such as the Akyem Abuakwa monarchy in the Eastern Region of Ghana. The Akan Ceremonial Dance

---

21 Boateng, Kete with KeteHene of Manhyia Palace.
22 Boateng.

Suite created for the ensemble by the late Professor Opoku includes singing Kete songs, Kete dance, and Fontomfrom. Researcher Paul Schauert recorded the ceremonial dance suite and a Kete performance by the Ghana Dance Ensemble that I refer to for analysis. In a 14-minutes and-38 seconds video titled "Performance: Akan Ceremonial Dance Suite" at the National Theatre in 2007,[23] we see how the amalgamation of ethnic representation was employed in this creation for the Akan ethnic group and for Ghana. The video (https://media.dlib.indiana.edu/media_objects/k06987653) starts with a Kete/Adowa song by the women performers, and then from 5m:54sec to 8m:27sec, we see two Kete performers. The drum ensemble of Kete is still draped in red and black cloth, which is symbolic to the Asante/Akan people, and the male performer dances with cloth tied at his waist level, as is required in Kete performance for men ,and the woman is clothed with wrapper and adorned with ornaments. From 8m:28secs to 14m:38sec is the performance of Fontomfrom, first by the king and then by the queen and the together as a duet. In a second video by Schauert titled "Performance: Kete"[24] ( https://media.dlib.indiana.edu/media_objects/sn009z020), we see one female dancer ushering guest to a function. The observed difference in Kete performance between Manhyia and the Global Dance Ensemble (GDE) lies in the contextual purpose of the dance. In the neo-traditional setting of the GDE, the performance is used to honor specific attendees of the function or context. In contrast, at Manhyia, where Kete is associated with the king, it either accompanies the king's movement or the king engages with the drummers in a greeting dance. The distinction reflects the hierarchical nature of the Manhyia performance, where the king is the central figure, and Kete doesn't accompany anyone else perceived as a dignitary higher than the king. This contextual foundation becomes crucial for analyzing the gestures performed by the GDE in the academic setting and those performed at Manhyia.

---

23 *PURL 1.2 Performance: Akan Ceremonial Dance Suite* (Ghana: Indiana University Press, 2007), https://media.dlib.indiana.edu/media_objects/k06987653.

24 *PURL 2.5 Performance: Kete* (Ghana: Indiana University Press, 2007), https://media.dlib.indiana.edu/media_objects/sn009z020.

# POSTSCRIPT: FUTURE OF KETE DANCE RESEARCH

In conclusion, this research explored the transmission of the Kete dance from the palace to the University of Ghana, examining it through the lenses of the Traditional and Academic dance categories. The study adopted an Afrocentric and phenomenological approach, emphasizing the agency of the Kete dancing body in shaping cultural ideals and philosophies within the Asante community. The research began by discussing Awuah's four categories of dance performance in Ghana, focusing on the Traditional and Academic categories for analysis. It highlighted the transition of Kete from the palace to the university, acknowledging the influence of the Ghana Dance Ensemble as a bridge between the Traditional and Academic categories. The research emphasized the need for a phenomenological standpoint to understand the role of these dance categories in the transmission of Kete. It demonstrated the efficacy of the black body in affirming cultural ideals and contributing to the propagation of Akan/Asante culture. The study highlighted the dynamic and evolving nature of indigenous dances, challenging static perceptions and advocating for a deeper exploration of the meanings generated through performance.

Through a phenomenological analysis, the research delved into the experiences of Kete performers, situating the holistic nature of performance mediums like music and dance within the intellectual framework of Asante culture. The Traditional and Academic categories were shown to influence the meanings generated in different contexts, emphasizing the importance of context-specific interpretations.

The research justified the potency of indigenous thought patterns manifested through performance gestures and underlined the significance of the African Genius concept in analyzing movement systems. It argued for the preservation of traditional structures in performance art to avoid distorting identity markers. The study also explored the Pan-Africanist paradigm, showcasing how Kete was employed in the development of a nationalist approach to governing independent Ghana. It advocated for an Afrocentric mode of inquiry, aligning with the researcher's focus and enabling a deeper exploration of indigenous perspectives.

Incorporating autoethnography, the research provided a retrospective exploration of the researcher's experiences as a Kete dancer in various categories, offering a balanced assessment of dance education and its challenges. It called for a reconsideration of the reductionistic leverage in neo-traditional dance performances and highlighted the academy's role in salvaging traditional dance forms. In summary, the research contributed to the discourse surrounding dances in Ghana by providing a conceptual framework for comparative analysis. It emphasized the nuanced functionality of Kete, showcasing its complexity rooted in cultural ideals and philosophies. The Afrocentric and phenomenological paradigms were deemed promising for expanding research into individual creative interpretations of indigenous knowledge, opening avenues for deeper exploration of lived realities in Ghanaian dance research.

# BIBLIOGRAPHY

Adeleke, Tunde. '"Black Americans and Africa: A Critique of the Pan-African and Identity Paradigms". *The International Journal of African Historical Studies* 31, no. 3 (1998): 505–36.
Adeleke, Tunde. *The Case against Afrocentrism*. The Case Against Afrocentrism, 2009. https://doi.org/10.5860/choice.47-7019.
Adinku, Ofotsu. *African Dance Education in Ghana: Curriculum and Instructional Materials for a Model Bachelor of Arts (Hons.) Dance in Society*. Accra: Ghana Universities Press, 1994.
———. 'Cultural Education in Ghana: A Case Study of Dance Development in the University System'. *Dance Chronicle*, 2004. https://doi.org/10.1081/DNC-120029926.
———. 'The Protection of Choreographic Works in Ghana'. *Matatu* 21–22, no. 1 (2000): 351–54. https://doi.org/10.1163/18757421-90000338.
Agyekum, K. 'The Sociolinguistics of Thanking in Akan'. *Nordic Journal of African Studies* 19, no. 2 (2010): 21.
Agyekum, Kofi. Akan language, movements, and music. Interview, Summer 2021.
———. 'The Pragmatics of Akan Greetings', 2008. https://doi.org/10.1177/1461445608091884.
Akyeampong, Emmanuel, and Pashington Obeng. 'Spirituality, Gender, and Power in Asante History'. *The International Journal of African Historical Studies*, 1995. https://doi.org/10.2307/221171.
Amegago, M. M. K. *An African Music and Dance Curriculum Model: Performing Arts in Education*. Carolina Academic Press African World Series. Carolina Academic Press, 2011. https://books.google.ca/books?id=zI0DtwAACAAJ.
Amegago, Modesto. 'An Holistic Approach to African Performing Arts: Music and Dance Curriculum Development and Implementation'. *ProQuest Dissertations and Theses*, 2000.
Ampene, K., A. A. Ampofo, G. K. Adjei, and A. K. Awedoba. *Discourses in African Musicology: J.H. Kwabena Nketia Festschrift*. African Studies Center, University of Michigan, 2015. https://books.google.ca/books?id=iDfNsgEACAAJ.
Ampene, Kwasi. *Asante Court Music and Verbal Arts in Ghana: The Porcupine and the Gold Stool*. Routledge, 2020. https://login.ezproxy.library.ualberta.ca/login?url=https://search.ebscohost.com/login.aspx?direct=true&db=cat03710a&AN=alb.9087114&site=eds-live&scope=site.
Anku, Willie. 'Drumming among the Akan and the Anlo Ewe of Ghana: An Introduction'. *African Music* 8, no. 3 (28 September 2009): 38–64.
Anthonio, Kofi. 'Exploring Indigenous Knowledge Through Music and Dance Practices of the Aŋlɔ-eʋe'. PhD, University of Ghana, 2021.

Anyidoho, Kofi, and Richard Rive. 'Writing Black'. *World Literature Today*, 1982. https://doi.org/10.2307/40137451.

Arthur, G. F. Kojo. *Cloth as Metaphor: (Re)Reading the Adinkra Cloth: Symbols of the Akan of Ghana*, 2001. https://books.google.com.br/books?hl=pt-BR&lr=&id=DuNFDwAAQBAJ&oi=fnd&pg=PT11&dq=cloth+as+METAPHOR&ots=4LXtHeezin&sig=gydsEMxBkNpI00UOmj667Qo4kus&redir_esc=y#v=onepage&q=cloth as METAPHOR&f=false.

'Asante Kete Drumming: Music from Ghana.' New York, NY: Lyrichord Discs, 2007. http://www.aspresolver.com/aspresolver.asp?WOMU.

Asante, M K. *Afrocentricity*. Trenton, NJ: Africa World Press, 1988.

———. *Afrocentricity, the Theory of Social Change*. Amulefi Pub. Co., 1980. https://login.ezproxy.library.ualberta.ca/login?url=https://search.ebscohost.com/login.aspx?direct=true&db=cat03710a&AN=alb.392106&site=eds-live&scope=site.

———. *An Afrocentric Manifesto: Toward an African Renaissance*. Wiley, 2007. https://books.google.ca/books?id=4hdyAAAAMAAJ.

———. *Meaning of my Kete*. Philadelphia, USA, 2021.

———. *The Afrocentric Idea*. Temple University Press, 1987. https://books.google.ca/books?id=H5txAAAAMAAJ.

Austin, J. L., J. L. Austin, J. O. Urmson, J. O. Urmson, and M. Sbisà. *How to Do Things with Words: Second Edition*. Harvard Paperback. Harvard University Press, 1975. https://books.google.ca/books?id=V43VS07TGEMC.

Avorgbedor, Daniel, and Kofi Agawu. 'African Rhythm, a Northern Ewe Perspective'. *Yearbook for Traditional Music*, 1996. https://doi.org/10.2307/767817.

Avorgbedor, Daniel K. 'Some Contributions of "halo" Music to Research Theory and Pragmatics in Ghana'. *Bulletin of the International Committee on Urgent Anthropological and Ethnological Research*, 1991.

Awuah, Eric. 'A Study of Amateur Groups' Re-Interpretation of Traditional Dances in Ghana: Role on Continuity and Safeguarding'. NTNU, University of Clermont Ferrand, University of Szeged, University of Roehampton, 2014.

———. 'A Study of Amateur Groups' Re-Interpretation of Traditional Dances in Ghana: Role on Continuity and Safeguarding1'. *Acta Ethnographica Hungarica*, 2015. https://doi.org/10.1556/022.2015.60.1.6.

———. 'Whose Dance Is This Again?' In *The Book of Everything You Want to Know about Open Air Museum*, edited by Nikola Kristovic, 148–52. Muzej na otvorenom, Staro selo, 2016. https://books.google.ca/books/about/Book_of_everything_you_wanted_to_know_ab.html?id=xB7CzQEACAAJ&redir_esc=y.

Ayittey, G. *Indigenous African Institutions*. Brill, 2006. https://books.google.ca/books?id=sW-wCQAAQBAJ.

Bakka, Egil, Andrée Grau, and László Felföldi. 'The Dance Event'. Trondheim: Choreomundus Master, 2013.

Bakka, Egil, and Gediminas Karoblis. 'Writng "a Dance": Epistemology For Dance Research'. *Yearbook for Traditional Music* 42 (3 August 2010): 167–93.

Bamfo, Napoleon. 'The Hidden Elements of Democracy among Akyem Chieftaincy: Enstoolment, Destoolment, and Other Limitations of Power'. *Journal of Black Studies* 31, no. 2 (11 February 2000): 149–73.

Banks, Ojeya Cruz. 'Of Water and Spirit: Locating Dance Epistemologies in Aotearoa/ New Zealand and Senegal'. *Anthropological Notebooks* 16, no. 3 (2010): 9–22.

Bannon, Fiona. 'Dance: The Possibilities of a Discipline'. *Research in Dance Education* 11, no. 1 (2010): 49–59.

Barbour, Karen. *Dancing Across the Page: Narrative and Embodied Ways of Knowing*. Bristol: Intellect Books, 2011. https://login.ezproxy.library.ualberta.ca/login?url=https://search.ebscohost.com/login.aspx?direct=true&db=e000xna&AN=1135592&site=ehost-live&scope=site.

Biney, Ama Barbara. 'Kwame Nkrumah: An Intellectual Biography.' SOAS University of London, 2007.

Boakye, Nana. *Kete with Nana Boakye*. Accra, Ghana, 2021.

Boateng, Nana Kwadwo. *Kete with KeteHene of Manhyia Palace*. Kumasi, Ghana, 2021.

Bob-Milliar, George M. 'Chieftaincy, Diaspora, and Development: The Institution of Nksuohene in Ghana'. *African Affairs* 108, no. 433 (1 October 2009): 541–58. https://doi.org/10.1093/afraf/adp045.

Bond, Karen. '"Me, a Tree" – Young Children as Natural Phenomenologists'. In *Back to the Dance Itself: Phenomenologies of the Body in Performance*, 205–32. Urbana, Illinois: University of Illinois Press, 2018.

Botwe-Asamoah, Kwame. *Kwame Nkrumah's Politico-Cultural Thought and Policies: An African-Centered Paradigm for the Second Phase of the African Revolution. Kwame Nkrumah's Politico-Cultural Thought and Policies: An African-Centered Paradigm for the Second Phase of the African Revolution*, 2005. https://doi.org/10.4324/9780203505694.

Brukum, N. J. K. 'The Northern Territories of the Gold Coast under British Colonial Rule, 1897-1956, a Study in Political Change'. University of Toronto, 1997. https://tspace.library.utoronto.ca/handle/1807/11542?mode=full.

———. 'The Voices of the Elite in Northern Ghana, 1918-1938'. *Transactions of the Historical Society of Ghana*, no. 7 (9 February 2003): 271–81.

C., A. W., and R. S. Rattray. 'The Tribes of the Ashanti Hinterland'. *The Geographical Journal*, 1933. https://doi.org/10.2307/1784589.

Carter, M. 'Telling Tales Out of School: "What's the Fate of a Black Story in a White World of White Stories?"' In *Interrogating Racism in Qualitative Research Methodology*, edited by G. R. Lopez and L. Parker, 29–48. New York: Peter Lang, 2003.

Charmaz, Kathy. *Grounded Theory: Objectivist and Constructivist Methods*. Thousand Oaks, CA: Sage, 2000.

Chawane, Midas. 'The Development of Afrocentricity: A Historical Survey'. *Yesterday and Today*, no. 16 (2016). https://doi.org/10.17159/2223-0386/2016/n16a5.

Collins, E. John. 'Ghanaian Neo-Traditional Performance and "Development": Multiple Interfaces between Rural and Urban, Traditional and Modern', 120–38. Leiden, The Netherlands: Brill, 2019. https://doi.org/10.1163/9789004392946_009.

Collins, John. 'Ghanaian Christianity and Popular Entertainment: Full Circle'. *History in Africa* 31 (2004): 407–23. https://doi.org/10.1017/s0361541300003570.

Connerton, Paul. *How Societies Remember. How Societies Remember*, 1989. https://doi.org/10.1017/cbo9780511628061.

Cornelius, Steven, and Habib Iddrisu. 'From Village to International Stage': In *Hot Feet and Social Change*, 228–48. University of Illinois Press, 2019. https://doi.org/10.5406/j.ctvswx837.18.

Cox, Gerry R., and Neil Thompson. 'The Akan of Ghana'. In *Managing Death: International Perspectives*, edited by Gerry R. Cox and Neil Thompson, 85–89. Cham: Springer International Publishing, 2022. https://doi.org/10.1007/978-3-031-05559-1_9.

Cudjoe, Emmanuel. 'Exploring Female Voices through the Togo-Atchan Dance as a Communicative Tool for Community Development in Togo-West Africa'. Choreomundus International Master Consortium, 2018.

———. 'The Contexts And Meaning In Asante Dance Performance: The Case Of Kete'. University of Ghana, 2015.

Davidson, Julia R. F. 'Listening to the Dancing Body: Understanding the Dancing Body as Performative Agent within the Choreographic Process Thesis Submitted in Partial Fulfillment of the Requirements for the Degree of Master of Arts in Dance Mills College Spring 2016 By', 2016. https://pqdtopen.proquest.com/doc/1781226761.html?FMT=ABS#:~:text=The performativity of dance relies, body (Franko%2C 2012).

DeFrantz, Thomas F. 'African American Dance - Philosophy, Aesthetics, and "Beauty"'. *Topoi* 24, no. 1 (2005). https://doi.org/10.1007/s11245-004-4165-7.

Dei, G. J. S., and S. Hilowle. *Cartographies of Race and Social Difference*. Critical Studies of Education. Springer International Publishing, 2018. https://books.google.ca/books?id=z559DwAAQBAJ.

Dei, G. J. S., and M. Lordan. *Anti-Colonial Theory and Decolonial Praxis*. Peter Lang Publishing, Incorporated, 2016. https://books.google.ca/books?id=CyWbDAEACAAJ.

Dei, George Sefa. *Indigenous Philosophies and Critical Education. A Reader- Foreword by Akwasi Asabere-Ameyaw*. New York, NY: Peter Lang Verlag, 2011. https://www.peterlang.com/document/1050926.

———. *Teaching Africa: Towards a Transgressive Pedagogy*. Explorations of Educational Purpose. Springer Netherlands, 2010. https://books.google.ca/books?id=BmjYy-PmEjcC.

———. 'The Role of Afrocentricity in the Inclusive Curriculum in Canadian Schools'. *Canadian Journal of Education* 21, no. 2 (1996).

Dei, George Sefa, and Marlon Simmons. 'Indigenous Knowledge and the Challenge for Rethinking Conventional Educational Philosophy: A Ghanaian Case Study'. *Counterpoints* 352 (2011): 97–111.

Denzin, Norman K., and Yvonna S. Lincoln. 'Introduction: Critical Methodologies and Indigenous Inquiry In: Handbook of Critical and Indigenous Methodologies Introduction: Critical Methodologies and Indigenous Inquiry', 2008. https://doi.org/10.4135/9781483385686.

Denzin, Norman K., and Yvonna S. Lincoln. *The SAGE Handbook of Qualitative Research*. Edited by Norman K. Denzin and Yvonna S. Lincoln. *Choice Reviews Online*. Sage Publications, 2005. https://doi.org/10.5860/choice.43-1330.

De-Whyte, Janice Pearl Ewurama. '(In)Fertility in the Akan Culture'. In *Wom(b)an: A Cultural-Narrative Reading of the Hebrew Bible Barrenness Narratives*, 53–75. Brill, 2018. https://doi.org/10.1163/9789004366305_004.

Duodu, Ampofo Emmanuel. 'Drumming and Dancing in Akan Society: A Study of Court Musical and Dancing Tradition'. Wesleyan University, 1972.

———. 'Topics in African Dance and the Related Arts'. *Legon Journal*, 1994.

Falola, Toyin. *The African Diaspora: Slavery, Modernity, and Globalization*. Boydell & Brewer, 2013. https://www.cambridge.org/core/books/african-diaspora/99E64922F04FD517890F5ABAD0E4C192.

Fanon, Frantz. *Black Skin, White Masks*. Grove Press, 2008. https://login.ezproxy.library.ualberta.ca/login?url=https://search.ebscohost.com/login.aspx?direct=true&db=cat03710a&AN=alb.4174166&site=eds-live&scope=site.

Felfoldi, Laszlo. 'Connections between Dance and Dance Music: Summary of Hungarian Research'. *Yearbook for Traditional Music* 33 (1 January 2001): 159. https://doi.org/10.2307/1519640.

Franko, Mark. 'Dance and the Political: States of Exception'. *Dance Research Journal* 38, no. 1/2 (2006): 3–18.

Fuller, Harcourt. 'Building a Nation: Symbolic Nationalism during the Kwame Nkrumah Era in the Gold Coast/Ghana'. University of London, 2010. https://login.ezproxy.library.ualberta.ca/login?url=https://search.ebscohost.com/login.aspx?direct=true&db=edsndl&AN=edsndl.oai.union.ndltd.org.bl.uk.oai.ethos.bl.uk.526756&site=eds-live&scope=site.

Giurchescu, Anca. 'The Power of Dance and Its Social and Political Uses'. *Yearbook for Traditional Music* 33 (18 February 2001): 109–21. https://doi.org/10.2307/1519635.

Greco, Mitchell J. 'The Emic and Etic Teaching Perspectives of Traditional Ghanaian Dance-Drumming: A Comparative Study of Ghanaian and American Music Cognition and the Transmission Process'. *ProQuest Dissertations and Theses*. Kent State University, 2014. https://login.ezproxy.library.ualberta.ca/login?url=https://www.proquest.com/dissertations-theses/emic-etic-teaching-perspectives-traditional/docview/1646474024/se-2?accountid=14474.

Gubrium, Jaber F, and James A Holstein. 'Narrative Practice and the Coherence of Personal Stories', 1998.

Hagan, George. 'Dondology: Music, Mind and Matter'. In *Discourses in African Musicology: J.H. Kwabena Nketia Festschrift*, edited by Kwasi Ampene, A A Ampofo, Godwin Adjei, and A K Awedoba, 456–77. Michigan: African Studies Center, University of Michigan, 2015.

Hale, Catherine Meredith. *Asante Stools and the Matrilineage*. Harvard University, 2013. https://dash.harvard.edu/handle/1/11004913?show=full.

Hall, Stuart. *Representation: Cultural Representations and Signifying Practices*. Culture, Media and Identities. SAGE, 1997. https://login.ezproxy.library.ualberta.ca/login?url=https://search.ebscohost.com/login.aspx?direct=true&db=cat03710a&AN=alb.1932763&site=eds-live&scope=site.

Hamera, Judith. 'Performance Studies in Critical Communication Studies'. In *Oxford Research Encyclopedia of Communication*, 2018. https://doi.org/10.1093/acrefore/9780190228613.013.640.

Hanna, Judith Lynne, and Theresa J. Buckland. 'Dance in the Field: Theory, Methods and Issues in Dance Ethnography'. *Ethnomusicology*, 1999. https://doi.org/10.2307/852643.

Herskovits, Melville J., and R. S. Rattray. 'Akan-Ashanti Folk-Tales'. *The Journal of American Folklore*, 1931. https://doi.org/10.2307/535628.

ICOM. 'Museum Definition'. ICOM Resources, 2007. https://icom.museum/en/resources/standards-guidelines/museum-definition/.

Kaeppler, Adrienne L. 'Dance Ethnology and the Anthropology of Dance'. *Dance Research Journal* 32, no. 1 (2000): 116. https://doi.org/10.2307/1478285.

Kaminski, Joseph S. 'Sound Barrage: Threshold to Asante Sacred Experience through Music'. *International Review of the Aesthetics and Sociology of Music* 45, no. 2 (1 December 2014): 345–71.

Kartomi, Margaret. 'Concepts, Terminology and Methodology in Music Performativity Research'. *Musicology Australia* 36, no. 2 (3 July 2014): 189–208. https://doi.org/10.1080/08145857.2014.958268.

Khokholkova, Nadezhda. 'Afrocentricity: The Evolution of the Theory in the Context of American History'. *Uchitel Publishing House* 15, no. 1 (2016).

Kibirige, Ronald. *Inherent Community-Based Agendas in Dancing and Dance-Musicking Traditions in Uganda.* Accra, Ghana: Department of Dance Studies, University of Ghana, 2021.

Koeltzsch, Grit Kirstin. 'The Body as Site of Academic Consciousness. A Methodological Approach for Embodied (Auto)Ethnography'. *Academia Letters*, 2021, 1–5. https://doi.org/10.20935/al3104.

Kringelbach, Hélène Neveu. *Dance Circles: Movement, Morality and Self-Fashioning in Urban Senegal.* Dance and Performance Studies. New York: Berghahn Books, 2013. https://login.ezproxy.library.ualberta.ca/login?url=https://search.ebscohost.com/login.aspx?direct=true&db=e000xna&AN=665967&site=eds-live&scope=site.

Kuwor, Sylvanus Kwashie. *Structures of Meaning in Ghanaian Traditional Dance Forms.* Accra, 2019.

———. 'The Impact of Adzido on Black Dance and Crosscultural Education in British Schools'. *Review of Human Factor Studies* 19, no. 1 (2013).

———. 'Transmission of Anlo-Ewe Dances in Ghana and in Britain: Investigating, Reconstructing and Disseminating Knowledge Embodied in the Music and Dance Traditions of Anlo-Ewe People in Ghana'. University of Roehampton, 2013. https://pure.roehampton.ac.uk/portal/en/studentTheses/transmission-of-anlo-ewe-dances-in-ghana-and-in-britain-investiga.

———. 'Understanding African Dance in Context: Perspectives from Ghana'. *The Journal of Pan African Studies (Online)* 10, no. 4 (2017): 47.

Kwakwa, Patience. 'Kwabena Nketia and the Creative Arts: The Genesis of the School of Music and Drama, and the Formation of the Ghana Dance Ensemble'. In *Discourses in African Musicology: J.H. Kwabena Nketia Festschrift*, edited by Kwasi Ampene, A A Ampofo, Godwin Adjei, and A K Awedoba, 480–506. Michigan: African Studies Center, University of Michigan, 2015.

Kwakwa, Patience A. 'Dance in Communal Life'. *The Garland Handbook of African Music*, 2008, 54–62.

Kwakwa, Patience Abenaa. 'Dance and African Women'. *Sage (Atlanta, Ga.)* 8 (1994): 10–15.

Kyei Baffour, Nana Kwame. Accra: Fieldwork in Ghana, 2021.

Langmia, Kehbuma. 'Debunking the Truth through a Video Documentary: A Case Study of Henry Louis Gates' "Wonders of the African World"'. *Journal of Third World Studies* 31, no. 2 (5 February 2014): 83–99.

Mauzé, Marie. 'Two Kwakwaka'wakw Museums: Heritage and Politics'. *Ethnohistory* 50, no. 3 (2003 Summer 2003): 503–22. https://doi.org/10.1215/00141801-50-3-503.

Mawuli, Cynthia Adjovi. 'Transmission and Embodiment of Heritage: An Analysis of Adinkra Symbology on Traditional Clothing in Ghana'. Central European University, 2019.

Mazama, Ama. 'The Afrocentric Paradigm: Contours and Definitions'. *Journal of Black Studies* 31, no. 4 (2001).

Merriam-Webster. 'Deformity Definition & Meaning', 2022. https://www.merriam-webster.com/dictionary/deformity.

Meyer, Birgit, and Kwame Anthony Appiah. 'In My Father's House: Africa in the Philosophy of Culture'. *Journal of Religion in Africa*, 1994. https://doi.org/10.2307/1581314.

Mfum-Mensah, Obed. 'The Impact of Colonial and Postcolonial Ghanaian Language Policies on Vernacular Use in Schools in Two Northern Ghanaian Communities'. *Comparative Education* 41, no. 1 (1 February 2005): 71–85. https://doi.org/10.1080/03050060500073256.

Mkabela, Queeneth. 'Using the Afrocentric Method in Researching Indigenous African Culture'. *Qualitative Report* 10, no. 1 (1 March 2005): 178–89.

Monteiro-Ferreira, Ana. *The Demise of the Inhuman: Afrocentricity, Modernism, and Postmodernism*. Albany: State University of New York, 2014.

Nance, C. Kemal. 'Brothers of the "Bah Yáh!": The Pursuit of Maleness in the Umfundalai Tradition of African Dance'. *ProQuest Dissertations and Theses*. Temple University, 2014. https://login.ezproxy.library.ualberta.ca/login?url=https://www.proquest.com/dissertations-theses/brothers-bah-yáh-pursuit-maleness-umfundalai/docview/1617432728/se-2?accountid=14474.

Nii-Yartey, Francis. 'Introduction to Contemporary African Dance'. Lecture Presentation, Department of Dance Studies, University of Ghana, 2010.

Nketia, J. H. K. 'Contextual Strategies of Inquiry and Systematization'. *Ethnomusicology* 34, no. 1 (1990): 75. https://doi.org/10.2307/852357.

Nketia, J. H. K. *Ethnomusicology and African Music: Modes of Inquiry and Interpretation*. Ethnomusicology and African Music: Collected Papers. Afram Publications, 2005. https://books.google.ca/books?id=CaafAAAAMAAJ.

———. *Reinstating Traditional Music in Contemporary Contexts: Reminiscences of a Nonagenarian's Lifelong Encounters with the Musical Traditions of Africa*. Regnum Africa Publications, 2016. https://books.google.ca/books?id=dJY5swEACAAJ.

———. 'The Interrelations of African Music and Dance'. *Studia Musicologica Academiae Scientiarum Hungaricae* 7, no. 1/4 (28 September 1965): 91–101. https://doi.org/10.2307/901416.

Nketia, J. H. K, and A. P. Merriam. 'Drumming in Akan Communities of Ghana'. *Ethnomusicology*, 1965. https://doi.org/10.2307/850333.

Nketia, J. H. K. 'African Music and Western Praxis: A Review of Western Perspectives on African Musicology'. *Canadian Journal of African Studies / Revue Canadienne Des Études Africaines*, 1986. https://doi.org/10.1080/00083968.1986.10804143.

———. 'The Poetry of Drums'. In *Voices of Ghana*, 2019. https://doi.org/10.2307/j.ctvbtzpxc.11.

———. 'The Role of the Drummer in Akan Society'. *African Music: Journal of the African Music Society* 1, no. 1 (1 December 1954): 34–43. https://doi.org/10.21504/amj.v1i1.225.

Nketsia, N K. *African Culture in Governance and Development: The Ghana Paradigm*. Ghana Universities Press, 2013. https://books.google.ca/books?id=dRDFoAEACAAJ.

Nkrumah, Kwame. 'The African Genius'. Accra: Institute of African Studies, University of Ghana, 1963.

Nyamuame, Samuel Elikem Kwame. 'History, Religion and Performing Yeve: Ewe Dance-Drumming, Songs and Rituals at Ave-Dakpa, Ghana'. *ProQuest Dissertations and Theses*, 2013.

Okrah, K. Asafo-Agyei. *Nyansapo (the Wisdom Knot): Toward an African Philosophy of Education*. African Studies. Routledge, 2012. https://login.ezproxy.library.ualberta.ca/login?url=https://search.ebscohost.com/login.aspx?direct=true&db=cat03710a&AN=alb.8775617&site=eds-live&scope=site.

Olokodana-James, Oluwatoyin. 'Trans-Sociological Hybridity: Conceptualizing African Contemporary Dance Identity'. In *Culture and Development in Africa and the Diaspora*, edited by Ahamad Sheuh Abdussalam, Aderibigbe Ibigbolade, Sola Timothy Babatunde, and Olutola Akindipe, 95–109. London: Routledge, 2020. https://doi.org/10.4324/9780429316296.

Olufunke, Oba. . Wilfrid Laurier University, 2018. https://scholars.wlu.ca/etd/2015/.

Opoku, Albert Mawere. 'Asante Dance Art and the Court'. In *The Golden Stool: Studies of the Asante Center and Periphery*, edited by Enid Schildkrout and Carol Gelber, 192–99. New York, NY: American Museum of Natural History, 1987.

———. 'Thoughts from the School of Music and Drama'. *Okyeame* 2, no. 1 (1964): 51.

Opoku-Amankwa, Kwasi. 'English-Only Language-in-Education Policy in Multilingual Classrooms in Ghana'. *Language, Culture and Curriculum* 22, no. 2 (1 July 2009): 121–35. https://doi.org/10.1080/07908310903075159.

Owusu-Ansah, Frances E, and Gubela Mji. 'African Indigenous Knowledge and Research'. *African Journal of Disability* 2, no. 1 (16 January 2013): 30. https://doi.org/10.4102/ajod.v2i1.30.

Paakwoh, C. *Rules in Kete Dance*. Kumasi, Ghana, 2021.

Patton, Michael Quinn. 'Two Decades of Developments in Qualitative Inquiry: A Personal, Experiential Perspective'. *Qualitative Social Work* 1, no. 3 (1 September 2002): 261–83. https://doi.org/10.1177/1473325002001003636.

Paulding, Ben. 'Asante Kete Drumming: A Musical Analysis of Meter, Feel, and Phrasing'. *ProQuest Dissertations and Theses*. Tufts University, 2017. https://login.ezproxy.library.ualberta.ca/login?url=https://www.proquest.com/dissertations-theses/asante-kete-drumming-musical-analysis-meter-feel/docview/1964391636/se-2?accountid=14474.

———. 'Kete for the International Percussion Community'. In *Discourses in African Musicology: J.H. Kwabena Nketia Festschrift*, edited by Kwasi Ampene, A A Ampofo, G Adjei, and A K Awedoba, 156–85. Michigan: African Studies Center, University of Michigan, 2015.

Petrie, Jennifer L. 'Music and Dance Education in Senior High Schools in Ghana: A Multiple Case Study'. *ProQuest Dissertations and Theses*. Ohio University, 2015. https://login.ezproxy.library.ualberta.ca/login?url=https://www.proquest.com/dissertations-theses/music-dance-education-senior-high-schools-ghana/docview/1769107898/se-2?accountid=14474.

*PURL 1.2 Performance: Akan Ceremonial Dance Suite*. Ghana: Indiana University Press, 2007. https://media.dlib.indiana.edu/media_objects/k06987653.

*PURL 2.5 Performance: Kete*. Ghana: Indiana University Press, 2007. https://media.dlib.indiana.edu/media_objects/sn009z020.

Quarcoo, Emmanuel. 'The English Language as a Modern Ghanaian Artifact'. *Journal of Black Studies* 24, no. 3 (9 March 1994): 329–43.

Rattray, R. S. 'The Tribes of the Ashanti Hinterland'. *African Affairs*, 1931. https://doi.org/10.1093/oxfordjournals.afraf.a101640.

Schauert, Paul. 'A Performing National Archive: Power and Preservation in the Ghana Dance Ensemble'. *Historical Society of Ghana* 10 (2007): 171–81.

———. 'A Performing National Archive: Power and Preservation in the Ghana Dance Ensemble'. *Historical Society of Ghana* 10 (2007): 171–81.

Schauert, Paul. *Opoku, Albert Mawere*. Oxford University Press, 2011. https://doi.org/10.1093/acref/9780195382075.013.1637.

Schauert, Paul. 'Staging Unity, Performing Subjectivities'. *Ghana Stduies* 15/16 (2013): 373–412.

Silver, Harry R. 'Beauty and the "I" of the Beholder: Identity, Aesthetics, and Social Change among the Ashanti'. *Journal of Anthropological Research* 35, no. 2 (14 January 1979): 191–207.

Thompson, Robert Farris. 'An Aesthetic of the Cool'. *African Arts* 7, no. 1 (12 February 1973): 41–91. https://doi.org/10.2307/3334749.

Welsh-Asante, K. 'African and African-American Dance, Music, and Theatre'. *Source: Journal of Black Studies* 15, no. 4 (1985): 381–403.

———. *African Dance: An Artistic, Historical, and Philosophical Inquiry*. Trenton, NJ: Africa World Press, 1996.

———. 'Philosophy and Dance in Africa: The Views of Cabral And'. *Source: Journal of Black Studies* 21, no. 2 (1990): 224–32.

Welsh-Asante, K., and E. A. Hanley. *African Dance*. World of Dance. Infobase Publishing, 2010. https://books.google.ps/books?id=uMcPuAEACAAJ.

Wiggins, Trevor. 'Personal, Local, and National Identities in Ghanaian Performance Ensembles'. In *Learning, Teaching, and Musical Identity: Voices Across Cultures*, 170–83. Indiana University Press, 2011.

———. 'Personal, Local, and National Identities in Ghanaian Performance Ensembles'. In *Learning, Teaching, and Musical Identity: Voices Across Cultures*, 2011.

Williams, R. *Marxism and Literature*. Marxist Introductions. Oxford: Oxford University Press, 1977. https://books.google.ca/books?id=7WHGAW7xnxIC.

Wilson, Margaret. 'Dance Pedagogy Case Studies: A Grounded Theory Approach to Analyzing Qualitative Data'. *Research in Dance Education* 10, no. 1 (2009): 3–16. https://doi.org/10.1080/14647890802697148.

Young, Robert. *White Mythologies: Writing History and the West*. Routledge, 2004. https://login.ezproxy.library.ualberta.ca/login?url=https://search.ebscohost.com/login.aspx?direct=true&db=cat03710a&AN=alb.8093928&site=eds-live&scope=site.

Younge, Paschal Yao. 'Enhancing Global Understanding through Traditional African Music and Dance: A Multicultural African Music Curriculum for American Middle Schools'. *Dissertation Abstracts International Section A: Humanities and Social Sciences*, 2008.

Younge, Paschal Yao. *Music and Dance Traditions of Ghana: History, Performance and Teaching*. Jefferson, NC: McFarland & Co., 2011.

# INDEX

1979 coup d'état regime 162
1992 Constitution of Ghana 78

*Abɔfoɔ agorɔ* xvi, 16, 135
Abibigromma Theatre Company 88, 117
*Abrafour* 58
Aburukuwa 56
Academic dance category 165
Accra 36, 41, 57, 88, 126, 144, 161
*Adaban* 58
Adabanka 55
*adabayɜ afunu* 161
Adeleke, Tunde 50–51
Adinkra symbols 28–31, 107–8
*Adinkrahene* 30
Adinku, Ofotsu 19, 36, 57, 71, 75, 121
Adowa xvi, xvii, 28, 162
African dance 3–4, 6, 9, 21, 31, 51, 122, 129, 133; forms 3–4, 14, 71
African epistemology 26
African Genius xxi, 49, 65, 70, 73, 76, 80, 165
African heritage 22, 48, 129
African Indigenous Knowledge Systems xxii, 2, 12, 38, 71, 76
African intellectual development 23
African movement systems 49
African neo-traditional dances 51
African personality 6–7, 9, 24, 39, 71, 77
African Philosophy of Education 149
African societies 3, 34, 129
African Youth Exchange Program 117
African-centered paradigm 21
African/Kete aesthetics 121–22, 129–31, 138
Afrocentric approach 10, 25–26, 29, 31, 33, 50
Afrocentric lens 15, 44
Afrocentric method 34
Afrocentric paradigm 5, 9, 11–12, 23, 33, 43, 51

Afrocentric theory 10, 30–31, 33–34
Afrocentric thought 50, 123
Afrocentricity xix, 11, 20–25, 32, 34, 43, 47–48, 50–51, 93
Afrocentrism 10, 21, 26, 44
Agogomu 55
Agyekum, Kofi 136, 140
Ahenemma Kete Group 45
*ahenkoa* 58
Akan aesthetics 131
Akan Ceremonial Dance Suite 19, 36, 162–63
Akan cosmology 31, 51, 99
Akan societies 122, 124–25
Akan symbolism 22
Akofena 31, 107–8
*Akwasidae* festival 53, 59
*Akwasikra* 151
Akyeampong, Emmanuel 17, 99, 123
Akyem Abuakwa monarchy 162
amateur dance category 18, 146, 151
Amegago, Modesto 5–6, 121–22, 128, 130, 138
*Amele* 60
*Amokom* 151
Ampene, Kwasi 13, 31
Ampofo-Duodu, Emmanuel 29
Anglican Missionary Church 114
Anglo-European methods of inquiry 10
Anthonio, Kofi 33, 35
Apentemma 133
Arthur, Kojo 28
Arts Council of Ghana 64–65
Asante, Molefi Kete 10–11, 20, 23, 25, 33, 43, 48, 50, 93
Asante Adae festival 62
Asante aesthetics 128–30
*Asante Asokore* 153
Asante cosmology 1, 16–17, 100
Asante dance movement systems 21

Asante Kete dance 34, 126, 147
Asante Mampong 96, 112
Asante percussion music 158
Asante philosophy 123
Asante Region 112, 126, 151
Asante spirituality 122
Asante/Akan culture xx, 55–56, 58, 123–25, 130–31, 138, 142, 157, 165
Asante/Akan people xv, xx, 28, 32, 54, 67, 99, 124, 130, 132, 135, 139–40, 159, 163
Asantehemaa 56, 59, 89, 154–55
Asantehene 19, 56, 61, 89, 154, 159
Asanteman 89
*Atsatsa* group 160
*Atumpan* drum 1
Aubin, Henri 4
Austin, J. L. 141
autoethnography xix, 45–46, 104
Awuah, Eric xix, 7, 39, 41, 61, 64, 66, 84, 109, 118, 121, 125, 140, 165
Ayittey, George 98

Bachelor of Arts (BA) 80
Bachelor of Fine Arts (BFA) 80
Baffour, Nana Kyei 16, 58, 155
Bakka, Egil 47, 142, 144, 149
Bamfo, Napoleon 97
beauty 129
black dancing body 3, 5, 12, 21–22, 47, 73
black genius 70
Boakye, Nana 58, 151–55, 157
Boateng, Nana Kwadwo 89–90, 155
Bob-Milliar, George 97
Bond, Karen 93, 103–4
Botwe-Asamoah, Kwame xxi, 40, 76

Carter, Melanie 25
Cartesian dualism 4
*chaochao* 55
chieftaincy 96–97
competence 130, 140
Conceptual Dance Knowledge (CDK) 81
Connerton, Paul 42
Consciencism 77
Contemporary Pedagogy 84
*Contexts and Meaning in Asante Dance Performance: The Case of Kete, The* (Cudjoe) xv, 14
Cox, Gerry R. xv
Crossley, Nick 104
Cruz Banks, Ojeya 47
Cudjoe, Emmanuel xv, xvi

dance competence 144
dance movements 124, 144
dance-musicking 14, 18, 50, 61–63, 80, 112
Davidson, Julia 139
deformity 159
DeFrantz, Thomas 129
Dei, George Sefa 26–27
Department of Dance Studies 7, 72, 80, 88–89
Dewey, John 52, 125, 149
Dominant 68
*Dondo* xvi
Dove, Nah 124
Duodu, Ampofo 12, 124, 141
*Dwennimmen* 108

epic memory 137–38
esotericism 99
ethnomusicology 43
Eurocentric lenses 27

Falola, Toyin 4, 6, 37–38
Fante New Town 87, 103, 106, 112–14
Felfoldi, Laszlo 142
Fontomfrom 28, 56, 162–63
Franko, Mark 7
"From Palace to the Academy" 151
Fuller, Harcourt 65, 71

gendered aesthetics 122, 126–27, 144
gendered movement 119, 121, 124, 128, 140–41
gestures xix, 54, 57, 127, 163, 165
Ghana Dance Ensemble (GDE) xvi, xix, 6–7, 13, 18–19, 37, 39, 44–45, 48, 52, 63, 65, 72, 77, 79, 84, 88, 117, 126, 147, 161, 163, 165
Ghanaian dance 9, 31, 63, 69, 90, 121
Ghanaian/African Holistic Nature 150
Giurchescu, Anca 142
Global Dance Ensemble (GDE) 163
*Granyo* 160
Greco, Mitchell J. 66
*Gye Nyame* 30

Hall, Edward 95
Hall, Stuart 128
Hamera, Judith 139
Hanley, Elizabeth 126
Heritage Africa Reality Show 117
holism 34
holistic approach 28, 34–35, 149

# INDEX

Hunter, Whitney 94
*Hweneye* 157
hybridity 18

improvisation 132, 145
indigenous knowledge systems (IKS) 10, 20, 33–35, 40, 44, 61, 84, 109
indirect rule 70
Institute of African Studies (IAS) 40–41, 63, 66, 75, 77, 84
International Council for Museums 106

Kaeppler, Adrienne 35
Kaminski, Joseph 16
Karoblis, Gediminas 47, 142, 149
Kete dance form xv, xxi, 15, 26, 31, 57, 88, 119, 121, 126–27, 141, 144, 146
Kete dance-music xvii, 2, 10, 31, 35, 149
Kete dancing body 51, 165
Kete drumming 56–57, 147, 153, 159
Kete drums 133–34, 156–59
Kete movement systems 20, 37
Kete music 15, 19, 36, 44, 56, 158–59
Kete performativity 139, 144
*Ketehene* 54, 154
Ketehene, Nana 53–54, 57, 59, 155–59, 161–62
*Kete*-Krachiɜ xvi, 16
Kibirige, Ronald 14
Koeltzsch, Grit 88, 98, 119
Kringelbach, Hélène 3–4
Kubik, Gerhard 66
Kumasi xx, 36–37, 87–89, 113, 115–16, 119, 161
Kumasi Cultural Centre 152
Kuwor, Sylvanus 11, 28–29, 49, 54, 71, 75, 80, 135, 149–50
Kwadum 54, 56, 133, 146
Kwakwa, Patience 38, 144–47, 161
Kyeremanteng, Baffour xvi, 16

Langmia, Kehbuma 21
linguistic routines 140
Lomax, Allan 20

*Managing Death: International Perspectives* (Cox and Thompson) xv
Manhyia palace 57, 69, 88–90, 153, 157, 162
Mauze, Marie 108
Mawere Opoku Dancehall 74
Mawuli, Cynthia 107

Mazama, Ama 23
menstruation 157
mere-transfer 68
Mji, Bubela 10, 33
Mkabela, Queeneth 10–11, 34
modernization 48–49
Mpesetea 56
*Mpintin* drum xvi
*Mpohor* 87
museums 65, 106–8

Nance, Kemal 46
national art forms 65
national identity 42, 69, 72, 85
National Theatre Movement 74
Nationalist Pedagogy 84
nationhood 44, 70, 112
*Ndehemaa* 160
neo-traditional dance music 39–41, 69
neo-traditional dance-musicking 44, 63
neo-traditional dances 7, 48, 72–74, 126, 144
Nii-Yartey, Francis 35, 39
Nketia, J. H. 12, 14, 19–20, 24, 37, 39, 41–44, 66, 72, 77, 128, 147, 161–62
Nkrumah, Kwame xx, 5, 7, 9, 20, 37, 39–42, 44–45, 48–50, 64–65, 70–71, 74–77, 122
*Nkyemkyemfour* 59–60
*Nseneakyɜ* 160
*Nyame Dua* 108

Oba, Olufunke 26
Obeng, Pashington 17, 99, 123, 158
*ɔdwanputua* 55
Odomankoma (God) 1, 112
"Odomankoma na ɔnwini kete!" (God assembled Kete dance-music) 1
Okrah, John 149
Okrah, Kwadwo 123, 125
Olokodana-James, Oluwatoyin 18
*Onyame* (the Supreme Being) 17, 99–100
Opoku, Albert Mawere xvi, 13, 17, 19–20, 35–37, 39, 41, 44, 72, 77, 127–29, 138, 140, 142, 144, 161–63
Opoku Ware II, Otumfour Nana xvi, 154, 162
Opoku-Boateng, Judith 88–89
"Order, Music/Communication, and Death" 31
Otumfuɔ (Asantehene) 56
Owusu, Frank 90
Owusu-Ansah, Frances 10, 33

Pan-African ideologies 42–43
Pan-Africanism 13, 41, 48, 50
Pan-Africanist movement 75
Pan-Africanist paradigm 165
Pan-Africanist revolution 9
*Parade* 55
Paulding, Ben 15, 18
"Performance: Akan Ceremonial Dance Suite" 163
"Performance: Kete" 163
permission asking process 68
pheno-choreological approach 149
political power 36, 50, 123, 125, 154
polyrhythm 136–37
postcolonial theory 24
postcoloniality 24
postindependence 5, 61, 84, 97
Practical Dance (PD) 81
Prempeh II, Otumfuɔ Nana Osei Tutu Agyeman 19, 36, 161
presentation technique 145
Professional, Academic, and Amateur xxi, 65–66, 69, 157–58
professional category xix
proverbs 28–29, 55, 110, 124

Rattray, R. S. 148
Rawlings, Jerry John 162
realization 62–63, 142
repetition 138
rhythmic foundations 144–45

sacred dances 65
Schauert, Paul 13, 163
School of Performing Arts 7, 72, 115–17
self-identification 38, 149
self-reflection 46
shoulders of eminence 2
*sika ɔdwan* 55

Silver, Harry 48–49
social construction of knowledge 125, 149
social dance events 62
social formation 64
social medicine 47
Speech Act theory 140
subpar dancer 145
*sum ne mogya* xvi, 16

*Tefre ayiyanda* 58
theory of concept and realization 47, 142, 150, 155
Thompson, Neil xv
Thompson, Robert Farris 130
times change 58
Traditional category xxi, 45, 64, 66, 69, 112, 126, 151, 159
traditional dances 7, 22, 29, 46, 51, 61, 67, 74, 77, 126, 145
Trans-Sociological Hybridity (TSH) 18
Turner, Victor 141
Twi language xx, 1, 8, 11, 24, 34

unity 58
University of Ghana xx, xxii, 1, 72–74, 79, 84, 113, 116, 147, 161, 165

Wassa Mpohor 95–96, 100, 108, 112
Welsh-Asante, Kariamu 63, 121, 126, 131, 133, 136, 138
Western educational system 5
Western investigative methods 34
Wiggins, Trevor 64, 66, 72
Williams, Raymond 64, 68–69
Wilson, Margaret 25

*Yamensa* 162
"Year of return" in 2019 68
Younge, Paschal 13, 135

Milton Keynes UK
Ingram Content Group UK Ltd.
UKHW041817041024
449024UK00001B/7